Tranquil is This Realm of Mine

Tranquil is This Realm of Mine

DHARMA TALKS AND WRITINGS OF
THE MOST VENERABLE NICHIDATSU FUJII

TRANSLATED BY

Yumiko Miyazaki

NIPPONZAN MYŌHŌJI

Nipponzan Myōhōji Publications
1127 Glenwood Ave., SE
Atlanta, GA 30316 USA

© 2007 Nipponzan Myōhōji

First Edition
Printed in the United States of America

Printed on acid-free paper certified by the Sustainable Forestry Initiative®.

Publisher's Cataloging-In-Publication Data
(Prepared by The Donohue Group, Inc.)

Fujii, Nittatsu, 1885-
  [Tenku yomonshu. English.]
  Tranquil is this realm of mine : dharma talks and writings of the most
venerable Nichidatsu Fujii / [Nichidatsu Fujii] ; translated by Yumiko
Miyazaki. -- 1st ed.

      p. : ill. ; cm.

  Includes bibliographical references.
  ISBN-13: 978-0-9791298-0-3
  ISBN-10: 0-9791298-0-X

  1. Fujii, Nittatsu, 1885- 2. Peace--Religious aspects--Buddhism. 3.
Nonviolence--Religious aspects--Buddhism. 4. Mahayana Buddhism. I.
Miyazaki, Yumiko. II. Title. III. Title: Tenku yomonshu. English.

  BQ4022 .F85 2007
  294.3   2006939071

All sumi-ink drawings and Japanese calligraphy, including the front cover,
by the Most Venerable Nichidatsu Fujii.

Front portrait photograph of the Most Venerable Nichidatsu Fujii as well
as photos on pages 47, 79, 111, 181 and 235 by Kunihiko Seto.

CONTENTS

FOREWORD

We offer this new translation of Dharma teachings and writings by the Most Venerable Nichidatsu Fujii, Founder and Teacher of Nipponzan Myōhōji, in deep and abiding gratitude for his words that continue to challenge, guide and lead in an age mired in chaos and violence.

Guruji, as he was more commonly known, passed away at 100 years of age on January 9, 1985. Japanese Buddhism counts anniversaries from the day of the event itself, and any year with the sacred numbers of three or seven is particularly significant. We humbly wish to mark the 23rd Commemoration of Guruji's passing with the publication of *Tranquil is This Realm of Mine*, the first book-length translation of Guruji's writings to appear in 27 years.

Born August 6, 1885 in Aso, Kyūshū Island, Japan, he became a Buddhist monk at age 19 in opposition to the tendencies of the time, which strongly encouraged a military career as the country rushed headlong into militarism under the guise of "modernization." At age 32 following much study and severe ascetic practice, he arrived at the realization that his mission—to spread world peace—would be accomplished through the practice of beating a drum and chanting Na Mu Myō Hō Ren Ge Kyō.

Guruji understood his life and mission through his discipleship to Nichiren Daishōnin, a 13th century Buddhist prophet and monk who first revealed the sacred mantra of Na Mu Myō Hō Ren Ge Kyō. Nichiren Daishōnin's ardent and uncompromising adherence to the teachings of the Lotus Sūtra led him through an extremely eventful life, which included severe persecutions and a near execution due to his challenge of the government and the religious leadership of his day. Relations between government officials and the clergy had had a corrupting influence on both. Furthermore, the chaos of the time spawned a multitude of religious schools that sought to answer the people's unease in various ways including occultism, formalism, individualism or simplistic teachings on salvation. Nichiren Daishōnin denounced all these practices for leading the people away from Buddhism's genuine founder, Buddha Śākyamuni, and his greatest teaching, the Lotus Sūtra. Nichiren Daishōnin firmly believed that the vitality of a nation and the welfare of the people and the land depended upon a government that upheld the genuine and deepest truth of Buddha Dharma. His prophet's zeal earned him powerful enemies. However, his courage and tender compassion for others also gained him a devoted following, many who were in turn persecuted for their loyalty. Guruji continually drew inspiration from this unique combination of profound faith, great learnedness, fierce devotion and deep compassion.

In order to fulfill a prophecy of Nichiren Daishōnin to bring the true spirit and teaching of Buddha back to India, Guruji first traveled there in 1931 to return countless times in the next 52 years. During his missionary work in India, he developed deep spiritual ties with the nonviolent independence movement and with Mahatma Gandhi, himself, who bestowed the name "Guruji" on him and who took up the practice of drumming and chanting which he continued for the rest of his life.

Guruji and his disciples have walked through all the continents beating the drum, chanting and offering prayers for peace. The atomic bombings of Hiroshima and Nagasaki in 1945 marked the dawn of the nuclear age, and Guruji recognized the grave danger in humanity's new and unprecedented capacity for self-annihilation. With characteristic resolve and unflagging commitment, he dedicated himself to a life-long campaign for the abolition of nuclear weapons, which he perceived to be the greatest evil of modern civilization and its science. His advocacy for abolition rested in the precept of not taking life, Buddhism's First Precept, which he understood as inviolable. His method was to walk throughout the world, praying to transform the great evil into great good through demilitarization and renunciation of war.

After World War II, Guruji also began the construction of Peace Pagodas as a means to build a universal, spiritual foundation for peace in this world. Peace Pagodas or stūpas enshrine holy relics of the Buddha. Guruji had first received such relics in Sri Lanka in 1933 and ever since aspired to erect a stūpa or Peace Pagoda whenever an opportunity arose. Today Peace Pagodas exist throughout the world and continue to be built by Nipponzan Myōhōji and others in a practice adopted directly from the Lotus Sūtra.

The 128 Dharma teachings and writings included in this book are from a slightly larger compilation of Guruji's teachings first published in Japanese as *Tenku Yōmonshū* in 1991. This collection was widely distributed to temples within the order to serve as a guide to the practice and to help the newly initiated to understand Nipponzan Myōhōji's mission and the reasons behind the practice. These Dharma talks had been directed mainly to Nipponzan Myōhōji monks and nuns, and the tone, at times, is one of a spiritual master instructing, guiding and occasionally admonishing his disciples. However, it also brings Guruji's penetrating insight on many topics including nonviolence, faith, service to others, war, materialism and his diamond-like, unshakable belief in the path to world peace through drumming and chanting Na Mu Myō Hō Ren Ge Kyō.

For this latter reason, we wanted to bring *Yōmonshū* to a larger audience for its message reaches far beyond the temple gates and contains a clarion call to heed the dangers of modern-day militarism, economic and environmental exploitation and to turn to genuine faith and practice. Our sincere and ardent wish is to bring Guruji's relevant and compassionate teachings to the West in the interest of world peace.

Yōmonshū was arranged almost entirely chronologically and, in this translation, we have maintained the original sequence. The only alteration has been to divide the individual teachings into Parts One through Ten and assign topic headings for each part from a title included in that section. This was done to attempt a more pleasing design and organization to the overall book. Admittedly, the sections can be seen as arbitrary designations. However, the topic headings chosen represent broad themes that appear throughout all of Guruji's extensive teachings spanning the better part of a century.

The original selections for the Japanese *Yōmonshū* were made by the late Rev. Higai Matsuya of Nipponzan Myōhōji. This translation is the work of a committee that included Rev. Toshihiro Yamaguchi of Nichiren School's Bukkōji Temple, Ven. Tenzin Priyadarshi of the Massachusetts Institute of Technology, Yumiko Miyazaki, the translator, as well as several members of Nipponzan Myōhōji.

Although many contributed to the creation of this book, without Ms. Miyazaki, it truly would have been impossible. Unquestionably she is the most qualified to translate Guruji's words, having served as his personal interpreter and as the primary translator of his writings into English. She has approached the translation of this work with devotion, zeal and a meticulous attention to detail and clearly shouldered the task as a great Bodhisattva practice. We are deeply indebted.

Editorial Committee
February 2007

TRANSLATOR'S NOTE

In October 1976, I was a novice interpreter accompanying a Japanese NGO delegation, which included A-bomb survivors, visiting the United States to petition the UN Secretary General for nuclear disarmament. As the delegation stepped into the J.F. Kennedy Airport lobby, an elderly Buddhist monk caught my attention. He was vested in a yellow monk's robe over a white kimono top and pants. Carrying a gnarled walking stick, he walked slowly but with a firm gait towards several monks and nuns there to greet him, who were similarly clad in robes of different hues of yellow. With palms pressed together, they fell to their knees three times saluting him and chanted, "Na Mu Myō Hō Ren Ge Kyō." I could not take my eyes off the most incredibly radiant smile on the elderly Venerable's face. I had never seen a person smile with every part of his face so that even his bushy white eyebrows seemed to be smiling. I wondered what could possibly make a person smile that way. It resonated deep in me and made me feel that I could believe in the goodness of man, an indelible moment in my memory. This was the Most Venerable Nichidatsu Fujii, or, as most of the English-speaking world came to know him, Fujii Guruji. He was 91 years old. I knew nothing about Buddhist doctrines or of his order nor had I heard him speak; but his smile filled my heart with pure joy and that was enough. The following nine years were a time of blessing that allowed me to be in the presence of greatness as his volunteer and self-appointed interpreter.

Guruji was a prolific writer and gave long Dharma talks after daily prayer sessions. This book is only the tip of the iceberg in materials waiting to be translated. *Tranquil is This Realm of*

Mine is an English translation of part of *Tenku Yōmonshū*, analects of Guruji's teachings including his oral sermons and writings that set forth core teachings and practices of Nipponzan Myōhōji. The titles of the individual Dharma talks are those used in *Yōmonshū*, though, with the exception of the written manuscripts, they were not necessarily titled by Guruji himself. Another book will follow shortly, which includes a greater number of Guruji's public speeches and writings.

I was faced with myriads of challenges. The early writings were particularly difficult to translate due to the abundance of Buddhist terminology, citations from scriptures and Nichiren Daishōnin's writings, as well as Guruji's eloquent, fluid and classical literary style. Also, Guruji frequently cited a wide variety of non-Japanese sources that had been translated into Japanese. In cases where I could not locate the original citation, I provided my own English translation. It was customary for Guruji to first cite the original words of Nichiren Daishōnin and follow with an explanation in simple, everyday language. For this reason, the English translation may appear at times redundant. I kept the style as is for it provides clarification in many instances. For Romanization of Japanese terms, I used a variant of the Hepburn system since it seemed the most intuitive and easily read by English speakers. Some examples are the use of "ō" instead of "oh" for a long o, "chi" instead of "ti," "tsu" instead of "tu" and "ji" instead of "zi".

Another challenge came from frequently used, common words with multiple meanings. For example, *kokoro* is a Japanese word that could mean heart, mind, soul, sentiment, emotion, intent and so on depending on the context. In most cases the translation of heart and mind was chosen. *Myō* was another extremely difficult word to translate. I understand it is a term that denotes sublimity, wondrousness, ethereality, inexplicability and mystery. It was suggested to me that the closest translation might be ineffable, yet sublime was chosen as the translation for *myō*, as in *myōhō*, the Sublime Dharma, because it conveys the sense of this Dharma, the Lotus Sūtra, as being the ultimate teaching, which was how Guruji and Nichiren Daishōnin understood it. Simple footnotes provide a contextual framework to facilitate the understanding of general readers. They are not meant to be thorough or complete. Some of the essays from my first translation of Guruji's writings, *Buddhism for World Peace*, offered to a smaller group of readers in 1980, were revised and included here. Given Guruji's broad and profound knowledge and practice, I am not certain if my English rendition captures even the bare essence of his words let alone the multiple layers of meaning or their grace, power and inherent tenderness. Language is modulated depending on the person using it, and limited understanding of the person on my part created inadequacies in the translation. However, I trust that Guruji's spirit will transcend all the inadequacies and potential errors and reach the hearts of the readers and inspire.

I have many people to acknowledge and thank, although I cannot list them all here. Rev. Toshihiro Yamaguchi of Nichiren School's Bukkōji Temple has initiated and funded this project and offered encouragement throughout. Venerable Tenzin Priyadarshi of the MIT Prajnopaya gave valuable advice and input on Buddhist terms in English and on the overall publication. Rev. Tenshin Shugei of Nipponzan Myōhōji offered insights and advice on the original text and provided context, while Rev. Gyōshu Sasamori facilitated communications with Rev. Shugei. Rev. Gyōkō Kurihara counseled me on content and footnotes. Gopa Maharathi proofread Sanskrit terms. Sister Denise Laffan displayed extraordinary patience in proofreading and worked with me through innumerable revisions. David Crockett Williams reviewed and provided comments on many of the initial drafts. Noe Minamikata and Hiroko Tanaka provided ideas and assistance in translating Japanese idiomatic expressions. Betty Jennings and Makoto Masui helped to research Mahatma Gandhiji's quotes. Michiko Sano, my mentor, gave me the assignment to accompany the delegation to the UN. Without her I would have never met Guruji. My son, Hiro, has continuously provided the much needed moral support over the last four years. Most of all, I was guided by Guruji's smile.

Yumiko Miyazaki
February 2007

Nichiren Daishōnin

Gohonzon [Principle Object of Veneration]

PART ONE

The Origin of Nipponzan

1

Yatsubuchi and Momonoo Cascades

Autumn, 1984

Atami, Japan

IT TAKES A PERSONAL EXPERIENCE to appreciate the profound Dharma and to decisively grasp the very essence of Nichiren Daishōnin's teachings. What does it take to have such an experience? After much reflection, I decided to cast aside all my learning in search of such an experience, and, at the risk of my life, secluded myself under waterfalls known for ascetic practices from bygone days. The rapid water cascading from the peak of Mount Hira[1] created eight waterfalls. I climbed to the highest of the eight and engaged in a week-long practice under it. Either I lose my life during this practice or I would gain the confidence for imparting the teachings of Nichiren Daishōnin in this Era of Declining Dharma.[2] That was my reason for choosing the basin of a waterfall seldom visited by anyone. Prepared to meet my death, I did not even bring candles. The clothes I wore were all I had. I dared not sleep even when night fell, but I laid on a relatively smooth surface created by the pounding water, exposed to its splash against the rocks. By the end of the week, mold covered the single-layered cotton undergarment I had on.

Although a week passed, I arrived at no resolve. It would have been easier had I died. I wondered what I should do and

---

1 Mount Hira is one of the mountains in the Hira Mountain range in Shiga Prefecture, located near Kyōto.

2 The teachings of the Buddha are said to spread in three consecutive periods after the demise of the Buddha Śākyamuni, namely, the Era of Genuine Dharma, the Era of Counterfeit Dharma and the Era of Declining Dharma.

decided to change locations to repeat the practice. As I started to descend the mountain without gaining what I had come for, I casually looked back. What I saw was a magnificent, multi-storied tower gate with a hanging frame. In vivid gold the two lines of calligraphy on the frame read, "The dual paths of learning and *budō*[3] forestall internal enemies." It urged me to remain vigilant so as not to be compromised by internal enemies when I set forth on the mission of spreading the Dharma and to find my own unique footing. This was the lesson I learned at the Yatsubuchi Cascade.

I returned to the temple in Katada in Ōmi[4] and from there started my quest afresh at various waterfalls where ancient seekers were known to have practiced. One such waterfall was where Reverend Honmyō Nichirin[5] practiced. I eventually arrived at the Momonoo Waterfalls located in the mountains of Tenri City. It was already late in autumn of that year. I felt pressed for time. I had already decided to set out on my mission to edify the people shouldering the great Dharma revealed by Nichiren Daishōnin at the beginning of the New Year. There was nowhere I could go after this. Bound and determined to have the great precept conferred to me as a disciple of Nichiren Daishōnin before I stepped out, I sequestered myself for a week in a small temple and practiced under the waterfall.

At dawn during the morning prayer on the last day of my practice, someone was ascending the mountain beating a drum. There was nothing out of the ordinary about this person. He

---

3 武道, The Way of the Martial Arts. Sword training has evolved from a sheer battle technique to a broader discipline that encompasses physical and mental discipline and seeks to develop individual character as well as technique.
4 Ōmi is the current Shiga Prefecture. Katada, located along Japan's largest freshwater lake, Biwa, has been an important location for transportation since ancient times due to its close proximity to Kyōto. Guruji had his first hermitage here before setting out on his mission to spread the Dharma.
5 Honmyō Nichirin 本妙日臨 [1793-1823]. At the age of 19, he was ordained in the Nichiren School and left a legacy of relentless practice and learning. At the age of 22, he vowed to study the entire Buddhist canon and practiced under a waterfall in Mount Minobu for seven days and nights.

looked no different from any layperson. I inquired who he was. His response astounded me. He said, "I am Bodhisattva Superior Practice."[6] Bodhisattva Superior Practice was carrying an *oizuru*[7] on his back. When I asked what he was carrying in his box, he answered, "Lord Buddha." He then passed by and continued to climb the mountain. This was the mysterious experience I had. I was not asleep, dreaming. Wondrously, Bodhisattva Superior Practice spoke those exact words to me and passed by. That's all that happened. It was a profound realization of the way Bodhisattva Superior Practice would practice when edifying the people in the Era of Declining Dharma. Right there and then was determined the course of action I was to take throughout my life. None of the academic learning on the Dharma I had up to that time was necessary. I came to the realization that all I needed to do was to walk about the Earth beating the drum, carrying Lord Buddha on my back. Thus I stepped out on my mission to spread the Dharma, including the practice in the capital of Japan to remonstrate the government and the Royal Family following the legacy of Kyōichimaru.[8]

---

6 Jōgyō-Bosatsu, 上行菩薩. In Chapter XV of the Lotus Sūtra, *The Bodhisattvas Who Emerge From The Earth*, when Maitreya [who is assured to succeed Buddha Śākyamuni] and other Bodhisattvas asked the Buddha to entrust them with the task of spreading the Lotus Sūtra after the Nirvāna of the Buddha, innumerable Bodhisattvas headed by Bodhisattva Superior Practice emerged from openings in the earth. The Buddha entrusted these Bodhisattvas, who were disciples of the Buddha from innumerable kalpas past, with the task after his passing.
7 笈摺. A wooden box carried like a backpack by itinerant monks that contains sūtras, robes, Buddhist altar fittings and utensils.
8 Kyōichimaru, 経一丸, is the childhood name of Nichizō, 日像, who became Nichiren Daishōnin's, 日蓮大聖人, disciple at the age of seven. Nichiren Daishōnin entrusted him when he was 13 years old with the mission to spread the teachings in Kyōto, the then-capital of Japan, and to remonstrate the government's wrong.

2

THE ORIGIN OF NIPPONZAN

September 18, 1983
Vienna Dōjō, Austria

THE PATH THAT LED to the founding of Nipponzan was indeed extremely challenging. I studied Buddha Dharma thinking that I could come to an understanding of something. I learned a few things, but nothing that enabled me to decide on the course of action to follow for the rest of my life. I had resolved to start out in the world as a bhikshu [monk] to deliver the Dharma at age 33. However, with no clear direction to pursue in my life as an ordained and a disciple of Nichiren Daishōnin, I did everything possible to determine my course, visiting various waterfalls, fasting and retreating alone to the mountains. There is a waterfall called Momonoo in the province of Yamato[1] in the mountains overlooking Tenri City, where virtuous monks from Nara[2] built dōjōs [place to practice the Way] in the past.[3] It was already the end of autumn, and I was pressed for time given my decision to step out in the world when the year changed and I turned 33.[4] I practiced under this waterfall and intently prayed while fasting. I experienced an inexplicable vision for the first time in my life. Strange as it may sound, I met Bodhisattva Superior Practice in

---

1 Currently Nara prefecture, originally coming from the name of place in the vicinity of Tenri City.
2 Nara was the capital of Japan from 710-794, seat of the Yamato Imperial Court.
3 The tradition of high monks and practitioners of mystic rites practicing under the Momonoo waterfalls goes back to ancient times.
4 Age counted by Japanese tradition reckons a child to be one year at birth, with another year added at every New Year. According to this method of counting, Guruji would have turned 33 the following New Year [1917].

my vision. He was carrying a child on his back and was walking towards me. I asked him who he was. He answered, "Bodhisattva Superior Practice." I further asked who the child was he had on his back. "Lord Buddha." He was walking, carrying Lord Buddha on his back beating an *uchiwa-daiko*.[5] That was the extent of the vision. I did not take this vision lightly and considered it a divine revelation. After I completed the fast, a devotee from Nara came to accompany me to his home. I shared with him that I made my resolve to practice by walking throughout the world. I placed the *Gomyōhan*[6] and a few changes of clothing in an *oizuru*, a rectangular box made out of paulownia wood. For nights when no shelter would be either offered or available, I cut a blanket in half and placed it on the top of the *oizuru*. An umbrella was attached to its side. Once the *oizuru* to carry on my back was ready, I wrote Na Mu Myō Hō Ren Ge Kyō with a brush on the front center along with my name. In the same manner, I wrote the single *gāthā* [verse] from *Exhortation to Hold Firm:*[7]

> Whether in villages or cities,
> Whenever there are those who seek the Dharma,
> We will go to them and
> Expound the Dharma bequeathed by the Buddha.

This was the attire I chose in my first step that gave birth to Nipponzan Myōhōji.

Whether in towns or villages, whenever there are those who seek the Dharma, I will go to them and chant the Odaimoku bequeathed by the Buddha. To this very day, I have practiced my initial vow to expound this Dharma to all the people far and wide. This *gāthā* from *Exhortation to Hold Firm* is what Nipponzan is founded on. You, too, are disciples coming from this origin; Nipponzan today is a result of those who walked about. Nipponzan has come a long way because of those who walked about.

5　団扇太鼓.　A hand-held drum in the shape of a round fan.
6　Writings of Nichiren Daishōnin.
7　Chapter XIII of the Lotus Sūtra.

3

THE SOUND OF THE DRUM

September 12, 1927
Excerpt from *Gyakku-Senryō*, Volume 2
Numazu, Japan

How far do the reverberations of the drum travel?
It is said to encompass the three-thousand-great-
thousandfold world.[1]

THE UNIVERSE WITH ten billion solar systems is said to
reverberate with the single sound of the drum. This is a Dharma
that a positivist mind fails to comprehend even in a hundred
thousand years. Sublime actions of emancipation are said to
manifest where the sound of the drum reverberates, extinguishing
the multitude of suffering and calamities of the human world and
the three lower realms of existence.[2][3]

The innumerable sufferings in the human realm include
the four kinds of sufferings,[4] the eight kinds of sufferings[5] and the

---

1 *Sanzen-daisen-sekai* 三千第千世界, *trisāhasra-mahāsāhasrāh lokadhātavah*;
trichioliocosm. A thousand worlds make a small one thousand world; a thousand
of these make a medium one thousand world. Often used to describe the whole
universe.
2 *Sanzu* 三途, also referred to as *san-akudō* 三悪道, the three lowest states of
existence: i) The realm of fire, hell, where fierce fire burns those who commit
wrong. ii) The realm of the sword, the realm of hungry spirits, where they are
tormented with swords or sticks. iii) The realm of blood, the realm of animals
where they fight and kill each other.
3 Konkōmyō-kyō 金光明経 Suvarnaprabhāsa-sūtra, Vol. 10.
4 四苦. The sufferings of birth, aging, illness and death.
5 八苦. In addition to the four sufferings, the suffering of being apart from loved
ones, of having to stay with those one hates, of not being able to have what one
wants, of being attached to the five elemental aggregates from which one's body,

"eighty-four thousand" sufferings.[6] The affliction of illness is one such suffering. However, these are all agonies that can undoubtedly be expunged by the single sound of the drum. Suffering and calamities in the human realm are essentially afflictions that are mild in comparison to those in the other lower realms. The realms in the Dharma realm[7] where suffering is most intense and excruciating are the worlds of hungry spirits, animals and hell. These are called *san-akudō* or *sanzu*. We are told that even the torment caused by committing heinous acts [through cause and effect] in the three evil realms is immediately extinguished by the single sound of the drum.

mind and environment are composed.

6 In Buddhism, eighty-four thousand is a symbolic number that refers to something unfathomable.

7 *Hokkai* 法界, *dharma-dhātu*. i) The realm or sphere of the ultimate reality. ii) The whole universe.

4

THE PRACTICE OF NON-CONFRONTATION

July 20, 1935
Bombay Dōjō, India

THERE IS A STAGE in the practice of the Bodhisattva called *jū-gyō*[1] or *jū-ekō*. The third stage in *jū-gyō* is known as *mui-gyakugyō*.[2] It can be described as adherence to the True Dharma[3] without receding. It is at the same time a practice of not confronting or going against any person. Never out of over-zealousness should we look down at the deeds and conduct of others or deride their state of confusion. Rather, we must cultivate the mind of playing ball with a child or listening to the elderly reminisce about the past. The seventh stage of *jū-ekō* is a level called *tō-zuijunichi-issai-shujō-ekō*.[4] It means to equally accept, harmonize with and minister to all people with a mind of equanimity. What is the reason for impartially accepting and ministering to the unenlightened, who engage in wrongdoing and know no virtue? It is a practice of embracing all people with great compassion, akin to a mother's heart that gives what her child seeks and shares the delight.

---

1 十行, 十廻向. There are ten levels, or stages of a Bodhisattva on the path to reach enlightenment. In Sanskrit these levels are called *bhūmi*. The list of ten *bhūmis* varies in different Mahāyāna texts, but the term *bhūmi* invariably denotes stages of attainment toward Buddhahood. The practices of the ten stages of profiting others are: i) joyful service; ii) beneficial service; iii) following with patience; iv) dauntlessness; v) no misconduct; vi) appearing in any form at will; vii) attachment to the void of existence; viii) acquisition of *zengon*, "root of goodness," which is difficult to obtain; ix)preaching the law; x) attainment of the middle way.
2 無違逆行. The practice of following without going against.
3 正法. "The True Dharma," the teaching of the Buddha, which conforms to the truth.
4 等随順一一切衆生廻回.

10

In edifying the people about the Dharma, a spirit of acceptance and non-confrontation yields more positive results than any argument or intellectual dialogue. When harmonious compliance and obsequiousness are considered to be the same, both we and others then lose the benefits of the Dharma. Seeing those who are obsequious should not make us depreciate the good practice of complying with others. Without confusing harmonious compliance with ingratiation, we must choose between the two. It is just like the Gaō's[5] beak that naturally divides water and milk.[6]

The practice of *shakubuku*[7] by Bodhisattva Never Despise was *tangyō-raihai*[8] [the sole practice of bowing and venerating the Buddha within others]. *Shakubuku* is nothing but the practice of harmonizing and ministering to others without confrontation. The term *shakubuku* somehow seems to evoke militancy. This should never be the case.

---

5 Legendary White Swan King who is known to possess a beak that is capable of separating milk from water.
6 Citing the analogy of Gaō with a beak capable of discerning milk from water, Guruji admonishes that we must be able to discern compliance from ingratiation, which may appear similar yet are very different in nature.
7 折伏. *Shakubuku* is to guide people to the Dharma and help them discern between right and wrong views.
8 但行礼拝.

Bokuyō [Sheep Farming] January 1, 1931. Singapore seaside. Gyōsho.

5

FRATERNITY OF MONKS IN HARMONY

July 25, 1935
Bombay Dōjō, India

IT HAS ALREADY BEEN 20 years since the order known as Nipponzan Myōhōji came into existence. It may not be too far-fetched to call it a group of ignoramuses, wrongdoers and thieves. There are no prestigious scholars, ministers or people of wealth among us. It must have been a wonder to many that we survived this far as a Buddhist order. We have somehow survived to this day only by chanting Na Mu Myō Hō Ren Ge Kyō. *Saiten-kaikyō*[1] has been the mission of my lifetime, yet not much has been achieved due to my limited abilities. Still, I am convinced that my endeavors will not be lost when the prophecy of the Lotus Sūtra that the True Dharma will spread throughout the world comes to fruition.

We are no more than unenlightened monks susceptible to wrongdoing. Nevertheless, we have been able to somehow achieve the great Dharma work that, in effect, can be described as aiding the vows of the Buddhas of the past, present and future. The ignorant, the wicked and the thieves of the order supported and cooperated in this Dharma work in complete unity. "I shall be

---

1 *Saiten-kaikyō,* 西天開教, is Guruji's vow to return Buddha's teachings to *Saiten*, the Western Heaven, which was also the fulfillment of Nichiren Daishōnin's prophecy. *Saiten* includes *Tenjiku,* 天竺, ancient India. At the time Guruji set out to the Western Heaven in 1930, the British colony of India covered a vast geographical area spanning from the Himalayas bordering on Tibet in the north to the South Indian Ocean, including Sri Lanka, to part of the Malay Peninsula, and westward to Hindu Kush Mountains.

pleased, and so will all the Buddhas"[2] must allude to this.

We must not be too fastidious and overly focused on the seemingly intolerable reality that lies before our eyes and make light of others. When the Bodhisattva Never Despise came across men and women who disparaged the Dharma, he immediately recognized the Buddha-nature in them and venerated them. Those who became the object of his veneration were ultimately and invariably led to engage in the Bodhisattva practice. The assurance of attainment of Buddhahood by the Bodhisattva Never Despise as he paid reverence was by no means false.[3] The four groups of Buddhists[4] who slander the Dharma were given assurances of their eventual attainment of Buddhahood, but nevertheless, they themselves rejected it as false. Their rejection is merely a superficial illusion. What is meant by embracing the Lotus Sūtra in the Era of Declining Dharma is entrusting oneself to the wondrous practice [of chanting Na Mu Myō Hō Ren Ge Kyō] extolled by the Buddhas of the past, present and future. Where else can we possibly find a better example of ordinary beings attaining Buddhahood in one's present body[5] in today's world than those who wear the robe and shave their heads?

The members of this order rejoice more than anyone else when I am praised. It is likewise the members of the order who grieve more than anyone when I am slandered. The members of the order are closest in sharing my sense of reverence in reciting the names of the Lotus Sūtra, Buddha Śākyamuni and Nichiren Daishōnin. We would not have become teacher and disciple without karmic connection. I have no intent to shun or reject anyone. Together with one mind and heart we shall spread the

---

2 Chapter XI of the Lotus Sūtra, *Beholding the Stūpa of Treasures* "This sūtra is difficult to keep, if anyone keeps it a short time, I shall be pleased, and so will all the Buddhas."
3 The Bodhisattva Never Despise venerated everyone he met and revered each one, believing he or she would become Buddha.
4 Buddhist monks, nuns, laymen and laywomen.
5 *Sokushin-jōbutsu* 即身成仏.

Odaimoku.[6] Together we shall face defamation and hardship. Together we must correct where we are in error. But, more than anything else, we must chant the Odaimoku. As long as we chant the Odaimoku we will be able to perform Dharma work even as we are. The heart of Tathāgata's[7] compassion is demonstrated in imparting guidance to all, excluding none, embracing all regardless of varied abilities and aptitude. This is exemplified by his teaching of enlightenment to be attained by the wrongdoers, animals, women and the two vehicles.[8] Enlightenment exists in our determination to succeed our father and Preceptor, Buddha Śākyamuni, as his children. Those who are ordained in Nipponzan Myōhōji must have been led by their aspiration to emulate me. Even if they do not become what I am today, they cannot be blamed. There are karmic obscurations from throughout innumerable kalpas[9] in the past that could prevent them. I shall overlook their current flawed conducts, focus on their aspiration for enlightenment, keep my eyes on the dawning of the ultimate truth and immerse myself in the practice of reverence in the tradition of the Bodhisattva Never Despise.

There is a lesson of "one mind, different bodies." A face with boils cannot be separated from the body because it is ugly. A hand cannot be placed on the head because it is dexterous.

---

6 Na Mu Myō Hō Ren Ge Kyo.

7 "One Who Has Thus Gone," the highest epithet of a Buddha signifying one who has reached the truth and has come to declare it.

8 A reference to the third and fourth states of mind out of the ten realms of living beings: Buddhas, bodhisattvas, *engaku*, *shōmon*, deities, human beings, *asuras*, animals, hungry spirits, hell. *Engaku* are those who attain enlightenment on their own but who do not spread the Dharma to others. *Shōmon* are those who are solely interested in their own enlightenment on hearing the teachings of the Buddha. The Lotus Sūtra is the first and one of two Mahāyāna sūtras that teaches enlightenment of *engaku* and *shōmon* along with the enlightenment of women and animals, and the only sūtra that teaches immediate Buddhahood of all beings.

9 Kalpa [Sk.] *kō* [Jap.] 劫. An immeasurably long period of time; aeons. Its length is metaphorically explained as the period required for one to empty a city full of poppy seeds by taking away one seed every three years. There are three increments of kalpa, small, medium and large.

Irrespective of the beauty or ugliness, one's body is nurtured as a whole. What it is acts in wondrous ways as it is! Certainly the good are not encouraged to do wrong, but the wrong must at least practice the Odaimoku, as they are, and rejoice in foreseeing the dissemination of the Lotus Sūtra in the future. Our relationship is not one bound by iron chains of good or evil. The five or seven characters of Na Mu Myō Hō Ren Ge Kyō are the iron chains that keep our order together. As long as we stay with the Odaimoku, we remain connected. Women, as they are, [just like men as they are], are also to engage in the practice of chanting Na Mu Myō Hō Ren Ge Kyō accompanied by the drum,[10] driven by the aspiration to liberate themselves together with all sentient beings that are afflicted from ill karma that manifests from previous lives by the law of cause and effect.

The practitioners of Na Mu Myō Hō Ren Ge Kyō walk the same right path sharing a common objective without even having to talk about it. Our founder, Nichiren Daishōnin, said in *Reply to Matsuno-dono*[11] that we are to venerate each other as set forth in the rite of Buddha Śākyamuni and Tathāgata Prabhūtaratna seated side by side in the stūpa.[12] The two Buddhas in the stūpa that we look up at in veneration must be the model of conduct we ultimately strive for to create harmony among the fraternity of us mendicant monks, who are monks in name only, unable to do justice to the Way.

---

10 *Gyakku-shōdai* 擊鼓唱題.

11 *Matsunodono-shō* 松野殿鈔. This letter is also known as the *Fourteen Slanders,* written by Nichiren Daishōnin on December 9, 1276 addressed to a devout follower, Matsuno Rokurō Zaemon.

12 *Nibutsu-byōza* 二仏並座. In Chapter XI of the Lotus Sūtra, *Beholding the Stūpa of Treasures,* a great stūpa adorned with jewels appeared in mid-air. The Buddha declares that within the stūpa is the whole body *śarīra* of a Tathāgata from a world in the east called Treasure Purity, and that the stūpa appeared to praise and attest to the veracity of the teachings of the Lotus Sūtra. Buddha Śākyamuni opens the stūpa revealing Tathāgata Prabhūtaratna [Abundant Treasures] seated on a lion throne. Tathāgata Prabhūtaratna offers half of his seat and invites Buddha Śākyamuni to sit by his side.

6

Faith

March 21, 1946
Excerpt from *Shinsui-Shōgo*[1]

WHEN FACING THE IMPERMANENCE and angst of life unable to find a sympathetic ear, one feels like a prisoner in a vast, isolated gaol. In such a state, religious faith is born out of seeking benevolence, rescue and protection from the kind father.[2] Anyone who desires to touch the true meaning of a life of faith while wallowing in the pleasures of worldly life is like looking for the North Star in the southern sky.

A sense of solitude tinged with bitterness is the invariable and universal consequence in coming to terms with and breaking away from temptations and errant views. From ages past, we find people arrive at faith out of this sense of alienation. Nothing brings joy, nothing engrosses, melancholy prevails stealing any desire to talk or listen; one desires only to be left alone. This state of despair and alienation, having absolutely no one to lean on, is requisite to faith. Reflecting deeply on the common, worldly life we take

---

1 心遂醒悟. *At Last Come to the Senses* was written by Guruji immediately after Japan's defeat in WWII in the midst of the nation's agony and despair. *Shinsui-shōgo* is a phrase in *The Duration of the Life of the Tathāgata* [Chapter XVI, Lotus Sūtra] in an analogy of the father, an excellent physician, who dispenses the superb medicine to his poisoned children to cure them of their delirium of distorted views caused by the poison. Seeing that some of the children would not take the medicine, as an expedient, he leaves for a remote country and sends a messenger home to inform them, falsely, of his death. The children think they have become orphans with no one to rely on, and the profound grief and isolation bring them back to their senses.

2 Reference to the benevolent father who saves the children and brings them back to their senses from the effects of poison with the superb medicine.

for granted, we learn that nothing can truly help. Treasures and riches piled high do nothing to alleviate the profound anguish or mutability of life. Having a wife, children and kin does not change the situation, on the contrary, it creates future agonies of separation by death, which is unconsciously denied. We discover our own helplessness in life, as if adrift in a small boat, tossed about by the waves and cut off from all rescue. To begin with, what are we living for? What does life bring? There is no answer. The only thing known is the inevitability of death. If that were the case, there is no recourse but to futilely let life come to end. If we hope to prevent life's cessation, we must enter into faith, which opens the gate to immortality.

Even more so when everything deemed to give meaning to life is lost—losing a father, a child, health, riches, distinction or honor—and the hour of death and extinction bearing down at alarming speed on wheels blazing with fire is the only thing certain, the deepest, heartfelt desire is not for reason or morals but only for a powerful hand offering extrication and protection.

Among those who do not know to ask for deliverance and protection at this time, more than a few brave death and extinction by their own hand to escape the fear of death and extinction. The vast, pure vow of the Bodhisattva Perceiver of the Voices of the World[3] aims to illuminate the darkness in the hearts of living beings isolated in despair with the light of emancipation and protection for all. The Bodhisattva clearly proclaimed and expounded this vow to save all in life-threatening circumstances, from the first calamity of conflagration to the peril of assault by foes and bandits. The Bodhisattva said to rest assured in the knowledge of this rescue for this is his vow, and, therefore, not to despair. Even if judged guilty in the secular world or accused falsely when innocent, let nothing be of concern. Whether guilty or not, the Bodhisattva ensures the rescue of everyone alike, severing all

---

3   Avalokiteśvara [Sk.], Kanzeon [Jap.], Kuan-yin [Chin.].

shackles, chains, fetters and stocks used for confinement.

Because faith values standards that are also provided by morals and laws, even schools of thought emerged which focused on discipline and observing precepts. Likewise, since faith values criticism of conventional wisdom and reasoning, even schools of thought that place importance on debate and theorizing came to be. However, faith is not a moral code, a law, common knowledge nor reasoning. It is a solution to the problems of life that is far more fundamental. It is a realm that transcends all else in worldly life. It works to emancipate human beings from life's despair and alienation, imbuing a sense of renewal and rebirth in a realm that transcends all else in worldly life. Faith is built on the mutuality of receptiveness and responsiveness,[4] of emancipating and being emancipated, between the Tathāgatha and human beings.

---

4 *Kannō* 感応. *Kan* is human beings' capability to receive the Buddha's saving power, and *ō* is Buddha's saving activity; it is the Buddha's responsive activity in conjunction with human's receptivity.

7

Faith of Compassion

1947
Excerpt from *Social Life*[1]

THROUGHOUT THE HISTORY of human culture, nothing surpasses the longevity and breadth of influence in society more than religion. Politics, economics, military force, revolutions and the like that comprise an important part of society, as well as kings, ministers and men of wealth who act within it, cannot compare with religion. Lasting and widely influential, religion relies on no other power or wealth. Those who practice religious teachings strive to nurture compassion and harmony in their hearts and minds, and religion's influence comes from nothing other than the virtue of veneration and prayer by seeing the Buddha in others and treating them with kindness as though they were one's own child. This was true in the past and will remain true in the future.

Those with compassion prosper for eternity; those without will invariably fall. The practicing of compassion and its incorporation into political and social systems is crucial in social life. To evoke compassion in the hearts of the people and to have it applied in politics and the military, it is essential to widely spread the religion of compassion. This is what is meant by *Risshō-ankoku*[2] [giving rise to the true teaching to create a peaceful nation].

---

1 *Social Life* 社会生活. An unpublished manuscript by Guruji.
2 立正安国.

8

Destiny of Religion

1947[1]
Excerpt from *Social Life*

IT IS NO COINCIDENCE that all religions to some extent have an overtone of self-centeredness as seen in ritual prayers to benefit an individual, pursuit of personal peace of mind and personal salvation. At a fundamental level, it involves a deep-rooted force that responds to the needs of biological life.

The True Dharma[2] and true faith can be established even within the self-centeredly-tinged desire for self-preservation. Religion, by its nature, is not bound by the state or society, but that is not a reason for state or society to altogether reject religion. Nichiren Daishōnin stated in *Risshō-ankoku-ron*[3] that, "If one wishes to have peace for oneself, one must first pray for the tranquility of the world."[4] When we pray for tranquility between heaven and earth, be it the tranquility of a society or that of a country, we are still firmly rooted in the law of self-preservation that seeks our own sense of security. However, when a religion

---

1 Republished in the January 1987 issue of *Tenku*.
2 *Shōbō* 正法, True Dharma, the teaching of the Buddha, which conforms to the truth.
3 *Risshō-ankoku-ron* 立正安国論 [*Treatise on Giving Rise to the True Dharma to Bring Peace to the Nation*]. It was written in the first year of the Bunnō Period [1260], and was presented to the former Shogun Regent lay Priest Saimyōji Nyūdō 最明寺入道 [Hōjō Tokiyori 北条時頼], the de facto ruler of the Kamakura Shogunate.
4 The original word here is *shihyō* 四表, meaning i) the four directions of a nation, ii) between heaven and earth, i.e. the world.

inclines towards personal salvation and negates emancipation of society and nation, the more that religion prospers, the more it becomes a religion that brings ruin to the nation. On the other hand, a religion solely biased towards the emancipation of the society and nation is destined to decline.

9

Life of Benevolence

1947
Excerpt from *Social Life*

CHARLES DARWIN, the leader in the theory of evolution, stated:

> Those most adept in the struggle for survival are neither those with the greatest physical strength nor those who are most cunning in nature, but rather those who are able to bring together both the weak and the strong to mutually cooperate, knowing and practicing ways to help and save each other for the well-being of the species or group.
>
> The most prosperous that preserve their species, raising the greatest number of offspring, are groups and species with the greatest number of sympathetic and benevolent members.[1]

Dr. Chardin,[2] an evolutionist, states that the final element of success in the struggle for existence is neither violent forces of tooth and claw nor oppression of others through deception. What surmounts force, deception and all other vices is the power of benevolence. Thus, animals that mutually help each other are proven to be stronger than those that simply seek to prevail in struggles.

According to these views on communal traits of species, the human society to prosper in the future is not one with rigid

---

1 Translator's rendition from a Japanese translation of the citation.
2 Most likely this is a reference to Pierre Teilhard de Chardin.

ethics and morals, not one confused by philosophers' empty theories and sophistry, and not one of insipid science, but a society in which a true life of benevolence taught by religion giving joy and alleviating suffering is easily practiced in all aspects of society. The Communist Party, which looks up to science as its guardian deity, also does not have the ability to lead humanity into the future because of its views against religion, the teacher of true benevolence and brotherhood. While applying historical views to life and the development of society, its constant use of struggle to achieve its ends invariably prevents it from prevailing in the common biological quest for survival.

From the above scientific conclusions of the evolutionists, one could infer that Japan is at the vanguard of human civilization with its recently established policy of complete demilitarization and renunciation of the right to war.[3] Japan is in accord with the purpose of life on Earth, which is the vigorous and sustained growth of approximately 1.7 million species of life that teem throughout the sky and Earth. It gives reason to believe in the prosperity of the Japanese people who have a noble mission to fulfill. This befits the name of Yamato[4] [Great Harmony] as its role among nations and is in keeping with the national name of Hi-no-moto[5] [the land where the sun rises] in assuming Japan's proper role in the culture of humanity. From the perspective of Buddha Dharma, Japan is now given the golden opportunity to take upon itself the Bodhisattva vow to justly build the Pure Land and engage in the practice of adorning the Buddha Realm. We must galvanize our spirits to rise to this awesome task.

---

3 Here Guruji is referring to Article 9 of the newly adopted Japanese constitution that declares renouncement of arms and the right to war as means to resolve international conflict.
4 大和.
5 日の本. One of the older records of Japan appears in a letter written by Shōtoku Taishi to the Emperor of China, Yangi [569-618 second Emperor of China's Sui Dynasty 隋煬帝]."The Emperor of the land where Sun rises [nihon/hi iduru] sends a letter to the Emperor of the land where Sun sets." More on Shōtoku Taishi in *Deeply Venerate the Triple Jewel*, p. 35.

10

Parasitic Life

1947
Excerpt from *Social Life*

THOSE WHO TAKE THE VOW and leave home to shave their heads, don monastic robes owing to the germination of the Buddha seed that had been planted;[1] who first venerate the Triple Jewel,[2] beat the Dharma Drum and chant the Sublime Dharma,[3] recite sūtras, study the writings of our founding teacher,[4] read Buddhist scriptures, attend religious ceremonies, pray to console the souls of the dead are those who engage precisely in the practices called for by a monastic. This does not constitute parasitic life. Rather it is a period in monastic life when he or she nurtures the physical body that houses the Buddha for the purpose of accomplishing the practices inculcated by the Buddha. However, parasitic life begins once he or she completes the required initial training, resides in a temple as its chief monk or nun and frequents the homes of even a handful of devotees. Monastics who acquire utensils and altar fittings in addition to receiving bare sustenance can be classified as relatively less objectionable among those who lead parasitic lives. Those who go so far as to adorn the temple are competent monks who have risen above the category of parasitic existence. One

---

1 The original Japanese term is *shukuzen-kunpotsu*, 宿善薫発, which describes how good deeds and merit accumulated over past lives sprout, nurture and grow with the coming of the opportune time which manifests them. Here this sprouting references the desire to enter monkhood.
2 The Triple Jewel is the Buddha, Dharma and Sangha.
3 *Myō-hō* 妙法.
4 Nichiren Daishōnin.

trait of a parasitic monastic is to intently pursue worldly interests, such as fame and fortune within the order. It is beneath them to become the head of a hermitage or of a humble temple. Going to inconvenient remote rural places is not to their liking. Going out on a mission to spread the teachings to unfamiliar places is the last thing they want to do. There are no guarantees for food, shelter, clothing, bedding or medicine in those places where one embarks to spread the Dharma.

The only assurance one has are the Golden Words of Buddha Śākyamuni contained in the sūtras. Those with little faith only perceive the assurance provided by the words of the sūtras as fictitious. Instead, they are more concerned with possible hardships, persecution and danger that accompany these missions. These are not places worthy for those admired as esteemed monks of great virtue and rank. Only novices and inexperienced people incapable of heading temples and monasteries belong in such places. Monks of high ranking and learning are the only ones qualified to be in charge of prominent temples and to lead the masses. They are driven by self-acknowledgement that they are indeed that person, and if they don't rise to the occasion, who will? Thus, by choice, they become chief abbots of renowned, grand temples and trivialize their peers and verdant practitioners as if they were dirt or servants.

Unlike the prosperous era of Buddha Dharma when priests of high virtue and learning appeared in large numbers like bamboo and reeds, these self-conceited monks today, who have not even assumed high ranks of monkhood, think of themselves as rare scholars and indulge in vain theorizing on unparalleled mysteries that they claim are still untapped. There is not an iota of mutual respect among these ordained or harmony and compliance with the multitude.[5] Neither the ordained nor laity have any regard for these monks. Consequently, the ordained become consumed in

---

5 Compliance here is to accept and harmonize with the people. Refer to *The Practice of Non-Confrontation*, p. 10.

the struggle for fame and fortune, and ultimately become the dog-like priests preached about in the Mahāparinirvāna Sūtra. The decline of the Buddhist order starts here.

11

Buddhist Sangha

1947[1]
Excerpt from *Social Life*

WHEN OPPRESSED BY THE STATE, those who refuse to abandon the lofty ideals and aspirations of humanity invariably transcend the state and nation and stand alone to endure persecution from the world, yet remain true to these high ideals with hope. This is when life of the supraworldly[2] unfolds. It is life in a different realm, a life of building peace and culture founded on faith without succumbing to sovereign authority or bending to prevailing public opinion. This is called *gyōji*, the practice and adherence to the true life of a Buddhist mendicant monk. This life of practice is not an aimless pursuit of lofty ideals and aspirations. From the very first step, initiates are called to renounce war openly and absolutely and, on their own, to completely disarm without being obliged by anyone. Even pocketing an inch of steel for self-defense is prohibited. Such a person will spare nothing be it treasure, country, castle, spouse, children, one's own head, eyes, marrow or brain.[3] By choice, every possession is offered for Buddha Dharma and other virtuous principles to the extent that even daily food to sustain life is left up to the generosity of others.

Slander, humiliation, verbal abuse, assault by swords,

---

1 Republished in January 1988 issue of *Tenku*.
2 *Shusseken* 出世間: i) to become free from the afflictions of the Triple World and enter the state of enlightenment, or a reference to that state; ii) a practice for enlightenment in pursuit of truth.
3 Reference in Chapter XXII of the Lotus Sūtra, *Devadatta* An expression used to represent the essence or entirety of oneself that is offered.

staves and stones—even the trials of the elements or hunger and thirst—are all completely borne without a trace of rancor or mind of reprisal. Contained within the single-minded devotion to the realization of ideals is the vow not to recede. When two, three, ten, a hundred-million-billion of such individuals stepped forward, the Buddhist Sangha finally formed and covered the Earth.

Almost 3,000 years have elapsed since the inception of the Buddhist order. The Buddhist Sangha experienced vicissitudes over time, buffeted by the changes in the status quo of societies and nations. As Buddha Dharma spread to the nations of Asia, it assimilated to different lands and different realities in people's lives. At any time and any place, Buddhism remained free from secular influences, consistently making clear where it stood. The first requirement of the Buddhist order is the acceptance of and adherence to the Three Refuges and Five Precepts. The first of the Five Precepts is the precept against taking life. Any war, large or small, invariably accompanies taking the lives of humans by fellow humans. The act of mass killing of human beings is called war. The sole mission of the sorcery called science is the discovery of weapons of mass destruction and killing. Even today, some still believe in the myth that the discovery, production and securing of high performance weapons of destruction and killing are requisites to preserving peace in the world. We must open our eyes to the fact that throughout history, any advancement in the sophistication of weapons resulted in intensifying the tragedies of war.

The precept against taking life in Buddhism applies to all living beings. The [Japanese] adage that "even an insect as small as an inch has a half-inch soul" is a lesson in sparing living beings from the suffering of death. The prohibition against taking life is the honor of the Buddhist order. The prohibition against taking life has been strictly held to be the inviolable supreme objective. Considering that those [Buddhists] who believe in this supreme objective have reached approximately 10 billion today, undoubtedly the divine transcendental powers of the Tathāgata are at work. The people of India hoisted the precept against taking life as their rallying cry and made it the number one prerequisite of their freedom movement. The Indian people are proud to protect and preserve their independence without relying on the sword. In contrast, nations of the world falter and are incapable of holding an unwavering belief in the renunciation of war, the greatest cause of human anguish in this iniquitous age of strife and confrontation. In light of this stark reality, we must uphold and cling to the belief in the invaluableness of the Buddhist order's precept against taking life in the interest of the ultimate human civilization.

PART TWO

Building a Peaceful Nation

12

TRANSFORMATION

October 1950
Excerpt from *Policies for Creating a Peaceful Nation*
Hanaokayama Dōjō, Japan

NICHIREN DAISHŌNIN founded the Hokke-shū[1] as a religion to emancipate the iniquitous Era of Declining Dharma. The code to disseminate this religion and thereby plant the seed of karmic causation for enlightenment is to chant and transmit the five or seven characters of Na Mu Myō Hō Ren Ge Kyō. Characteristically, people in the iniquitous Era of Declining Dharma are said to widely commit the five deadly acts[2] or ten evil acts.[3] Cold-bloodly killing a sovereign or parent without remorse; cursing sages; disparaging religion and morality, applauding the condemnation as if it were an honorable deed. After all, no aspiration to attain Buddhahood is held by these people. The four evil realms of hell, hungry spirits, animals and *asura*[4] are seen as given conditions of social life. However, this realm of ours needs to be made tranquil and the society of humans peaceful and pure, as if it were filled with celestial beings. To that end first and foremost, we must bring radical transformation deep into the hearts and

---

1 法華宗. Also known as the Nichiren School.
2 五逆 *Gogyaku*. The five deadly acts are killing one's father, killing one's mother, killing an *arhat*, causing the Buddha's body to bleed and causing disunity in the Buddhist order.
3 十悪 *Jūgyaku*. Taking life of living beings, stealing, committing adultery, telling lies, uttering harsh words, uttering words that cause enmity between two or more persons, engaging in idle talk, greed, anger and holding distorted views.
4 Demigods. The realm of *asuras* is considered a state of constant fighting.

minds of the people. Just as darkness shuns the light and illness stymies the absorption of nutrients, people in the iniquitous era do not readily accept and have faith in the True Dharma. Instead of embracing joy and peace in their hearts and minds, people in the evil era harbor great enmity caused by hatred, malice, indignation, and covetousness. Class struggles and world wars are eruptions of the mind of enmity. The mind of great enmity originates in the depths of the human mind and heart. It is a deep-seated abomination. Unlike class struggles or world wars that employ materials and propaganda to achieve their ends, the True Dharma of Na Mu Myō Hō Ren Ge Kyō singularly employed arouses this great enmity and eradicates it. At times this is called *shakubuku* because it breaks open the solid husk that covers the hearts and minds of the people. It is also referred to as "imposed poison" since the people do not joyfully accept it. This practice [of chanting Na Mu Myō Hō Ren Ge Kyō to unwilling recipients] is called "planting the seed in the mind field of the eighth consciousness."[5] Sowed seeds always germinate. There will come a time when these people also attain Buddhahood by Na Mu Myō Hō Ren Ge Kyō. It is namely, the transformation of humanity.

---

5 *Hasshiki-shinden-no-geshu* 八識心田の下種. The eight consciousness are visual consciousness, auditory consciousness, gustatory consciousness, tactile consciousness, mental consciousness [the function of which is to discriminate objects], ego-consciousness [the function of which is to perceive the subject portion of the eighth consciousness and erroneously regard it as one's ego, thereby creating ego-attachment], and *ālaya* consciousness [the foundation consciousness of one's existence, which stores all potential energy for the mental and physical manifestations of one's existence].

13

DEEPLY VENERATE THE TRIPLE JEWEL

December 17, 1950
From the lecture *The Principle of Building A Peaceful Nation*
Fukui City, Japan

CIVILIZATION IS NOT ABOUT installing electric lights, having airplanes or producing nuclear weapons. What defines civilization in its entirety? It is not to kill; not to destroy; not to wage war. It is about people holding one another in mutual affection and respect. There is nothing else that defines a viable human civilization. The foundation for these conditions in our communal life is not to be found in the enactment of laws nor in institutions but in religious faith that nurtures tenderness and integrity in our hearts. In Article 2 of the constitution [of Seventeen Articles], Shōtoku Taishi[1] defined how to achieve a peaceful nation as envisioned in Article 1. In the interest of building a peaceful nation, Article 2 states, "Deeply venerate the Triple Jewel. The

---

1 Umayado no ōji 厩戸皇子 [574-622 A.D.], literally the prince of the stable door, is commonly known as Shōtoku Taishi 聖徳太子 [Crown Prince Shōtoku]. He was born the son of Emperor Yōmei and Empress Anahobe Hashihito no Himemiko of Tatar ancestry. He was a statesman and served as regent for the first reigning empress, Empress Suiko, during the Asuka period. He is credited with bringing peace and harmony to the Japanese nation, which was a quagmire of warring political factions in its prehistorical period, through his proclamation of Japan's first Seventeen Article Constitution. That constitution prescribed the philosophic and religious principles on which the Japanese Imperial government has been based for 1,500 years. He introduced the Buddhist religion through the founding of the Shitennōji and later Hōryuji temples; initiated scholarly pursuit with the founding of institutions of higher education; wrote many treatises such as his History of Japan; and created social programs to benefit the average citizen. From the International Buddhist University, www.shitennoji.ac.jp/ibu/english/

Triple Jewel is the Buddha, the Dharma and the Sangha. . . . How could any one in any era not hold it in high esteem?" This religion does not offer emancipation from the ills only to a certain era. No matter when it is, who it is, it impels veneration. For the sake of all sentient beings, there is no guiding principle other than the Triple Jewel, which is the Buddha, the Dharma and the Sangha.

While there are various religions in the world, if we are to create nations of genuine peace, the only viable path is profound reverence in the Triple Jewel. The Triple Jewel is the ultimate of all religions, the path that takes us to the height of human civilization. "How could any one in any era not hold it in high esteem?" The Triple Jewel remains relevant in the world today in the work of building peaceful nations, and not one of the three can be absent. Its dignity has been kept intact. The Japanese Constitution that declares renunciation of war and demilitarization was required of us by the United States. In fact, it is an expedient that came externally. Celestial beings and good guardian deities of Buddha Dharma caused this to happen because Japan, lost in a war craze that infected everyone from the Imperial family to ordinary citizens, needed to revert to the spirit of Shōtoku Taishi's constitution. What is true and imperishable illuminates all eternity.

14

THE BENEFIT OF THE BODHISATTVA NEVER DESPISE

January 27, 1951
Excerpt from *Tranquil is This Realm of Mine*
Hanaokayama Dōjō, Japan

CHAPTER XXI of the Lotus Sūtra, *The Divine Transcendental Powers of the Tathāgata* states,

> Just as the light of the sun and moon
> Can dispel the darkness,
> So this person walking through the world,
> Can disperse the gloom of the living.[1]

Light cast by the sun and moon dispels all darkness in our world. Yet, darkness in the hearts and minds of humankind, as well as darkness in our society, cannot be dispelled even with the light shed by the sun and the moon. Darkness in society, darkness that nestles in the human heart and mind can only be dispelled by the blood and tears of compassionate practitioners of the True Dharma, who bear the unbearable and accept the pains of sacrifice. Those who step up to offer themselves for this sacrifice would be the nation of India and her people, who gave birth to Buddha Śākyamuni, Nāgārjuna[2] and Vasubandhu;[3] and the nation

---

1 Translator's own rendition based on the Chinese of Kumārajīva.
2 Nāgārjuna is one of the prominent philosophers of Mahāyāna Buddhism and the propagator of Mādhyamika School of Buddhism. He was born in a brāhmana family in South India around the second or third century AD.
3 Vasubandhu, born in Purusapura, Gāndhāra [modern day Afghanistan] in the 5th century AD, was among India's prominent Buddhist philosophers.

of Japan and her people, who embraced the Genuine Dharma left by the Tathāgata and transmitted his legacy in the Era of Declining Dharma to shine the great light of liberation on the peoples afflicted by the five poisons. India is likened to the light of the moon and Japan to the light of the sun. India's mission and likewise that of Japan are not only to dispel darkness in society but also the darkness in the hearts and minds of humans, which is the cause of war in this world. Their mission is to protect life by prohibiting the taking of life.

In their mission of peace—call it nonviolence or *ahimsa*, passive resistance or not taking life—is the passive precept to forestall evil. *Tangyō-raihai* [the singular practice of bowing and venerating the Buddha in others] is the active precept of cultivating good. Killing evil humans does nothing to forestall their evil thoughts. Precisely for this reason, every trial, war and like attempts to counter evil become meaningless acts of beastly barbarity. We can dispel evil in the minds of humans, no matter how egregious, when we truly understand and venerate them at the risk of our lives.

Tangyō-raihai presumes profound faith and devout conduct and is the one and only practice that has the benefit of liberating the formidable enemies of the One Vehicle.[4] Only this act of veneration has the power to transform their errant views that pervade this iniquitous age of the Era of Declining Dharma. This is taught as the "divine benefit of the Bodhisattva Never Despise."[5]

---

4 Ichijō 一乗, Ekayāna, the One Vehicle; the single path to enlightenment. Buddha Śākyamuni emphasizes in the Lotus Sūtra that he taught many vehicles as expedients and that ultimately there is only one vehicle as revealed in the Lotus Sūtra.
5 Cited in *Kangyō-hachiman-shō* 諫暁八幡鈔 [*Remonstration of Great Bodhisattva Hachiman*] by Nichiren Daishōnin, written on December 1280 at Mount Minobu.

15

ASPIRATION FOR WORLD PEACE

September 7, 1952
Hanaokayama Dōjō, Japan

RISSHŌ-ANKOKU-RON[1] was written to forewarn and subdue[2] the calamities of war, namely, the catastrophes of imminent civil and international[3] wars about to befall Japan. All teachings and guiding principles in society that lead to war are collectively called pernicious doctrine. In that sense *Senjakushū* from the past is a pernicious doctrine,[4] as are communism of present day Soviet Union and American liberalism. Cataclysmic natural disasters are better endured than the tragedy of war. The ravages of war are the most intolerable tragedies in human society. There are aspects of natural catastrophe that cannot be prevented by human resolve and are beyond our control. However, war is never inevitable so long as human beings decide not to kill. It never happens by chance without our knowledge. War is always preventable should humanity so choose.

When war is averted, there is peace. The desire for peace and happiness in life is innate to humans, and it is the most fervent

---

1 Reference footnote 3 in *Destiny of Religion*, p. 21.
2 The original term used here is *jōbuku* 調伏, taming and subduing, controlling [evil].
3 A reference to the Mongolian invasion.
4 撰択集. Written by Hōnen in 1198, this treatise is thought to provide the core teaching of the Jōdo School. It teaches that chanting the name of the Amida Buddha is the way to enter the Pure Land following death. The translator is not certain of Guruji's intent in identifying *Senjakushū* as pernicious doctrine. Possibiliy it was considered the antithesis of *Risshō-ankoku-ron,* which places importance on the interests of the entire nation and, ultimately, the world.

longing of humanity today. The aspiration of world humanity to build peace rests now on the Great Asian continent. The aspiration of the Great Asian continent to build peace now depends on Japan. Japan's aspiration to build peace is dependent on firmly establishing the conviction of its 84 million people to relinquish arms and the right to war. This commitment to demilitarization and renunciation of war cannot come without the rise of Buddha Dharma.

16

Spiritual Pillars

April 3, 1953,
Hanaokayama Dōjō, Japan

THE NEARLY COMPLETE LOSS of spiritual pillars among individuals, societies and nations is the origin of fear and vice in the contemporary human. This is due to widely spread notions such as "knowledge is power" and "justice is predisposed by the sword." Mahatma Gandhi's criticism that "politics and economics that become distant from religious faith are like the corpse of a dog that has no other use but to be buried" is an exact reference to this. An individual, society or nation that loses its spirituality is willfully drawn into the whirlpool of struggle for existence driven by animal instinct and by blindly complying with the "law of the survival of the fittest"—the law of the jungle. Murder, destruction, rape and plunder are legitimized, and all of the various scientific discoveries and inventions are made to serve the purposes of war. Even religion and morality are used as arguments to justify war. Accordingly, not a shred of scruples or regret is shown in executing war in which even nuclear weapons—i.e., weapons of mass destruction, weapons that raze cities and are extreme in their indiscriminate brutality and inhumanity—are freely used.

In such an environment created by modern civilization, people can barely protect their own safety, and eventually there may no longer be a way for any sentient being to live on the surface of the Earth. A number of civilizations have appeared on Earth since the ancient Egyptian civilization, whose remnant is memorialized by the pyramids. Every one of these civilizations collapsed without being able to sustain themselves. Strange as it may seem, even modern civilization gives us the premonition that it has reached the apex of fear and vice, compelling us to envision the possible ultimate annihilation of humanity and the decimation of civilization.

From ancient times, just as spiritual pillars were the first to be built at the rise of every civilization, similarly, the decline of religion and morality with the destruction of spiritual pillars is a salient phenomenon that precedes the fall of every civilization. In the *Requital of Gratitude*[1] Nichiren Daishōnin illustrates this:

> The Zhou dynasty lasted 700 years because of the great emphasis King Wen[2] placed on propriety and filial piety. The short lived Qin dynasty[3] was a consequence of the tyranny of its first Emperor.

---

1 *Hōon-jō* 報恩鈔. Written on July 21, 1276 at Mount Minobu after receiving notice of the death of his master, Dōzen-bō.
2 King Wen [1099-1050, BC] was the founder of the later Zhou Dynasty in China.
3 A short dynasty with a span of 15 years, 221-207, BC.

17

THE PROMISE OF SPRING

July 1953
Excerpt from *Requisition of Land*
Shibuya Dōjō, Tōkyō

THE ENTIRE WORLD is currently frozen in a military mindset. This military mindset has served no other purpose for humanity than to create fear. Humanity is eagerly searching for an alternative path to alleviate the fear. No matter how arduous and narrow this path may be, there is no other way for humanity to rid the fear but to seek a different path. This alternative path is to elevate overall spirituality and moral values. No matter how small our influences may be, all the more because of our inadequacies, we cannot afford to be idle. We must be the vanguard of spiritual advocacy and defenders in creating peace. This is the common goal of humanity and the way to bring emancipation to the modern times. Who can believe that when the time comes, even the harshest winter that hardens everything into solid ice yields to the gentle sprouting of vegetation stirred by the spirit of creation? With the quickening of the spirit of creation, eventually ice will thaw. This heralds the beginning of spring, the winter solstice.[1] In time, winter solstice will likewise greet human society.

Just as the height of winter is the prelude to spring, the fear that shrouds humanity can be seen as a harbinger of peace, leading

---

1 The original term used here is *ichiyō-raifuku* 一陽来復, a term deriving from the Chinese I Ching, the *Book of Changes* meaning the winter solstice. According to the lunar calendar, the spirit of incipient creation starts to stir with the winter solstice.

43

to a sudden upsurge of spiritual vigor sprouting in the hearts and minds of humanity. Only with such spiritual conviction can we overcome the trials we face in this perilous time. Humanity's challenge in the latter half of the 20th century is to choose between extinction and great unity through reconciliation. It is in turn a choice of victory for violence or for human spirituality.

Haru [Spring] February 1959. Nichidatsu.

18

THE SOURCE OF PEACE

August 2, 1953
Excerpt from *Geki [Manifesto]*
Shibuya Dōjō, Tōkyō

THE TRUE SOURCE OF PEACE is not found in politics or in economics but in a heightened ethical conduct and regard for religious faith. Similarly, the true cause of war is not in politics or economics but solely in the decline of ethical practices and in the derision of religious faith. The source of peace exists within our innate Buddha-nature; the source of war, likewise, is nothing more than avarice and anger in the human heart and mind. Religion nurtures inner peace in the minds of individuals and shows the path to eradicate the source of war from the mind.

Nichiren Daishōnin called this *Kanjin-honzon*. When we are able to discern the object of reverence that is intrinsically sacred in our mind and recognize the innate divine entity that exists in our minds this very world of ours is the Eternal Pure Land, bereft from the three calamities[1] and free from the confinements of the four kalpas.[2]

---

1 They are the calamities of fire, wind and water during the kalpa [aeon] of destruction that may destroy the world.
2 The four kalpas referenced here are periods of cosmic change, i.e., the kalpas of formation, existence, destruction and non-existence. These four as a complete cycle constitute a mahākalpa [large kalpa].

PART THREE

Bodhisattva Practice

19

IGNORANT MONKS

July 21, 1955
Excerpt from *The Ill-Informed*

DO NOT KNOWINGLY ESPOUSE the Dharma unsolicited, even with some knowledge. Moreover, even when asked, do not respond to questions regarding the Dharma if the questioner holds anger in the heart and is pointlessly attempting to argue with the teachings for the sake of argument. Do not, likewise, expound the Dharma to those who are without joy on hearing it. The Odaimoku is called the quintessential Dharma of mystery[1] for it is not to be expounded indiscriminately.

There is no benefit in expounding the Dharma to ordinary beings in the Era of Declining Dharma, particularly to those with distorted views. Instead, we are to chant Na Mu Myō Hō Ren Ge Kyō, bow to them in reverence and walk away. When met with groundless arguments, abuse and violence by arrogant and conceited minds, it is wiser to avoid them and to run far away rather than to face them head-on. If our only response is to bow, show veneration, chant Na Mu Myō Hō Ren Ge Kyō and move away to avoid confrontation, the arrogant among the four groups of Buddhists[2] will invariably revile us as ignorant monks and despise us.

In the previous Era of Declining Dharma during the time of King Majestic Voice Tathāgata,[3] Bodhisattva Never Despise was

---

1 *Hiyō-no-hō* 秘要の法.
2 The four groups of Buddhists are monks, nuns, laymen and laywomen.
3 Reference made in Chapter XX of the Lotus Sūtra.

reviled as an ignorant monk by monks and others of arrogance. *Ongikuden*[4] states that, "Those like myself are also reviled and called ignorant by arrogant monks and others." When cursed as ignorant monks we are in the footsteps of these past sages, and it is by no means a disgrace. On the contrary, the monastics who are not reviled as ignorant, but rather become pretentious scholars, who behave knowingly as though they are versed in the Dharma, should truly be ashamed as disciples of Nichiren Daishōnin.

---

4 御義口伝 *Record of the Orally Transmitted Teachings*. A two-volume text attributed to Nichiren Daishōnin transcribed by a disciple during his life of seclusion at Mount Minobu, January 1, 1278.

20

The Quintessential Practice of the Lotus Sūtra

August 25, 1955
Excerpt from *Ignorant Monks*
Hanaokayama Dōjō, Japan

The quintessential practice of the Lotus Sūtra is that of *tangyō-raihai* as exemplified by the Bodhisattva Never Despise. The objects of his worship were not icons, wooden statues, nor sacred images of the various Buddhas and guardian deities. Nor were they images of Buddha Śākyamuni or sacred inscriptions. In the Era of Declining Dharma,[1] his veneration was justly directed towards wrongdoers who, affected by the most potent of the three poisons,[2] constantly engaged in conflict and verbal assaults towards the conceited[3] four kinds of Buddhists.[4] Unless these people can be made "upright in character, gentle in mind"[5] and encouraged to venerate and speak highly of one another, human life cannot possibly be peaceful and tranquil. The lifelong bodhisattva practice exemplified by Bodhisattva Never Despise was not that of building temples, enshrining Buddha statues, reciting sūtras, exegesis on the sūtras' arcane meanings, encouragement of

---

1 Buddhism was predicted to spread through three time periods: the Era of Declining Dharma [*Mappō* 末法] is the last of the three.
2 The three poisons are covetousness, anger and delusion.
3 Those who are excessively conceited with a false sense of enlightenment.
4 The four kinds of Buddhists are monks, nuns, laymen and laywomen; or male mendicants, female mendicants, male novices and female novices.
5 Citation from Chapter XVI of the Lotus Sūtra, *The Duration of the Life of the Tathāgata*.

offerings, practicing precepts or engaging in charity work. His was the singular practice of consciously bringing himself before the four groups of people, the arrogant multitiudes, who flooded the streets and to salute them with joined palms. This single practice of veneration and praise of others quells the conflagration of strife and arguments and uniquely dispirits the violence caused by arrogance and conceit. Veneration and admiration can be practiced among close friends, between mortal enemies and in the home. There is no place in this vast human community where veneration and admiration cannot be practiced. Veneration and respect for others are the essence of practicing the Lotus Sūtra, and the secret to peace in the world.

When the body bows in veneration, the mouth utters words of praise. When the body is expressing veneration and words of praise are uttered toward others, contempt and arrogance have no place in the heart. Only with humility and respect can one's body express veneration and one's mouth utter words of praise.

The teaching in the chapter *The Bodhisattva Never Despise* is to venerate and praise others by believing in the innate sacred nature that exists equally in the hearts of even supercilious men and women in the Era of Declining Dharma. What is called morality or philosophy for the most part distinguishes good from evil, but lacks the teaching of veneration of the wicked. Veneration of the wicked is the unique hallmark of the Lotus Sūtra, the practice of the quintessential Dharma that does not perceive duality of good and evil. It is the virtue of the Bodhisattva practice. An old proverb applies here: "Hold the teaching of Bodhisattva Never Despise in your hearts, utter his words and let your body emulate Bodhisattva Never Despise's veneration."

After all, the crux of the essential practice of the Lotus Sūtra is to guide us human beings, who are filled with ill karma and delusion, to attain Buddhahood as we are and to immediately transform this human world into the Pure Land.

21

Modern Enslavement

August 1955
Excerpt from *Nuclear Technologies and the Future of Humanity*

INVERSION OF THE HEAVENS and earth is the state of the Era of Declining Dharma. As predicted in the Lotus Sūtra, when people's minds become perverted, they cannot see the Buddha, "who yet remains near." People lose sight of the true savior, the entity that should be the sacred object of faith, and instead worship money as God on earth, although it was initially nothing more than a means of trade. An aberration sets in, and it seems as if people are ruled by money. Finally, in the stage of financial capitalism, individuals, the state and even the world are chained down by money, and true freedom is lost. The reason why Japan has no choice but to follow the United States is due to the shackles of financial capitalism. Workers have become slaves to machines; capitalists have become slaves to the pursuit of profit. Everyone in civilized societies has been enslaved. The sweet wine of civilization brought about such vagaries. Modern civilization is now being affected by this poison and is thrashing around in agony. The superb medicine kept by Buddha Śākyamuni specifically for the Era of Declining Dharma is the five or seven characters of Na Mu Myō Hō Ren Ge Kyō. The Lotus Sūtra states:

> This superb medicine I now leave here.
> You may take it and have no fear of not getting better.

If we were to simply chant Na Mu Myō Hō Ren Ge Kyō without

adhering to the precepts of not taking life and the practice of offering,[1] how could that possibly make us Buddha or transform this world into a Pure Land? This is the question that would naturally come to anyone's mind. The answer is, all we need to do is chant Na Mu Myō Hō Ren Ge Kyō. We must chant Na Mu Myō Hō Ren Ge Kyō for those to hear who do not chant it. We must constantly chant Na Mu Myō Hō Ren Ge Kyō with great compassion and without neglect for those who close their mouths, cover their ears and refuse to chant or hear it.

---

1 *Fuse-haramitsu* 布施波羅密 *dāna-pāramitā.*

22

PRIMAL LIFE

March 1957
From *2,500 Years after the Parinirvāna of the Buddha*
Shibuya Dōjō, Tōkyō

PRINCE SIDDHĀRTHA[1] sat cross-legged on a bed of *kuśa'* grass[2] under the bodhi tree. He severed himself from all ignorance and delusions and devoted himself to consummating the ultimate Incomparable Enlightenment. Thereby, he entered the ultimate unshakable[3] state of profound ecstasy.[4] Without employing any measures of self-sustenance or defense, he cultivated great compassion towards Māra's[5] army. The wondrous great transcendental power that subdued all of Māra's army was, in fact, Prince Siddhārtha's immeasurable compassion, which equally renders all weapons of murder and destruction useless. This transcendental power is in every human being. It is known as *shitsu-u-busshō* [Buddha-nature inherent in all sentient beings].[6]

---

1 Prince Gautama Siddhārtha, name of Buddha before renouncing the world.
2 Shade plant belonging to the lily family. It is called *kichijō-sō* [吉祥草] in Japanese. It is given this auspicious name to indicate that propitious things happen when the flowers bloom.
3 Vajra [diamond, symbolic of firmness and unshakablility].
4 *Daizenjō* 大禅定, mahā-samādhī, meaning the ultra-mundane experience translated as "absorption" or "ecstasy".
5 Māra is the personification of evil. Māra sent three daughters, Tanha [desire], Rāga [lust] and Arati [aversion] to seduce Siddhārtha into breaking his concentration and vow not to move until he found a way to eradicate suffering by achieving Annuttara Samyak Sambodhi, Unsurpassable Highest Enlightenment. Māra is the lord of misfortune, sin, destruction and death, and is the ruler of desire and death, the two evils that chain humans to the wheel of ceaseless rebirth.
6 悉有仏性.

We, bhikshus and bhikshunis, the disciples of the Buddha, have been sent to free this era 2,500 years after the Parinirvāna of the Buddha. What are we to do in the midst of Māra's great army of brutal weapons of murder and destruction starting with nuclear weapons? The sūtra expounds that, "Before long he will make a seat of grass and sit at this place of his enlightenment and subdue Māra's army."[7] We likewise need no submarines or airplanes to defeat the Māra today or, for that matter, any schemes for self-defense. We shall find shade offered by the leaves of a tree provided by nature, make ourselves a cushion out of grass found by the roadside and sit. We must beat the drum of Great Dharma while single-mindedly endeavoring to attain Great Immeasurable Compassion. Liberation from the harm of the ultimate machine of civilization is found in the ultimate "primality" of life in nature. The Lotus Sūtra clearly states that the sublime sound of the drum of Great Dharma shall subdue Māra's army and free all living beings from the ocean of old age, sickness and death.[8] In other words, it shall emancipate all living beings from the calamity and unnatural death caused by nuclear weapons.

---

7 Chapter XXIII of the Lotus Sūtra, *The Previous Life of the Medicine King*.
8 Chapter XXIII of the Lotus Sūtra, *The Previous Life of the Medicine King*.

23

GYAKKU-SHŌDAI[1]

March 1, 1957
Excerpt from *2,500 Years Following Buddha's Nirvāna*
Shibuya Dōjō, Tōkyō

ORIGINALLY, DRUMS WERE instruments to accompany songs, dances and entertainment. Becoming absorbed in the drum tends to defeat aspiration for the Way, causing one to a lapse into self-indulgence. For this reason, the Tathāgata prohibited listening to and beating the drum, and therefore, those who follow the Theravāda tradition are wary of this instrument and refrain from beating it or even hearing it from others. However, once the drum becomes the vehicle for disseminating and promoting the Great Dharma of Na Mu Myō Hō Ren Ge Kyō, it is justly the drum of the True Dharma. It resounds with the sublime reverberation of the Celestial Drum, planting the Buddha-seed and fostering the Bodhi-mind for those who respond with joy in their hearts upon hearing it; as the Poisonous Drum, it subdues all evil thoughts by severing the root of ignorance deep in the core of the heart[2] for those who respond with enmity and incur a mind of anger upon hearing it. Thus, those who beat the Great Dharma drum in the era 2,500 years following the Nirvāna of Buddha Śākyamuni are those who will, without doubt, prevail in the Dharma battle to

---

1　擊鼓唱題.　The chanting of the Odaimoku accompanied by the beating of the drum.

2　*Ganpon-no-mumyō* 元品の無明. The last category of inherent, fundamental ignorance that can only be severed by the wisdom of the Buddha.

defeat Māra.[3]

Not only are they not in violation of the precepts as bhikshus, Buddha's disciples, on the contrary, they are called precept-keepers, adhering to the rigorous code laid down in the Lotus Sūtra.[4] This is what is meant by the golden words of the Buddha, "Such a one is named precept-keeper."[5] Those who do not beat the drum of the Great Dharma 2,500 years after the Nirvāna of the Buddha are called violators of the precepts laid down in the Lotus Sūtra and would not prevail in the battle with Māra in the iniquitous Era of Declining Dharma. This is because the rules for emancipating living beings differ depending on the times. The hallmark characterizing the difference between those disciples of the Theravāda and Mahāyāna traditions are those who beat the Great Dharma drum and those who do not in the 2,500 years following the Nirvāna of the Buddha. This comes from the differences in the sūtras and disciplines that are adhered to.

The Buddha Dharma of Japan, a Mahāyāna tradition, is not marked by the chanting of the "Three Refuges and Five Precepts"[6] morning and evening, but rather by the chanting of Na Mu Myō Hō Ren Ge Kyō whether we are moving, sitting or lying down. Be it Mahāyāna or Theravāda, there is no question that the first rules observed when entering the Way of the Buddha are the Three Refuges and Five Precepts. The Buddha Dharma of Japan

---

3 *Gōma* 降魔, to quell the demons. Māra is the lord in the Realm of Desire who takes away the wisdom-life of all beings. Defeating Māra in this context is to correct and prevail over social injustice, exploitation, violence and war. The Dharma battle is engaged through beating the celestial/poisonous drum. Introduction of the Lotus Sūtra states, "And defeating the army of Māra/and beating the Dharma drum."
4 The practice of beating the drum and walking about the world based on the passage of *The Divine Transcendental Powers of the Tathāgata*.
5 Chapter XI of the Lotus Sūtra, *Beholding the Stūpa of Treasures*.
6 *Sanki-gokai* 三帰五戒. At the time of initiation, one first takes the oath of the Three Refuges and then that of the Five Precepts. The Three Refuges are: taking refuge in the Buddha, Dharma and the Sangha [the Buddhist order]. The Five Precepts are: not to kill, not to steal, not to commit adultery, not to tell lies and not to take intoxicants.

neither denies nor views the Three Refuges and Five Precepts as unnecessary. It simply does not chant the Three Refuges and Five Precepts in Pali. Based on the most profound, unsurpassed Mahāyāna teachings of the Buddha, a different kind of Three Refuges is taught[7] when taking refuge in the Buddha, Dharma and Sangha. In lieu of the five precepts, Na Mu Myō Hō Ren Ge Kyō is chanted. Na Mu Myō Hō Ren Ge Kyō embodies all the merits of Buddha Śākyamuni for preaching and emancipating every living being, as well as merits resulting from his practice as a Bodhisattva, which created cause for his enlightenment;[8] likewise, it is the merit of the precept against taking life manifested in characters. The Five Precepts in the era 2,500 years following Buddha's Nirvāna is namely the five and seven characters of Na Mu Myō Hō Ren Ge Kyō. The immeasurable life span of Buddha Śākyamuni, who always resides at the Divine Eagle Peak, is attributed to the merit of the precept against taking life, which is based on the supremely profound Mahāyāna teachings of the Buddha.

---

7 The Three Refuges are sought: in Buddha Śākyamuni, the True Teacher, who attained Enlightenment in the immeasurable kalpas in the past; in The Great Equality One Vehicle, Myō Hō Ren Ge Kyō; and in the Disciple of the Eternal Primoridal Buddha, Superior Practice [Nichiren Mahā Bodhisattva].
8 *Ingyō-katoku* 因行果徳.

24

The Teachings of Nichiren Daishōnin

October 12, 1957
On the anniversary of the death of Nichiren Daishōnin
Ikegami Dōjō, Tōkyō

WE MUST LOOK at Nichiren Daishōnin's life as a whole. *Risshō-ankoku* is the summation of his entire life. That was his life, nothing less. His was a life that sought to restore the Genuine Dharma to bring peace to the nation. When the nation is in turmoil, what can be done to save it? This is the one and only question we need to concern ourselves with throughout our lives. Any other incidentals—building temples, temple sitting, visiting devotees to perform memorial services—are all matters that lead us away from our true destiny and besmirch the very purpose behind the Bodhisattvas'[1] mandate by the Eternal Primeval Buddha to appear in the Era of Declining Dharma. We would then be no more than thieves or animals cloaked in a monk's robe. Nichiren Daishōnin never encouraged such things nor did he himself set such an example.

Nichiren Daishōnin's ardent vow to remonstrate the Shogunate and save Japan from national crisis is what prompted his return from the Land of Sado[2] to Kamakura.[3] The government

---

1 *Honge-no-bosatsu* 本化の菩薩. Reference to the Bodhisattvas Who Emerge from the Earth who are disciples of the Eternal Buddha, entrusted with the transmission of the Lotus Sūtra.
2 The current Sado Island, which is the largest island in the Sea of Japan. Nichiren Daishōnin was exiled to Sado for condemning the government.
3 Capital of Japan during the Kamakura shogunate, Japan's first samurai government, from 1185 to 1333.

solicited him to perform ritual prayers to repel the national crisis, but faith is not to be compromised. He refused to cooperate. He believed Shogun Hōjō's faith was not with the True Dharma. Nichiren Daishōnin once again left Kamakura stating that the sūtras provide limited evidence and thereby are of little persuasion,[4] but that his remonstration would be understood when Mongolia strikes Japan. Mount Minobu became his abode. He could have owned a temple had he so desired. The government's offer in return for his ritual prayers was one thousand *chō*[5] of fertile land and the position of the chief priest of Aizendō, which enshrines the deity who subdues war and evil. He did not accede. Nichiren Daishōnin spent the rest of his life in Mount Minobu in privation, enduring cold and hunger. This is what faith is.

The practice of the Lotus Sūtra is to reprove the state. I would not say that building temples is worse than becoming a thief, but it is not what the Bodhisattvas who are disciples of the Eternal Buddha are meant to do. There are much more crucial matters we need to attend to. The issue is the intangible distress of the nation as a result of the people's afflictions. Our calling is to contemplate on how to free the people of these afflictions. Whether we have the power to do so or not is beside the point. Whether or not we have the ability or influence, we must chant the Odaimoku and take on ourselves the task of resolving the crisis that confronts the nation. This is the teaching of Nichiren Daishōnin.

---

4 Buddhist theology consists of theoretical evidence, evidence in writing [sūtras] and evidence found in reality. Here Nichiren Daishōnin is indicating that sūtras cannot provide enough evidence to convince a doubting mind, yet what he predicts will be proven true when Mongolia invades Japan, providing factual evidence.
5 *Chō* is a unit of area and in those days said to be approximately 2.9 acres. One thousand *chō* signifies a large area of fertile land, ordinarily a status enjoyed by a feudal lord.

25

COMPASSION—THE PRECEPT AGAINST
TAKING LIFE[1]

July 15, 1958
Shiobara Hot Springs, Japan

THE MERIT OF THE PRECEPT against taking life, i.e., the compassionate heart and mind, protects all sentient beings. It is a moral standard so supreme that it instills fearlessness in all that lives. It transcends by far the violent immorality of so-called "self-defense." At the same time, it is the great transcendental power that disarms bitter enemies at the most fundamental level. However, even with our heart and mind of compassion, i.e., our vow to uphold the precept against taking life, it may be impossible to bring immediate repentance and transformation in those with blazing enmity or brutality. We then will risk losing our body and life because of our adherence to the precept. In that moment, whether we choose violence out of a reluctance to lose our body and life, or offer our body and life to preserve the precept of nonkilling, depends on the depth of our faith and vow toward the precept.

Every Jataka tale[2] of the Bodhisattva practice in Buddha's previous lives during three asamkhyeya-kalpas and one hundred

---

1 In May of 1958, an ethnic insurgency involving Tamils shook the nation of Sri Lanka. Udakandawala Saranankara Thero, an elder of the Sri Lankan Buddhist Sangha, wrote to Guruji for his advise, and this is an excerpt of Guruji's eight-page response.
2 *Honshōtan* or *honjōtan* 本生譚, stories on the earlier lives of Buddha Śākyamuni's practice as a Bodhisattva.

regular kalpas[3] are morals in forsaking one's flesh, limbs or life, which are all too precious to lose. King Śibi[4] offered his body to save the life of a pigeon. The flesh and limbs sacrificed by King Śibi ultimately became the sublime, indestructible diamond material body[5] of Tathāgata Śākyamuni. When such Jataka tales of a Bodhisattva are put to practice in human societies, the entire Triple World[6] becomes the domain of the Buddha. When these Jataka tales are seen as amusing fables and of no consequence by the four groups of Buddhists, then the Three Refuges and Five Precepts turn into vexing, burdensome formalities imposing useless restrictions that will certainly be lost and grow obscure for a modern humanity marked by self-indulgence and abandon. No matter how many times the Three Refuges and Five Precepts are thought and chanted morning and evening, Buddhism that is incapable of protecting human life is nothing but a fossilized corpse.

---

3 According to the Theravāda tradition, a Bodhisattva is required to practice the six *pāramitās* [charity, observing precepts, perseverance, assiduity, contemplation and wisdom] for three countless kalpas to become a Buddha and train an additional period of 100 kalpas in order to attain the 32 marks of a Buddha.

4 尸毘王. Ruler of the kingdom of Śibi known for his philanthropy.

5 *Shikishin* 色身. Physical form of a Buddha

6 *Sangai* 三界, *trayo dhātava*. The three realms of the world of transmigration where the unenlightened cannot escape from the cycles of birth and death: the realms of desire, form and non-form.

26

NIPPONZAN'S MODE OF PRACTICE

December 8, 1958
Excerpt from *Shakubuku*

THE ESSENCE OF THE LOTUS SŪTRA'S practice of
shakubuku is clearly depicted in Chapter XX of the Lotus Sūtra,
The Bodhisattva Never Despise. The mode of practice is not reading
or reciting the Lotus Sūtra or any other scriptures on the teachings
expounded by the Buddha in his lifetime, let alone becoming an
exegete or lecturing on them. It is to consciously approach anyone
we see and engage in *tangyō-raihai*. Any lecture or *shakubuku* that
does not place ultimate importance on *tangyō-raihai* is akin to
studying the analects of Confucius and having no understanding
of them.

The method of practicing *shakubuku* exemplified by
Bodhisattva Never Despise was not to slight or to scorn others,
but on the contrary, to hold profound respect for others. Bowing
in veneration with palms together[1] is the bodily expression of
this practice. Its oral component is to loudly recite the twenty-
four characters[2] of "I deeply revere you. I dare not make light of
you." The mental component of the practice is to believe in the
attainment of Buddhahood by all sentient beings.

The mode of the practice of *shakubuku* we are to inherit
is to embrace the heart and mind of non-contempt exemplified
by Bodhisattva Never Despise, to utter the *gāthā* of Bodhisattva

---

1 *Gasshō-raihai* 合掌礼拝.
2 Reference to the twenty-four Chinese characters of the passage.

Never Despise through our mouth and to express veneration emulating Bodhisattva Never Despise with our body. Having said that, we currently chant the five or seven characters of Na Mu Myō Hō Ren Ge Kyō with the same intent in place of the twenty-four characters that describe the words uttered by Bodhisattva Never Despise.

The true purpose of the birth of the Preceptor, Buddha Śākyamuni, was to edify human beings on conduct for the sake of bringing peace and tranquility to human society. The fundamentals of right and wrong had been laid down for human conduct, and the Buddha beseeched us to take the vow to do good and to cease doing wrong. These are the precepts laid down in Buddha Dharma. Some precepts are meant solely for the ordained and others apply to all, from kings and ministers to the general public. Precepts are external rules of conduct. Buddha therefore specifically opened the gate to the teaching of contemplation[3] to discipline the mind against self-indulgence and against the inability to quieten the mind, thereby showing the path to enhancing life through contemplation. This is the teaching of wisdom.[4] Buddhist teachings are categorized into the three disciplines of precepts, meditation and wisdom. However, all three disciplines originate, are sustained by and culminate in one's ardent faith. All sentient beings indisputably become Buddha. This was Bodhisattva Never Despise's faith. It was, at the same time, Bodhisattva Never Despise's wisdom. *Tangyō-raihai* is Bodhisattva Never Despise's way of practicing the precepts. The passage of the sūtra that consists of twenty-four characters, "I deeply revere you..." was the contemplation cultivated and advocated by Bodhisattva Never Despise.

How are we to dispel the pervasive terror of our time in

---

3 *Zenjo*, 禅定 *dhyāna*. Contemplation or meditation. Sometimes it is understood as an ultra-mundane experience and translated as "absorption" or "ecstasy."
4 *Prajñā*. One of the six pāramitās. The mental function that enables one to perceive without error and to distinguish between what is true and what is false.

the Era of Declining Dharma, which is entrenched in strife and confrontation? We must practice *tangyō-raihai* before we ever fight; we must invoke the belief that all enemies will eventually become Buddha before fearing their weapons; and we must enunciate our profound respect towards our enemies before harboring resentment or hatred against them. As such, the Bodhisattva Never Despise's mode of practice is true to the reason for Buddha's advent in bringing emancipation to the evil age of five defilements.[5] This is precisely the mode of practice at Nipponzan Myōhōji.

---

5 *Gojoku* 五濁. The five defilements are: i) defilement of the period; ii) defilement of views; iii) defilement by evil passions; iv) defilement of sentient beings and; v) shortening of life.

27

Resurrection

January 1, 1959
Article from Shizuoka Newspaper, Japan

THE LIBATION DRINK for celebrating good luck on New Years day is called *otoso*, which signifies a drink that resurrects even the dead. It is for this reason it is taken at the beginning of the year as a good medicine for rejuvenation and longevity. Resurrection is the greatest of man's physical desires.

Chanting Na Mu Myō Hō Ren Ge Kyō is the tenet of Nichiren Daishōnin. Among the various titles of sūtras delivered by Buddha Śākyamuni, we find the prefix of *dai*, meaning great or large, including the Great Perfect Wisdom Sūtra[1] and the Sūtra on the Buddha of Eternal Life,[2] but no other [except the Sūtra of the Lotus Flower of the Sublime Dharma] incorporates the word "*myō*" [ineffable, sublime]. It is explicated that all of these various sūtras are for treating those that are living and possess a mind; they cannot treat those without a mind or the dead. It is also said that the title of Sublime Dharma is bestowed on the Lotus Sūtra for its ability to thoroughly treat not only those living beings with a mind, but to equally treat the dead or those without a mind.

---

1 Dai-hannya-kyō 大般若経 Mahāprajñāpāramitā Sūtra. It is a collection of sixteen sūtras, both short and long, which set forth the doctrine of *prajñapāramitā*, i.e., Perfection of Wisdom.
2 Dai-muryōgi-kyō 大無量寿経 The Larger Sukhāvati-vyūha. The principle sūtra in the Jōdo-shū [Pure Land School], which describes the vows of Buddha Amida.

To chant the "*myōhō*"[3] [sublime Dharma] reflects the spiritual aspiration of human beings that seek immortality. The ill-fated threat of imminent destruction of humanity's approximately two billion abounds from the Arctic Circle and well beyond into outer space. Modern civilization, including its science, politics and military power, lacks the means to eliminate this threat. Transforming the heart and mind of individuals, in other words, the unseen spirit of each and every one of us, is the only means that can make it happen.

---

3 妙法.

28

Convulsion of Nature

On the first anniversary of the Kano River disaster[1]
October 10, 1959
Mishima Dōjō, Japan

IN LIGHT OF THE ever-escalating damages caused by extraordinary natural disasters in recent years and days, we cannot be satisfied with simply devising countermeasures. We must prevent the ultimate calamity—acts of war—which inevitably follows scourges of unprecedented natural convulsion as its portent. All acts of war arise from a single thought in the heart and mind of man and are executed through the hands and feet of man. When compassion, which values the lives of others and laments their anguish, awakens in the heart and mind, acts of war will eventually cease. A mechanism to evoke compassion in the hearts and minds of men needs to be built and measures taken to prevent war in our societies. People must take the initiative to cultivate compassion in their own hearts and minds.

Despite potential shortcomings or harm Buddhism may have, its essence is nothing other than to teach compassion and to provide guidance for a social life that never condones murder or destruction. This is called the precept of not taking life.[2] If we fail to adopt radical spiritual measures at this time, I am deeply concerned that the future of Japan, or for that matter, the future of world humanity, might be that of destruction and annihilation.

---

1 Flood disaster of Kano River in Izu Peninsular in September 1958 caused by a typhoon resulting in deaths of over a thousand people.
2 *Fusesshō-kai* 不殺生戒 *ahimsā* [Sk].

29

A Good Dream

January 31, 1966
Kudan Dōjō, Tōkyō

GANDHIJI WROTE that people might say he's dreaming upon hearing that independence can be achieved through peaceful means. To the contemporary mind it sounds like nothing more than a dream. He did not mind that it was a dream. It was as if he was seeing a dream while awake in broad daylight: an awakened, noble dream. It was an exalted dream of humanity prospering into the future. He encouraged his people to dream, to hold a good dream, so that they may feel their morality soar instead of being encumbered by the hardships of exploitation and enslavement.

It was truly a dream in those days. Independence without firing a single bullet, without killing a single person in the oppressive, ruling colonial power was truly just a dream in the history of revolutions in this world. Gandhiji made that dream come true. Its virtue is overwhelming. It is an enormous beacon that illuminates the path to be taken by humanity.

Buddhism is a world of dreams. Nichiren Daishōnin said that a nation would become peaceful by the chanting of Na Mu Myō Hō Ren Ge Kyō. No one believed such a thing. Believing it was a dream. But this dream was one with the clear objective that by chanting Na Mu Myō Hō Ren Ge Kyō peace would be brought to the nation and to the world. No one can rule out the possibility of this dream coming true. When we look around to see what other paths are realistically available to make this world a peaceful place, killing is all we actually see.

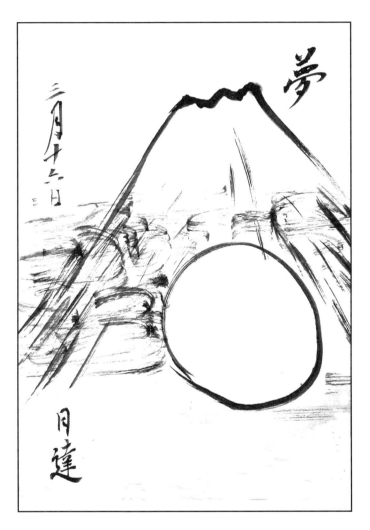

Yume [Dream] March 16. Nichidatsu.

30

THE BODHISATTVAS WHO EMERGE
FROM THE EARTH—1

May 25, 1966
Kudan Dōjō, Tōkyō

UPON THE REALIZATION of his mission as Bodhisattva Superior Practice, Nichiren Daishōnin initiated the chanting of the Odaimoku.[1] In *Letter to Reverend Myōmitsu*[2] he writes, "What caused me to start to chant? I began to utter Na Mu Myō Hō Ren Ge Kyō as though I was speaking in my dreams, without being fully conscious of what I was doing. Whether it is ultimately a good thing or not, neither I nor anyone else knows for sure."

I also have learned to chant the Odaimoku, but it came to me naturally. It was not something I arrived at after elaborate theorization. I just came to chant the Odaimoku unbidden. Digressing from the Odaimoku for a moment, I heard of Nichiren Daishōnin's reputation as a great man. I thought it would be fascinating to study about him, and that naturally became my motivation to become a monastic, not that I had a genuine appreciation for the Odaimoku. Once I joined a temple with the Nichiren School, chanting the Odaimoku was required. Without

---

1 In Chapter XV of the Lotus Sūtra, *Bodhisattvas Who Emerge From the Earth*, when Maitreya [who is assured to succeed Buddha Śākyamuni] and other Bodhisattvas asked the Buddha to entrust them with the task of spreading the Lotus Sūtra after the Nirvāna of the Buddha, innumerable Bodhisattvas headed by Bodhisattva Superior Practice emerged from openings in the earth. The Buddha commissioned these Bodhisattvas, who were revealed to be Buddha's disciples from the immeasurable kalpas past, with this task after his passing.
2 A letter written in 1276 to Reverend Myōmitsu, a devotee who supported Nichiren Daishōnin through his time in Mount Minobu.

really knowing whether it was a good thing or not, I chanted it because that is what was done. That was how it was. It is about *en* [karmic connection]. I started to chant not because I was able to intellectually comprehend it with what I know in this lifetime, but it was something I came to do naturally. This is taught as residual connection[3] created in our past lives. There is a limit to things we can comprehend based on knowledge of this life alone.

I started to chant the Odaimoku for reasons I am not even aware. Once I started, I found no reason to stop and have continued to chant. That is how it is. If it were through wisdom we come to chant, there are those who are wiser than us, yet they do not chant. The Odaimoku cannot be chanted through intellect. There are people who lecture on the Lotus Sūtra, and still these people are unable to chant the Odaimoku.

The chanting of the Odaimoku is said to be the good karmic consequence from our past lives. Ososhi-sama[4] said that those who are thus graced are the Bodhisattvas Who Emerge From the Earth. "The Daimoku is hard to chant if not for the advent of the Bodhisattvas Who Emerge From the Earth." Whether temporarily or in one's sleep, the chanting of the Odaimoku is the work of none other than the Bodhisattvas Who Emerge From the Earth.

We are born into the transitory world of humans. However, when we chant the Odaimoku, whether temporarily or in our dreams, if we believe in the words of Nichiren Daishōnin, we are ourselves one of the Bodhisattvas Who Emerge From the Earth. In a world entrenched in evil in the Era of Declining Dharma, the Bodhisattvas Who Emerge From the Earth are entrusted with the mission to transform our *shaba*[5] world into the Pure Land. "The

---

3 *Shukuen* 宿縁. Relationships from past lives.
4 御祖師様. A reference to the founder of a school of Buddhism, i.e., Nichiren Daishōnin.
5 娑婆. Transliteration of the Sanskrit word *sahā*, "endurance"; also translated *a nindo* 忍土, "the land of endurance," the world in which Lord Buddha preaches the Dharma; the world we live in, where people must endure various afflictions and pain.

Daimoku is hard to chant if not for the advent of the Bodhisattvas Who Emerge From the Earth." Nichiren Daishōnin firmly believed in these words of his. We, too, must believe in them.

When this can be done, no matter how foolish we may be in flesh, we are able to chant the Odaimoku, which is to be spread by Bodhisattva Superior Practice to bring peace to our domain and its people in the turbid Era of Declining Dharma. That is what proves the advent of the Bodhisattvas Who Emerge From the Earth.

As long as we chant the Odaimoku, we must have unfaltering faith in the True Dharma of *Risshō-ankoku* and be well prepared to extricate the people from the afflictions of this world. The inexplicable blessings of the Odaimoku can be appreciated if we consider that to be the mission that brought us to this world, a promise waiting to be fulfilled. When we ponder on the intent of Lord Buddha leaving the Odaimoku for the present Era of Declining Dharma and the significance of Nichiren Daishōnin appearing in this world, what are we to do but chant the Odaimoku, which is hard to do except for the retinue of the Bodhisattvas Who Emerge From the Earth? We must bring liberation from the sufferings of this world and shed light on its darkness as shown in the teachings of *Risshō-ankoku*.

31

Bodhisattva Practice

June 4, 1966
Kudan Dōjō, Tōkyō

THE BODHISATTVA PRACTICE in Buddha Dharma is to feel the anguish of the people firsthand and to reflect on a way to free them from their suffering. However, there is not much we can do standing alone in the midst of demons wielding the power of military and economic might. Yet one thing we can do is to pray. No matter how rampant the forces of demons may be, we shall spread the just path of emancipation of Lord Buddha. With this single act of chanting Na Mu Myō Hō Ren Ge Kyō, we can pray, pray and continue to chant until we draw our last breath without yielding to power, economic might or any other obstruction. This is not like chanting a simple song. "I, Nichiren, do not cry, but my tears flow incessantly."[1] These tears embodied through our voice become Na Mu Myō Hō Ren Ge Kyō. When realizing that our body must serve in finding the path of emancipation from suffering for the people of the world, we are then capable of sustaining our chant of this phrase of prayer wherever we are in the ocean of suffering.

---

1 *Shohō-jissō-shō* 諸法実相鈔 [*The True Aspect of Existence*]. Written by Nichiren Daishōnin on May 17, 1273 addressed to Sairen-bō from Sado Island.

32

Entering Monkhood

March 30, 1968
Kiyosumi Dōjō, Japan

THE POLICY of the Meiji government[1] was to enrich the nation and to possess a strong military.[2] It maintained that farming brings affluence to the nation. I therefore entered an agricultural school with the intention of becoming a farmer and growing lots of rice. As I was studying, I became torn between spending the rest of my life farming or pursuing something even more worthwhile. An instructor of the agricultural school was a graduate of the Sapporo College of Agriculture.[3]

Dr. Clark,[4] who came from America, founded the Sapporo College of Agriculture and became its first president. All he brought with him were Bibles. Someone asked him what he would teach. He said he would teach the Bible. "Anything else?" "Nothing else." The Bible was all he taught. Among his students were those who later became top Christian leaders of the Meiji era including Kanzō Uchimura.[5] When students visited Dr. Clark, he would talk

---

1   Japan's government from 1567-1911. This period marked a transition from a feudal warrior society to a modern society modeling the West.
2   *Fukoku-kyōhei* 富国強兵.
3   Sapporo College of Agriculture is the present day University of Hokkaido.
4   William Smith Clark [1826-1886] was the third president of Massachusetts Agricultural College [the present day University of Massachusetts] from 1867 to 1879. He was invited to Japan by its government from July 1876 to May 1877 during his sabbatical to help establish the Imperial Agriculture College in Sapporo and became its first president.
5   内村鑑三 [1861-1930]. Founder of the No-church Christianity movement and intellectual of the Meiji and Taishō era [1911-1925].

to them about the teachings of Jesus Christ instead of farming. Students listened with fascination. Kanzō Uchimura thought very highly of Nichiren Daishōnin's *Risshō-ankoku-ron*. He came to believe that Nichiren Daishōnin was an unrivalled prophet in the world. He had thought there were no prophets among Japanese Buddhists. But goodness! Nichiren Daishōnin was the greatest prophet he had ever known! This was absolutely amazing to him.

After I read something to that effect, my views gradually changed. I realized that be it growing rice or researching insects, these are all decent things to do; there are many good things I could be doing in life. But studying Nichiren Daishōnin was even better. With this realization I lost interest in producing rice. I wasted no time in going to a temple and became a novice monk.

33

NONVIOLENCE IN ACTION

May 25, 1968
Excerpt from an article in *Buddhist Times*, Tōkyō

NOTHING IS RESOLVED by policies favoring war. Having said that, putting nonviolence into practice is not for the timid of heart. The martyred Dr. Martin Luther King was a believer in Gandhiji. Nonviolence demands extraordinary courage. It takes uncompromising faith in human beings and unwavering confidence in spiritual values to believe that there is Buddha-nature even in evil men and a resolve to sacrifice oneself for them. It requires dauntlessness that refuses to succumb in the face of power. It is a path beset with hardship. Just as in the analogy in the Lotus Sūtra of the wealthy man whose house is on fire, there is only one gate from which we can escape. This single gate open for humanity to escape the conflagration that consumes the threefold world[1] is none other than nonviolence. However, for the wealthy man with all his powers, dragging the children out of the burning house was not what would save them. That is the nature of religion. The path for genuine universal liberation is there for humanity to choose with courage, faith in humanity and spiritual values.

---

1 *Sangai* 三界, *trayo dhātava*. The world of unenlightened human beings, divided into three worlds: the world of desire, the world of form, and the formless world.

PART FOUR

Buddha Dharma of Japan

34

Odaimoku—1

September 9, 1968
Kiyosumi Dōjō, Japan

According to Ososhi-sama,[1] those who keep the Lotus Sūtra in the Era of Declining Dharma are Bodhisattvas Who Emerge From the Earth entrusted with a special mission. These true disciples of Lord Buddha from infinite past kalpas who had accepted the task of bringing emancipation to sentient beings in the Era of Declining Dharma are born into this age assuming the appearance of human beings. When we come to a profound appreciation of our revered mission of liberating the people of this era through chanting the Odaimoku, we are inspired to go about the worlds in the ten directions[2] chanting the Odaimoku, even for a day.

One of the joys taught in Buddha Dharma is the joy of pondering on matters like this. It is known as "tranquil bliss."[3] Among the people we meet will be those who find pleasure in chanting the Odaimoku. We shall share the joy by chanting the Odaimoku with them. When I am in India simply beating the drum, the Indian people more than any others feel an affinity towards me. Even in the United States people start to have empathy with me when I chant the Odaimoku. No matter where we go, no

---

1   Nichiren Daishōnin. Refer to footnote 4 in *Bodhisattvas Who Emerge From the Earth—1*, p. 73.
2   *Jippō-sekai* 十方世界, the worlds in the ten directions, i.e., the four cardinal points, the four intermediate directions, and up and down.
3   *Jakumetsu-no-raku* 寂滅の楽, tranquil bliss.

one objects when the Odaimoku is chanted with absolute faith in its service to the world. We shall persevere. In time there will be people who greet it with joy. That is what it means to be Buddha's disciple designated with this task from the immeasurable past. We must save this world together with these people who are joyous in hearing the Odaimoku. By save, I'm not referring to politics. All we do is to walk about chanting the Odaimoku. Nipponzan's job is to have unyielding faith in the Odaimoku. It does not matter who you are or who you become to spread the Odaimoku but just to chant it. This should be our one and only joy. When we go against the will of the guardian deities and incur their displeasure, it will be of no avail no matter how hard we work. Unless we are completely immersed in faith for the Odaimoku and engage our bodies in the Bodhisattva practice—stūpas will not be built by skill alone! At present I am no longer of much service to anyone. But just by chanting the Odaimoku, it shall spread. As it spreads, we would have to start building a makeshift hut. Once it is completed, a stūpa then needs to be built. These are all means of expedience to guide the people to the Dharma. Our only true focus is to spread the Odaimoku. The members of Nipponzan are in a position to freely go wherever they so choose to spread it. We will chant the Odaimoku until we draw our last breath and make that our joy. Where we go or where we die is of no concern.

Buddha Dharma of Japan—1

December 10, 1969

ONE WHO CHANTS Na Mu Myō Hō Ren Ge Kyō through the mouth, beats Na Mu Myō Hō Ren Ge Kyō with the hand drum, venerates with Na Mu Myō Hō Ren Ge Kyō though the body and holds Na Mu Myō Hō Ren Ge Kyō in the mind and heart with profound veneration; who walks through villages and cities, circulating back and forth through the worlds of ten directions, solely praying for *Risshō-ankoku*, this one is a practitioner of the Buddha Dharma of Japan. Buddha Dharma of Japan is the teachings of the Buddha first chanted and spread by Nichiren Daishōnin in Japan more than 750 years ago. Generally, the five or seven characters of Na Mu Myō Hō Ren Ge Kyō are said to be the title of a sūtra named Lotus Flower of the Sublime Dharma, yet it is nothing of the sort. It is expounded in the chapter of *The Divine Transcendental Powers of the Tathāgata* of the Lotus Sūtra that "all the teachings of the Tathāgata, all the sovereign transcendental powers of the Tathāgata, all the ineffable essential treasuries of the Tathāgata and all the profound workings of the Tathāgata, are all proclaimed, demonstrated, revealed and expounded" in the five or seven characters of Na Mu Myō Hō Ren Ge Kyō. Na Mu Myō Hō Ren Ge Kyō is the sum total of the arcane, sovereign, transcendental powers of the Tathāgata. It is an exceedingly profound Dharma imparted to Nichiren Daishōnin as the five or seven characters of Na Mu Myō Hō Ren Ge Kyō by the Preceptor, Buddha Śākyamuni, out of boundless compassion to accommodate the infants, meaning the ordinary humans of the Era of Declining Dharma, with a Dharma that can be readily received and kept.

36

The Great Mandala of Ten Realms of Beings[1]

Autumn Equinox, 1971
Excerpt from *Sandai-Hihō-Mondō-Shō*[2]
Rajgir Dōjō, India

THE GOHONZON[3] delineated in calligraphy by Nichiren Daishōnin embodies the following two passages from the *gāthā* in *The Duration of the Life of the Tathāgata* of the Lotus Sūtra:

Then I together with all the Sangha
Appear on the Divine Eagle Peak.

As such, this Gohonzon encompasses the spheres of all sentient beings[4] as well as the realm of non-sentient beings.[5] It is all encompassing including self and others, the four holy ones[6] and the six worlds.[7] It is a great mandala depicting the ten realms of existence exactly like the actual world we live in. We must recognize and venerate the Buddha-nature and the Buddha-body within the people who harm, kill and are avaricious, living in states such as

---

1 The ten realms of existence are hell, the worlds of hungry spirits, animals, *asura* [a demon fond of fighting by its nature], human beings, celestial beings and deities, the worlds of Shōmon [*srāvakas*: disciples of the Buddha who attained the stage of arhat], Engaku [*pratyekabuddhas*: solitary Buddhas], Bodhisattvas and Buddhas.
2　三大秘法問答鈔. *Questions and Answers on the Great Dharma of Three Mysteries.*
3 Honzon is the principle object of veneration.
4 *Shujō-seken*, 衆生世間.
5 *Kokudo-seken*, 国土世間.
6 *Shishō*, 四聖, the four kinds of sages, i.e., *srāvaka, pratyekabuddha*, bodhisattva and Buddha.
7 *Rokudō*, 六道, the six worlds in which the souls of living beings transmigrate: hell, the worlds of hungry spirits, animals, *asuras*, human beings and the heavens.

those of the hungry spirits or animals.

This *sahā* world we live in is replete with suffering caused by the cycle of birth, illness, aging and death as well as war, plunder, power and oppression. These various afflictions are shadow images painted by the brushes of delusions and perversion in one's own mind. When the delusions causing plunder and killing cease, this very domain of ours is inherently the Land of Eternal Tranquil Light.[8] "Tranquil is this realm of mine"[9] is the original state of this *sahā* world. If the United States were to withdraw all of its troops from Vietnam, the heavens and earth of Indochina are peaceful as they are. As such, the great mandala revealed by Nichiren Daishōnin depicts the genuine form and mind of the ten realms of existence as a Honzon for us to embrace and venerate. That is to say, Nichiren Daishōnin's great mandala of the ten realms of existence is a representation showing us that the domain we live in is essentially the Land of Eternal Tranquil Light, a sacred place, and that the people who live there fundamentally deserve veneration.

---

8 *Jakkōdo* 寂光土. According to Tendai Daishi [founder of Ti'en-Ta'i School of Buddhism] this "Land of Eternal Tranquil Light" implies it is eternal because Buddha Dharma is eternal, tranquil because it is bereft of delusion and suffering, and light, which signifies wisdom.
9 The Lotus Sūtra, Chapter XVI, *The Duration of the Life of the Tathāgata.*

37

THE TROUBLE WITH FAME AND FORTUNE

January 6, 1973
Orissa Dōjō, India

FAME AND FORTUNE are common causes of trouble in the secular world. They also make their way into Buddha Dharma. The true meaning of the Buddha Dharma is destroyed by attachment to money, but compromising for public acclaim holds the danger of the Buddha Dharma becoming a tool for fame and power. We must be on guard. History shows that even monks of high rank or virtue who come to serve the interest of the government are fleeting in their influence. Religion must continue to live on in the minds and hearts of the people. Praise and reputation gained through compromise with power do not resonate with the people.

What really touches the minds and hearts of others in religion are the inner hardships that are endured by those who practice the teachings. When this is felt heart to heart, religion lives on. Whether we can build stūpas or temples is irrelevant. There is no need to go out of our way to find acquaintance with presidents, prime ministers or the like. All we are to do is to hone ourselves on spiritual issues at all times. If our minds and hearts are distorted, arrogant or "dissolute and set on the five desires,"[1] no matter whether the president comes or the prime minister comes, what we do is no longer Buddha Dharma. It is a matter of the mind and heart. We must be vigilant.

---

1 Chapter XVI of the Lotus Sūtra, *The Duration of the Life of the Tathāgata*.

38

THE ETERNAL AND EVER PRESENT TRIPLE JEWEL

February 25, 1973
From the speech given at the Land Breaking Ceremony
of the Lumbini Stūpa, Nepal

STŪPAS, WHICH ENSHRINE the relics of the Buddha, Buddha halls[1] that enshrine Buddha statues and scriptures, and the Sangha[2] that serves stūpas and Buddha statues as well as reciting sūtras, are the three prerequisites for the restoration of the Buddha Dharma. Even if Buddha statues and scriptures exist, without the Sangha jewel to serve, study and disseminate the Buddha Dharma, it will not flourish and be spread through the Era of Genuine Dharma, the Era of Counterfeit Dharma and the Era of Declining Dharma. The Sangha jewel is likened to firewood, and the benefits of the Buddha Dharma are like fire. Without the Sangha jewel, stūpas, Buddha statues and canons of scriptures cannot benefit the people. Similarly, the Sangha is akin to the earth, and stūpas, Buddha statues, and sūtras are like trees and grass. Without the Sangha jewel, Buddha Dharma will not be able to provide its benefit to sentient beings. The three jewels combined —the Buddha, the Dharma and the Sangha—are referred to as the one and inseparable Triple Jewel. When the Triple Jewel is one and intact, Buddha Dharma becomes eternal and ever present. This is taught as "The Ever Present Triple Jewel."[3]

"The Ever Present Triple Jewel" is an assurance that no

---

1 *Butsuden* 仏殿, caityas.
2 Monastic community 僧伽.
3 *Jōjyū-sanbō* 常住三宝.

matter how great suffering and affliction may be in the human world, no matter how imminent the threat of humanity's extinction may be, the power to extricate ourselves will always be there. The means to bring refuge will always be there, and human beings instrumental in bringing refuge will always come forward.

39

KŌKUYŌ-SHARI
MAKE OFFERINGS TO MY ŚARĪRA[1] FAR AND WIDE[2]

August 6, 1973
Rajgir Dōjō, India

THE CHAPTER OF *The Bodhisattva Medicine King* in the
Lotus Sūtra says:

> My good son! I commit the Buddha Dharma to you.
> . . . I also entrust to you any relics that may remain after
> my extinction. Let them be disseminated and offerings
> made to them far and wide. Let some thousands of
> stūpas be erected.[3]

From his birth in Lumbini Gardens to his passing at Kushinagara,
the Preceptor, Buddha Śākyamuni, universally benefited sentient
beings in the entire Indian continent with the Dharma expounded
during his life of 80 years. However, the great compassion of the
Tathāgata[4] was not limited to his guidance extended over those 80
years. It has and will continue to offer refuge to all sentient beings
from distress, sorrow, suffering and affliction throughout the one
thousand years of the Era of Genuine Dharma, one thousand
years of the Era of Counterfeit Dharma and ten thousand years of
the Era of Declining Dharma following the Buddha's Parinirvāna.[5]

---

1 *Shari* 舍利, relics of Buddha Śākyamuni.
2 Chapter XVI of the Lotus Sūtra.
3 Chapter XXII of the Lotus Sūtra.
4 Thus Come One or Thus Gone One.
5 This idea of "ten thousand years of the Era of Declining Dharma" was proposed
by Nangaku [Chinese. Nan- yueh or Hui- ssu 慧思], the second patriarch of the

The Buddha left behind two Tathāgata-bodies[6] to benefit sentient beings. One is Buddha's teaching called Dharma-body *śarīra*.[7] The Dharma-body is embraced, recited, explicated and transcribed from sūtras. The second Tathāgata-body is the physical *śarīra*,[8] Tathāgata's bodily relics. The physical *śarīra* is widely enshrined in stūpas in many countries and receives veneration and offerings.

The chapter *On the Nature of the Tathāgata* of the Mahāparinirvāna Sūtra says:

> If one desires to venerate the Dharma-body *śarīra*, one must venerate the stūpas of the various Buddhas. Why? It is out of the wish to guide and emancipate all sentient beings. [9]

One who merely recites and explicates the Buddhist canon, claiming them to be the way to honor the Dharma-body *śarīra*, is prone to lose sight that the Dharma is made sacred by the one who expounded it and consequently fails to venerate stūpas that enshrine the relics of the Preceptor, Buddha Śākyamuni. One who does not venerate the stūpa enshrining the relics of the Buddha is eventually liable to lose deference for the Dharma-body *śarīra*, meaning the sūtras, and runs the risk of aimlessly reading and reciting the sūtras, making them a tool for hollow arguments.

Chapter XI of Mahāprajñāpāramita-śāstra[10] says:

> Question: Those such as Devadatta[11] and Hata[12] also

Chinese Ti'en-T'ai school of Buddhism in Sui Dynasty.

6 *Nyorai-shin*, 如来身,Tathāgata-kāyā.

7 *Hosshin-shari* 法身舎利.

8 Saishin-shari 砕身舎利. The term in Japanese denotes fragmented bodily relics.

9 Translator's version.

10 *Ta-chih-tu-lun* [*Commentary to The Great Perfection Wisdom Sūtra*]. A 100-fascicle commentary on the Mahāparañāramitā-sūtra attributed to Nāgārjuna and translated by Kumārajīva into Chinese.

11 A cousin of the Buddha Śākyamuni. He was initially a follower but later left the order and attempted to take Buddha's life by sending a fierce elephant to trample him.

12 A disciple of Buddha Śākyamuni who was known to say one thing but

preached the Tripitaka,[13] Shizō,[14] Śrāvaka Dharma[15] and the teachings of Mahāyāna. Nevertheless, they went to hell. How could this be?

Answer: Devadatta had seriously distorted views.[16] Hata was guilty of false talk. Their preaching was not a pure offering of Dharma in the interest of the Way. They taught out of interest in winning recognition, respect and offerings. Devadatta fell to hell alive for his evil thoughts; and Hata fell to the evil path upon his death. Furthermore, to expound the teachings of the Buddha by mouth alone is not *Dharma-dāna* [the offering of expounding the Dharma].[17] *Dharma-dāna* is to always expound the Dharma to all with a pure and good heart. Just as offerings of materials are not called precious virtues unless given with a pure heart, so is *Dharma-dāna*. It is not *Dharma-dāna* unless offered with a pure and good heart.

In this connection I would like to point out the following to those who profess faith in the Mahāyāna teachings, claiming to venerate the Dharma-body *śarīra*. One may study Tripitaka and Shizō, preach to others based on Śrāvaka Pitka from early Buddhism and Mahāyāna Bodhisattva scriptures known as the genuine

---

immediately contradict himself. The Translator could not identify the name of 呵 多 [Hastaka? Hata?].

13 The three branches of the Buddhist scriptures, including sūtras [teachings], vinaya [monastic code] and abhidharma [commentaries]. It refers to the entire collection of Buddhist writings.

14 *Tripitaka* and *dhārani* together make *Shizō* 四蔵. *Dhāranī* are mystic syllables that sustain and protect those who recite them.

15 *Śrāvaka* means a disciple of the Buddha. Those who listen to the Buddha's teaching and attain enlightenment.

16 *Jyaken* 邪見, *mithyā-drsti*. A point of view, which negates the law of cause and effect. Accordingly, the theory of the four noble truths is not accepted.

17 *Hōse* 法施, *Dharma-dāna*. One of the three offerings, which are material, spiritual and fearlessness [almsgiving, expounding the Dharma and bestowing confidence].

Kōkuyō-shari [Make Offerings to My Śarīra Far and Wide] Nichidatsu.

Single Buddha Vehicle,[18] but if one derides the stūpas enshrining Buddha's physical *śarīra*, not venerating and worshiping them but instead speaks ill of them, one would be following the footsteps of Devadatta, and is doomed to fall into incessant hell.

The chapter of *The Bodhisattva Lion Roar* in the Mahāparinirvāna Sūtra says:

> If [Buddha's] body was that of miraculous birth,[19] how could there be bodily relics? The Tathāgata breaks his body into pieces and offers his fragmented ashes to nurture the virtues of sentient beings. This is the reason why the Tathāgata does not assume a transformed body. Not a single Buddha among the various Buddhas goes through metamorphic birth.

If the eternal, ever-present Tathāgata-body that resides in this world is a theoretical, non-substantial void, then sentient beings would not be able to see or hear it deliver the Dharma and have it cause them to make offerings. The reason for the Buddha leaving his physical *śarīra* is so that stūpas may be erected to nurture the virtues of all sentient beings after his passing through their veneration and offerings. The era when people no longer embrace, read and recite the sūtras—the Dharma-body *śarīra* of the Tathāgata—is called "the era of concealment of Buddha Dharma."[20] When there are no longer people who venerate and make offerings to stūpas, it is referred to as "the world deprived of Buddhas."[21] Today the world is degenerating into a place where Dharma is concealed, a world deprived of Buddhas.

Rajgir began to decline and fall to ruins approximately 1,000 years ago, eventually turning into a jungle where no one

---

18 *Ichi-butsujō* 一仏乗, *Ekayāna*: same as One Vehicle, the single path to be taken to enlightenment by all living beings.
19 The four forms of birth are from the womb, moisture [moss], egg and miraculous.
20 *Byakuhō-onmotsu* 白法隠没.
21 *Mubutsu-sekai* 無仏世.

except venomous snakes and ferocious animals lived. However, during the five years since the emergence of the Rajgir Stūpa, several hundreds of pilgrims from near and far visit daily. The construction of Jain and Sikh temples followed, and Rajgir has regained its reputation as a major spiritual city whose influence spread throughout the Indian continent leading to voices calling for the restoration of Buddha Dharma. Year after year the number of pilgrims from abroad visiting Buddhist ruins grew dramatically to several tens of millions. Consequently, the construction of a road that connects Buddhist ruins for pilgrims was planned. In merely five years, Rajgir was restored from the devastation of more than 1,000 years and is on its way to flourish, reminiscent of the era of great King Bimbisāra.[22]

---

22 King Bimbisāra was the first royal patron of the Buddha and the founder of the Magadha kingdom. It is said that he sent 500 carts of food and other necessities daily as offerings to the Lord Buddha and the newly created order of over 1,000 monks.

40

Do Justice to the True Worth of Religion

November 1973
Issue of *Tenku*
Prepared for Kakasaheb Kalelkar's[1] Birthday Celebration

In its essence, nonviolence or peace cannot be fostered through politics or arms but only through purely spiritual cultivation and training. Spiritual cultivation and training have always been the practice of people of religion from ancient times. However, monastics and other religious practitioners tend to be absorbed in sectarian rituals or research and propagation of doctrine and have a diminished sense of responsibility in creating societies of peace and nonviolence within a nation or the world. Sectarian differences in form or doctrine have nothing to do with the true worth of religion. The innate true worth of religion is, first and foremost, the precept against taking life, secondly, the precept against stealing, followed by the third, fourth, fifth precepts and so on. There should be no religion that cannot work together in embracing and advocating the precepts against taking life or stealing. When applied to the modern world, the precept against

---

1 A close associate of Mahatma Gandhi, a great prose-writer, personal essayist of the highest order, beautiful travelogue writer and freedom fighter, Dattatreya Balakrishna Kalelkar [1885-1981] was lovingly known as Kakasaheb Kalelkar in Gujarat and all over India. Guruji met Kakasaheb on the train to Wardha when he first visited Gandhiji and ever since cherished a life-long friendship. Among all of Gandhiji's associates, Guruji had the closest association with Kakasaheb. He attended various Dharma-works of Nipponzan Myōhōji throughout Japan as a guest, and several members of Nipponzan Myōhōji and Sarvodaya studied under him.

taking life calls for complete renunciation of war; the precept against stealing calls for actions against exploitation. The precepts that prohibit taking life and stealing are not issues that only concern individual religious practitioners or their denomination, but have immediate relevance to the world as the foundation of world peace and the prosperity of humanity. Religion, on its own authority, rejects war and prohibits exploitation. The modern world recklessly affirms war and killing to secure vested interests and legitimizes exploitation and stealing. This is the seemingly hopeless affliction of the modern world. Religious practitioners of the world must unite efforts in the interest of curing modern civilization of its grave disease and do justice to the true worth of religion.

41

REMONSTRATE THE GOVERNMENT

March 7, 1974
New Delhi, India

BUDDHISM DEFENDS the authority of the Dharma[1] expounded by the Buddha. We must never disgrace the virtues of Lord Buddha. We are not in the business of currying favor with governments but of correcting the course of their actions. We will unite and guide the power of the people to that end. This is what Buddha Dharma is about. It is not about building temples or stūpas. Its essence is to right the wrongs of the defining policies of the state. As the first step, we build temples like this or stūpas. However, there are monks who cannot even do that. These are people who merely eat themselves out of their resources. If building temples or stūpas were all that needed to be done, piling stones on top of each other would suffice. We must at least do that. And if we can, we must move in the direction that would reverse the course of ultimate delusion that plagues world humanity.

---

1 The ordained who practice the Lotus Sūtra protect the authority of the Dharma, going beyond worldly authority.

42

Odaimoku—2

March 8, 1974
New Delhi, India

WE WERE CRITICIZED and suffered persecution, but throughout all this one thing remained unchanged. We kept chanting Na Mu Myō Hō Ren Ge Kyō. This is one aspect of my mind that never wavered under any circumstance throughout my life. As a human being, I have always met hardships by chanting Na Mu Myō Hō Ren Ge Kyō.

Na Mu Myō Hō Ren Ge Kyō is a word. The Bible describes the beginning of creation.[1] It starts out saying, "In the beginning was the Word." What was the Word? At this time, no one seems to be able to tell what the Word is. We don't know what this Word is. ". . . the Word was with God and the Word was God." I felt this to be incredible. I feel that when the peoples of the world seriously ponder on this "Word," they will come to chant the Odaimoku. If I'm asked what this Word is, I am ready to answer without any hesitation that it is the single word of Na Mu Myō Hō Ren Ge Kyō. I don't know whether it would be accepted. The last judgment will be rendered by history.

I will bring this Word on my upcoming visit to the United States. You also chant the Odaimoku, but not many know what it is. If one chants to make a living out of monkhood or chants because one cannot make a living, one will eventually not be able to chant this Word with all of one's heart. The Word will not live

---

1 Here Guruji is referring to the opening verse from the Gospel of St. John.

in such a person. ". . . the Word was with God and the Word was God." This needs to be experienced in order to be comprehended. For the Word to be kept by a human being, the Word manifests as a human being. What is revered as noble about human beings lies in our capacity to keep the Word.

Humanity is now searching for ". . . the Word was with God and the Word was God," because the fate of doom that cannot be prevented by any person is approaching. We cannot remain unconcerned in the face of imminent ruin. Humanity must be saved. Seeking to be saved is to seek the "Word that was with God." Is there or is there not such a thing? We don't know. However, there is no other way but to seek it. If we are human beings who think, we cannot tolerate life that merely consists of eating to stay alive and eventually die. That is not satisfying. We must bring deliverance to all. We must offer the Word that has the power to deliver. This Word that is offered by humankind will, in itself, bring deliverance to humankind. Salvation comes in this form of God manifesting through human beings. Thus, we shall spread the Word.

43

THE PRINCIPLE OF WORLD PEACE

April 8, 1974
Usuki Peace Pagoda, Japan

ECONOMY IS THE ISSUE in today's world. Differently put, "economic development" is the doctrine of greed. The economic development of one country proportionately impoverishes another country. Military power and nuclear weapons do not serve humanity either. Military and economic forces control politics. Here is humanity's impasse. Humankind is looking for a breakthrough to this quagmire, yet there is no one to show the way out, a way to ensure peace if humanity were to believe in it.

Liberalism[1] is "plunder-ism." Communism also sanctions tools of war. No matter how developed it may be, a nation that sanctions theft and murder can never serve to bring happiness to humanity. Buddhists are those who adhere to the precept of "never to take life." If one is to become a Buddhist, the teachings of Lord Buddha require the vow of not taking life. This is what we need today.

Peace shall prevail in the world when we no longer kill or take from others and instead make offerings to sustain the lives of others. The time is upon us to re-examine this simple teaching. Short of this, words out of the mouth of any president or prime minister are essentially idle talk for pillage and murder. Humanity is bound to perish unless this simple principle for world peace taught by Lord Buddha is believed. Now is the time to believe.

---

1 Here the reference is to the theory in economics that emphasizes individual freedom from restraint and is usually based on free competition, the self-regulating market and the gold standard.

44

ENLIGHTENMENT OF ICHINEN-SANZEN

April 25, 1974
Ground-breaking Ceremony of the Tagonoura Peace Pagoda
Shizuoka, Japan

ONE OF THE CENTRAL TENETS of Nichiren Daishōnin's teachings is that of the "Enlightenment of *Ichinen-sanzen*."[1] A single person becoming a Buddha in complete isolation from others is not good enough. When one attains Buddhahood, this very domain[2] we live in must together be transformed into the Pure Land. This is known as the "enlightenment by the realm of non-sentient beings."[3] Human beings live in communities of people. Therefore, a single person attaining Buddhahood in seclusion somewhere deep in the mountains does not suffice; one must seek to become Buddha together with the people of the community whom one sees daily. This is called the "enlightenment by the realm of sentient beings."[4] At the same time, our hearts and minds must become Buddha. Our hearts and minds can somehow follow the path that leads to Buddhahood if we aspire towards it. But how are we to achieve enlightenment of the physical domain we live in?

The realm of non-sentient beings, the physical environment

---

1 一念三千. Three thousand realms contained in a single thought. Each of the *jikkai* 十界 [ten worlds, i.e. hell, the world of hungry spirits, animals, *asuras*, human beings, world of deities and heavenly beings, the world of shamon, engaku, bodhisattva, and Buddhas] of existence includes the other nine in itself.
2 *Kokudo* 国土.
3 *Kokudo-seken-no-jōbutsu*, 国土世間の成仏. One of the three categories of realm.
4 *Shujō-seken-no-jōbutsu*, 衆生世間の成仏.

where people live, is being destroyed. The term currently used for this is environmental destruction. Living here does not entitle us to destroy the land. Human beings ought to simply live in nature. Birds do not destroy the trees they live in. Fish do not pollute the water they live in. Human beings are the only ones living on the surface of the Earth that do terrible things like cutting down trees or clearing the land without regard for other beings. In recent times, pursuit of profit under the pretext of industrial development has made people completely indifferent to any ill effects or sacrifices they may cause. In a world filled with such people, one's own enlightenment does not suffice. The three thousand states of existence, that means all forms of existence, need to attain enlightenment, and our domain become the Pure Land. What is the first step to make Japan the Pure Land? No one believes the environment talks. However, just as a person has a spirit, even a single speck of dust has a spirit. Everything and every one must become Buddha while alive, not in the world hereafter. The land thus transformed and enlightened is called the Pure Land. Each and every one of us—every child, woman and man—must become Buddha. This is the "enlightenment by the realm of sentient existences." In days gone by, people looked to Mount Fuji as the heart of this country. Mount Fuji has been the inspirational center in molding the peaceful and noble Japanese outlook on life.

45

THE STATE AND CONGLOMERATES

May 21, 1974
Inauguration Ceremony of Sendai Peace Pagoda
Miyagi, Japan

MODERN EUROPEAN CIVILIZATION, which has dominated the world, found its way to Japan as well. The European civilization is characterized by materialism, in which spiritual issues are trivialized. Faith is therefore regarded as inconsequential. The modern civilization is also known as the civilization of science. It is a civilization that has developed through research of the physical world. The modern state is its outcome. The modern state is a laboratory for science. For one, it is a laboratory of murderous machines, including nuclear weapons. All murderous weapons are by-products of the European civilization of science. Another aspect is its industry. Utilization of machines resulted in mass industrialization. Poverty was to be eradicated as a function of industrialization and its abundant production. However, this was not the case. The United States of America is a nation of wealth. Yet, its wealth is concentrated in and controlled by a handful of people, providing no benefit to others. The military-industrial complex created the modern state, which has become its playing field. Its arsenal has developed to a level sufficient to bring humanity's decline and devastate the world. The myriad of goods produced by industry is remaking the world where eventually no people, birds, fish or any other life can survive. The civilization of science has culminated in sophisticated weaponry and intensive production and has become an affliction to humanity and a curse to the heavens and earth. What must be done if humanity hopes to survive? The answer lies in the practice of generosity as taught in Buddhism. It is a teaching that encourages us to offer food to the hungry and to clothe anyone who is cold.

Humanity is on course to extinction. No complicated rationalization is necessary to prevent it. All it takes is to sincerely adhere to the solemn, singular precept espoused by Buddha Śākyamuni, which is not to take life. This precept cannot be imposed from above. It can only be followed when one believes in the sacredness of this teaching and puts it into practice. The spreading of the Buddha Dharma is the spreading of the practice of generosity as a way to liberate humanity. In a country where we see such a practice, social structures will not force the poor to steal from others. The teaching of generosity is found neither in the prevalent economics nor in Marxist Communism. In this respect, neither one receives a passing grade in creating global peace. Instead of teaching to make offerings to others, the only thing taught is to take from others to feed oneself. The creation of arsenals and industrial corporations are inevitable outcomes of the existence of the state. In this process, the poor are exploited and humanity is threatened. Sooner or later the modern institution of "the state" needs to be reformed. Unless the state is transformed to explore ways to live in peace, its very existence is a curse to humanity.

We have built a peace pagoda here. Perhaps some people will gather to venerate it. Reverence is where world peace starts. We will make offerings to those who visit. Let us start building global peace from what we do here. We may succeed. We may not. In either case, the teachings that Buddha Śākyamuni left to emancipate the modern times have nothing to do with arms or industrial development but to "offer what we have to others" and "not to take life." Why can't modern states adhere to such simple basic teachings? Governments that cannot abide by them should step down.

46

The Triple Emanantions of the Buddha

May 24, 1974
Kudan Dōjō, Tōkyō

THE CHAPTER OF *The Duration of the Life of the Tathāgata* expounds that the Buddha's existence is "forever here and forever remaining." There are three perspectives or three ways to view the Buddha who is forever here and forever remaining. First, there is what is called the Buddha realm that basically encompasses everything, that is to say, the entire universe. It is known as Dharma-body.[1] The Dharma-body of the Buddha cannot be seen or reached. Human beings recognizing the presence of this Buddha attempt to correct the wrongs in this world, guiding the world in the right direction toward peace and happiness. In other words, those living in the human world perceive or are enlightened to the Buddha in the form of the Dharma-body. This awakening on the part of the human being to the Dharma-body is called the Reward-body.[2] It is the Buddha who manifests to reward the accumulation of practice and wisdom. This is one aspect of the Buddha described in *The Duration of the Life of the Tathāgata*. The Buddha revealed in *The Duration of the Life of the Tathāgata* is the Buddha who attained Buddhahood in the human world by being enlightened to the Dharma-body Buddha. However, the Reward-body Buddha also possesses the body of wisdom and virtue that is totally unrestricted, and, for that reason is somewhat distant from the human world.

---

1 *Hosshin* 法身, *Dharmakāya*.
2 *Hōjin* 報身, also known as Accommodative-body.

The Buddha, known as the historical Buddha Śākyamuni, born in the human world, who experienced all the things of a human being including illness, studying, growing up and getting old, is called the Response-body Buddha. This is the Buddha who appears in response to the capacities of the people to emancipate them at their respective levels. The existence of the Response-body Buddha is what enables us to believe in the Reward-body and the Dharma-body, which are invisible to our eyes. Being born into the human world, the Response-body Buddha showed a finite life span of 80 years and took the appearance of passing away, although he never passed away. Other facets of the Response-body are the Buddha statues and portraits. They are all manifestations of the Response-body Buddha. They are manifestations of the Buddha appearing for the sake of emancipating the people. The Response-body Buddha manifests through the mediums of wood, paper or metal. It is fascinating if you believe this to be true. If not, you will never know. Once a dōjō comes about in the United States, statues of Ososhi-sama as well as Lord Buddha will appear, and therein will be their presence. When the teachings of the Buddha cease to exist, there will no longer be Buddha statues, stūpas, temples or the monastic community.

The Response-body Buddha appears to save this world, assuming different forms depending on the capacities and disposition[3] of the people of that time. Accordingly, the Buddha takes forms like this [a Buddha statue] or becomes a tree, plant or a person as a way to save that era. This is the Response-body. There is a teaching known as *sōmoku-jōbutsu*.[4] A generally accepted interpretation is that even trees or grass become the Buddha. However, from the perspective of the Buddha, it is "the Buddha who manifests as trees or grass." It is not the trees or grass that

---

3 *Kikon* 機根, is the propensity of capacities of human beings.
4 草木成仏. Plant life and all others in the natural environment can become Buddha since all sentient and non-sentient beings possess Buddha-nature.

become the Buddha, but it is the Buddha that becomes trees or grass. The same Buddha manifests as Buddha statues and appeared as Lord Buddha in the human world. The Buddha manifests in our Bodhisattva practice and as us, the ordained. These are all the diverse appearances the Buddha assumes in order to free the world. This is the Response-body of the Buddha, who appears in different times, different places and as different people. We cannot take this matter lightly. Where there are no Buddha images or temples, there is no Buddha Dharma. When that happens, Buddha Dharma cannot liberate the people.

47

TATHĀGATA NA MU MYŌ HŌ REN GE KYŌ

September 22, 1974
Utsunomiya Dōjō, Japan

NA MU MYŌ HŌ REN GE KYŌ is displayed in the center of
the jeweled stūpa flanked by Lord Buddha, who is the Response-
body Buddha born in this *sahā* world to preach the Lotus Sūtra,
and Buddha Prabhūtaratna,[1] who attested to the truth of the Lotus
Sūtra. Some claim that this Honzon is a Dharma Honzon based on
the view that Na Mu Myō Hō Ren Ge Kyō is a Dharma. However,
it should be seen as a person. It represents Lord Buddha who
attained enlightenment infinite countless kalpas ago,[2] and who, at
the same time is Buddha Śākyamuni, Buddha Prabhūtaratna and
the emanated Buddhas in the world of ten directions. This source
Buddha is Myō Hō Ren Ge Kyō, thus saluted by the name Na Mu
Myō Hō Ren Ge Kyō. This Honzon is not Dharma. Dharma is what
someone espouses or what exists from the past. However, that is
not what we are talking about. The source of Buddha's action of
freeing sentient beings is Na Mu Myō Hō Ren Ge Kyō. The chapter
of *The Duration of the Life of the Tathāgata* of the Lotus Sūtra
provides its ground. If we see the Honzon as Tathāgata Myō Hō

---

1 Taho Buddha 多宝仏 or Abundant Treasures Buddha appears in a Stūpa of
Many Treasures, which is suspended in midair in Chapter XI of the Lotus Sūtra,
to fulfill his vow made in the distant past to appear whenever the Lotus Sūtra is
preached to praise and attest to the truth of the teachings delivered.
2 *Kuon-jitsujō* 久遠実成. Also known as Buddha Śākyamuni of Honmon, Eternal
Primordial Buddha or Buddha revealed in *The Duration of the Life of the Tathāgata*,
whose original attainment of Buddhahood was many hundreds of thousands of
billions of nayutas of kalpas ago.

Ren Ge Kyō, it is a Person Honzon. The chapter of *The Divine Transcendental Power of the Tathāgata* also provides grounds for this. These two chapters of the Lotus Sūtra identify Tathāgata Myō Hō Ren Ge Kyō. Tendai-daishi[3] interpreted that Tathāgata Myō Hō Ren Ge Kyō is the totality of the Buddhas in the ten directions, the Buddhas in the past, present and future. Ososhi-sama cites this in *Ongikuden*. This Tatāgatha encompasses every Tatāgatha, the Original Buddha, Buddhas in manifestation and the like. This is who Tathāgata Myō Hō Ren Ge Kyō is.

As such, here this Tathāgata is represented as Myō Hō Ren Ge Kyō with Buddha Śākyamuni, Buddha Prabhūtaratna and emanative Buddhas in the worlds of ten directions as attendants. While the person and the Dharma cannot be separated, the representation of the person as Tathāgata Na Mu Myō Hō Ren Ge Kyō is used while still sustaining oneness of the person and the Dharma.[4] The most accurate grounds for this is the Lotus Sūtra, yet there are also frequent references in the Parinirvāna Sūtra that "the Tathāgata is the Dharma." Taking birth in the world of human beings makes the Tathāgata a person. It is the appearance assumed to free sentient beings. The source that emancipates sentient beings is the Original Buddha.[5] We pay homage to this Buddha as Tathāgata Na Mu Myō Hō Ren Ge Kyō. Assuming the appearance of a person could be misperceived as being subjective, which would allow for comparability. It is taught that the Buddha

---

3　天台大師. Also known as Chih-i [538-597], the third patriarch in the lineage of the Chinese T'ien-t'ai [Tendai] School. He lived during the Chin and Zui Dynasties and is regarded as the founder of the Tendai School in China. He is an author of many commentaries and books including the *San-ta-pu* [*Sandaibu*], which are the three commentaries on the Lotus Sūtra. Another well-known work is *Mo-ho-chih-kuan* [*Makashikan*], a 20-fascicle work that explains the various aspects of meditation.

4　What Guruji is referring to here is the teaching called *Ninpō-ichinyo* 人法一如, the indivisibleness of the person, i.e., Tathāgata and the Dharma. However, emancipation by the Dharma cannot be brought to sentient beings without the person. That is why the aspect of the person, the Tathāgata, is brought to the forefront.

5　*Honbutsu* 本仏.

revealed in *The Duration of the Life of the Tathāgata* appeared as Buddha Śākyamuni temporarily for the sake of the people who are without virtue in the Era of Declining Dharma. This is who Na Mu Myō Hō Ren Ge Kyō Tathāgata is. Na Mu Myō Hō Ren Ge Kyō Tathāgata is simple but cannot be readily understood, thus revealing itself to be Buddha Śākyamuni. This is known as the teaching on "revelation of the true aspect of the Response-body Buddha."[6] The Buddha who was born in this world of human beings is himself the Original Eternal Buddha.

---

6 *Ōjin-no-kenpon* 応身の顕本.

PART FIVE

Great Dharma Work

48

To Initiate the Dharma Work

October 13, 1974
Tama Dōjō, Tōkyō

BUILDING STŪPAS is a practice taught in the Lotus Sūtra. Practicing of the Lotus Sūtra is the monumental movement of *Risshō-ankoku* espoused by Nichiren Daishōnin. In spite of this, some in the order do not participate. They think of this work as mere construction, as workers building temples and stūpas. Stūpas can never be built with this mindset. Things have been opening up for Nipponzan today solely because our movement for global peace, the movement for *Risshō-ankoku*, resonates with the people. I see temples in which monks are practicing monastic life just as a means of making a living, even within Nipponzan. These people are indifferent to Dharma-work initiated by others and are intent on making a living and saving money for themselves. This is mundane to the utmost. Tremendous Dharma-works can be achieved if everyone were to bring their savings together and spend it for the Dharma-work initiated by others. This is the kind of Dharma-work we engage in at Nipponzan today. Our Dharma-work arises out of nothing. Dharma-work is materialization into form. It takes financial resources to do that. The only way to materialize Dharma-work is for everyone to bring their hearts and minds together to help where help is needed. You can get away with not being involved if you so chose. Many of you act as if these Dharma-works are not your business. That should not be. I can somehow serve as the fulcrum for our efforts while I am still alive and with you. However, when I am gone, having lost the fulcrum,

I can easily envision many of you starting to make monkhood into a profession. When that happens, it will render Nipponzan meaningless. Then all of you would have to return to secular life and make a living as construction workers.

49

RŌHACHI

December 1, 1974
Rajgir Dōjō, India

DECEMBER IS CALLED *rōgetsu*.[1] This practice is performed over an eight-day period at the beginning of December, thus it is referred to as *rōhachi*.[2] We have completed today's practice of *sesshin*,[3] a practice to quiet the mind, put everything aside and be totally immersed in chanting the Odaimoku. Perhaps it does not matter when it is done, but we observe *rohachi-sesshin* in December. December marks the end of the year. This practice is the year's final, decisive battle with the demons. Should we lose in this practice, the merits accumulated through our practice this year would be in vain. We must not succumb to the demons during this week. This brings us to the close of the year. Another year is around the corner. We will prepare ourselves today for our battles with the demons in the year to come. This week serves to deepen our confidence in our vision and in our ability to perform the Dharma-work that needs to be carried out. Our successful practice of *rōhachi-sesshin* this year shall open the doors to satisfactory Dharma-work in the coming year. I say this with absolute confidence based on my experience of engaging in this practice year after year.

Now, what is this battle against the demons? For one, it is desire. We will correct the way we view food, the source that

---

1 臘月. December according to the Japanese lunar calendar.
2 臘八. Hachi is the number eight in Japanese.
3 摂心.

sustains our lives. We can then detach our minds from the desires for food and instead focus on other issues. When we prepare three meals a day, the whole day is spent on shopping, cooking and cleaning up. Buddha Śākyamuni chose not to prepare food in order to free us from the desire for food. Of course he could not continue to work and teach should he starve to death, therefore, he received just enough alms to sustain his life.

Living beings take food one way or another. Birds fly scavenging for food, and humans provide for animals like cats and dogs. If monks were to be provided for by others unwisely, we would be no different from cats and dogs. We would turn into parasites living off of others. Buddha Dharma declines when such monks grow in number. These monks do not benefit society. Increase in the puppy population would be better in comparison. Monks are to detach themselves from the desire for food and instead rely on others to provide them with the means of sustenance. It is daunting to become an ordained without absolute faith that somewhere in this human world there are people who would sustain us. When we have complete faith in it, everyone feeds us. The food that we receive might be leftovers given to their cats or dogs. However, even in this case, this sustenance for the first time awakens our gratitude towards food, towards our own life and towards all sentient beings that help to sustain our lives

Children of the wealthy, children who grew up in prominent families know no sense of indebtedness and gratitude. Those born into poverty and raised by the kindness of others grow up to do good things. The world today is at an impasse caused by the prevailing theory of economics. There is no sense of gratitude no matter how much one receives. Monks do not work for the basic needs for sustaining life, such as clothing, food or shelter. We eat without cultivating the fields or spinning yarn. If we value our life, we know to be grateful. Monastic life exists to show the world this sense of gratitude. When a monk who does not make money lives without being occupied by thoughts of want for food, toilet paper, oil or anything else, but rather ponders other noble things in life, and if one sees that this monk is grateful for a small amount of food offered—even leftovers given to one's cat—the world becomes a peaceful place. Among other things, Nipponzan is poor. Because we are destitute, we know what to be grateful for.

50

Civilization of Science

May 8, 1975
Excerpt from *Buddha Dharma of Japan*
On the Dedication of the Paris Dōjō

HUMANITY COMPRISED of three billion people is compelled to live in the "Western civilization." The civilization of the West is that of science, machines, murder and war. Europeans developed the civilization of science, and everywhere they went was rife with invasion, war, conquest and domination. How many of the world's hundred plus nations, large and small, existing today have not been subjected to invasion and domination by Europeans?

The civilization of science has not only driven the Europeans to frantic invasion and conquest, but has also led them to wreck irrevocable destruction on the natural environment because of their belief in the supremacy of economic development. Everything from air to water has been contaminated, rendering the environment harmful and unfit for sustaining life, and underground natural resources have been depleted through unsparing exploitation. The civilization of science is, after all, a civilization of violence. Regardless of any progress, it does not advance human spirituality in morality or religion even one step but, on the contrary, causes spiritual degradation and turmoil. The civilization of science is a cursed civilization.

51

May 8, 1975
Excerpt from *Buddha Dharma of Japan*
On the Dedication of the Paris Dōjō

KANJIN-HONZON

HUMANS CAN BE PHYSICALLY sustained on bread alone, yet life based on needs and wants of the flesh is devoid of joy and gratitude. Dissoluteness leads to societies without order, where ferocious, brute and animal-like indolence prevail, a society marked by robbery, rape and murder. New York in the United States and other major cities are prime examples. Courts and jails are of no use. Eventually pervasive crimes will require entire cities or the whole country to be turned into a prison. Social life there is extremely dangerous with no effective means to counter violence. Success in traveling to space or building submarines to explore the ocean floor will not bring peace to America. These phenomena reflective of the spiritual degradation are caused by the heart and mind of Americans.

The fundamental flaw in the western civilization is its incessant research of external matter, which likewise treats humans as matter. Spiritual activities that should intrinsically be esteemed are also considered a function of matter, resulting in a failure to discriminate right from wrong, good from evil. This results in a view towards life and living where humans, animals, rubbish, feces and urine are all deemed more or less the same as far as matter goes. No wonder slighting or murdering others are not considered grave crimes. Others who should be praised are condemned.

To protect and emancipate humanity from the fear brought on by the conflagration, war and bloodshed of the non-virtuous modern age and to bring tranquility, all people must be taught of the presence that is intrinsically to be venerated. It exists in the heart and mind of humans. It is what generates respect towards others in our heart and mind. It is called *Kanjin-honzon*. To actualize the heart of respect towards others, our body bows in reverence. This is called *tangyō-raihai*. To express the heart of respect towards others, we utter the phrase of commendation through our mouth. This is called *tanshin-kushō*. These constitute the Dharma of the Three Great Mysteries[1] of the Buddha Dharma of Japan. The Dharma of the Three Great Mysteries of the Buddha Dharma of Japan teaches that people are intrinsically to be esteemed. The awakening to the four kanji characters of "intrinsic reverence [本来尊重]" is the one and only religion that will bring deliverance from the anguish of modern humanity.

---

1 *Sandai-hihō* 三大秘法.

52

FOR REASONS CAREFULLY CONSIDERED

January 4, 1976
Atami Dōjō, Japan

OSOSHI-SAMA'S LATTER YEARS at Mount Minobu were nine dreadful years of suffering that almost cost him his life, perhaps surpassing even his near beheading at Tatsunokuchi. He would build a makeshift hut, but a gust of wind would blow it down, and then he would build it again. Ososhi-sama, writing of his life at the hermitage, said, "Moonlight shone in from the ceiling; the wind blowing in from the cracks of the wall rolled the scrolls of the sūtra." In the winter, his "clothing was thin, and food gone." We must all think hard about why he entered Minobu in his latter years, "for reasons carefully considered." After careful consideration, he chose life at Minobu to set an example of a life of one who holds the Dharma for disciples and devotees who would come after him. It is absolutely astonishing. The life at Minobu was not imposed on Ososhi-sama, but was a life of his own choosing.

The Lotus Sūtra will exert its power for the first time to save the modern times. If I wear fine clothing like this and *tabi*, perhaps I am not qualified to be Ososhi-sama's disciple. I do not wish to wear *tabi*, fine clothing or indulge in tasty food as long as I live, but rather to follow in Ososhi-sama's footsteps. That's what it takes to save the current world. Being old as I am, I cannot even walk without help, let alone save the world. Nevertheless, I am nursing myself along while rueful and apologizing for what I have become as Ososhi-sama's disciple. Any deadlock in our Dharma-work or inability to guide people to the Dharma comes from the error in the way we conduct ourselves. Fault must be found in ourselves that the stūpa does not materialize.

53

LIFE OF SERVICE

February 10, 1976
Atami Dōjō, Japan

MR. DAISUKE TAKAOKA, Chair of the Japan-Indian Association, told me that when he met Gandhiji, Gandhiji pointed to Rev. Gyōryō Maruyama, who was attending to him, and explained to Mr. Takaoka how he owed his life to this monk. Gandhiji was not too sturdy a man, and illness frequented him. On one such occasion, Rev. Maruyama, in prayer for Gandhiji's recovery, fasted and burned his arm as an offering.[1] One cannot know if that is why Gandhiji recovered, but he felt a debt of gratitude for the sentiments behind it and said Rev. Maruyama saved his life. This is incredible. Buddha Dharma spread in India because of things like this. Gandhiji was that kind of person. Those close to him learned of his sentiments, and everyone honored the monks from Japan. This is what Buddha Dharma is about. Even if we were to ardently explicate the doctrines of the Buddha Dharma of Japan, it would not have impressed Gandhiji.

Buddha Dharma is not about theories. Buddha Dharma is nothing other than to serve others with a sincere heart. Buddha Dharma will decline when monks, taking care of only themselves and disregarding service to others, grow in number. These monks serve no purpose in society. We are here to save the lives of others in this world, not in their afterlife. With a willingness to serve

---

1 A practice that takes after the example of Bodhisattva Medicine King in Chapter XXIII of the Lotus Sūtra who burned his body as a supreme offering to the Lotus Sūtra.

others and the world, the ordained can be in harmony with others. Harmony is not created when one puts one's own needs first. Buddha Dharma is of no service to society without concordance. Otherwise, it means that monks merely make a living without concern for others. The power that made Nipponzan rise from nothing to what it is today lies in what I just mentioned. Rev. Maruyama was a senior member of the order, but those who came after him were able to follow him. There are monks who no one follows despite their seniority in age or length of time since ordination. The only way to lead and create concordance among the multitude is by serving others. No matter how arduous one may practice the Buddha Dharma on one's own, it is meaningless without service to others. Buddha Dharma is to serve others without sparing oneself.

54

The Practice of the Odaimoku

February 2, 1977
Sri Pada Dōjō, Sri Lanka

Yōmon-shō[1] contains the *gāthā* in praise of the Buddha.[2] The congregation of the Bodhisattvas extolled the virtues of Lord Buddha. Amidst their praise is a phrase, "The sacred voice [of the Buddha] is akin to the roars of thunder." A voice powerful enough to be likened to the reveberation of roaring thunder is required. By the dedicated chanting of the Odaimoku, our voice gradually grows stronger. A strong, loud voice comes from the abdomen. Those who chant with voices from the depth of their abdomen can enjoy this practice. When the Odaimoku is chanted just through the lips, it becomes tedious. Appropriate force cannot be applied on one's abdomen with bad posture. The Odaimoku is enunciated by engaging our entire body. However, the abdomen is the primary part of the body involved. If you have pain anywhere in your body, you cannot produce a loud voice since it reverberates there. A loud voice can be produced when we engage our entire body. That, in turn, allows the practice to be performed with ease. This is a practice of our own volition. We do not do it as a favor to someone. When the Odaimoku is chanted with vigor, we can enjoy this practice. Those who cannot enjoy it spare their voice. Nichiren Daishōnin taught in *Requital of Gratitude* to "chant without sparing the voice."

---

1 要文抄. A compilation of excerpts of essential teachings from the Lotus Sūtra and the writings of Nichiren Daishōnin prepared by Fujii Guruji for daily use by Nipponzan Myōhōji.
2 The Sūtra of Innumerable meanings, Chapter I, *Virtues*.

55

BUDDHA-NATURE IN ALL CREATION

February 8, 1977
Sri Pada Dōjō, Sri Lanka

KANJIN-HONZON-SHŌ[1] [*Treatise on Seeing the Essential Object of Veneration in the Heart and Mind*] is considered to be the most important writing of Nichiren Daishōnin among the numerous treatises he authored in his lifetime. As the title *Kanjin-honzon* denotes, the text reveals that the sacred being exists in the heart and mind. In reply to a question doubting the presence of the Revered One in the heart and mind, Nichiren Daishōnin pointed out that a person's face never remains the same but displays a diverse range of expressions reflecting one's state of mind and heart. Anger, joy, insipidness, dissatisfaction or cajolery all show through one's facial and physical expressions. Joy is a reflection of the realm of heavenly beings existing in the heart and mind of humans. "Tranquil is this realm of mine, ever filled with celestial beings" is a passage from *The Duration of the Life of the Tathāgata* of the Lotus Sūtra. Every being, be it human, dog, cat, bird, horse or cattle, possesses ten realms of existence within its heart and mind. A manifested world in which beings live with joy in their hearts and minds is the realm ever-filled with celestial beings.

---

1 観心本尊鈔. Written by Nichiren Daishōnin on the fourth month of Bunei Period [1273] at Sado Island during his exile. Commonly known by this title, its official title is *Nyorai-metsugo-gogohyakusai-shi-kanjin-honzon-shō* 如来滅度後五五百歳始観心本尊鈔鈔, *Treaties on Seeing the Essential Object of Veneration in the Heart and Mind Revealed for the First Time in the Fifth Five Hundredth Year Period Following the Nirvāna of the Tathāgata*. The original manuscript is still retained together with *Risshō-ankoku-ron* at the Nakayama Hokekyō-ji Temple.

When I went to India, at first I saw no joy, but rather avarice and self-abasement in every person I came across. Despite spending three years in India, I saw no one expressing joy. In time, an opportunity arose to visit Mahatma Gandhi's ashram. A group of people heading to Gandhiji's ashram boarded the train with me. My experience traveling on a third-class ticket up to that time had been analogous to the transportation of animals in freight trains. The moment you board someone tried to pick a fight with you. It became hard to even stay onboard without being pugnacious. However, on that occasion the atmosphere on the train was inexplicably gentle. When I arrived at Gandhiji's ashram, every one was showing joy. I was able to finally see faces and an environment where joy abounded. It resonated in me and brought joy to my heart.

Rakan-sama [an arhat] attained enlightenment alone in a forest. At a time like this, the realm of *rakan-sama* is not readily manifested in the human world, yet we cannot say that it does not exist. Why? Because Buddha Śākyamuni became the Buddha while taking the appearance of a human being. However, we are taught that Lord Buddha is not the exception, but that every one of us can attain Buddhahood as well. This is the teaching of equality and great wisdom of the Lotus Sūtra. What happens to those who do wrong? They too will become Buddha. Eventually everyone becomes one and the same.

We cannot manifest the realm of the Buddha at this time. It is concealed. However, one practitioner of the Lotus Sūtra known as Bodhisattva Never Despise went about bowing and revering everyone with all his heart, including those who held enmity towards him and beat him. "You will eventually become Buddha, please treasure yourselves and practice." Bodhisattva Never Despise not only saw that they had the heart and mind that will eventually make them Buddha, but also envisioned them in their ultimate stage of attaining Buddhahood. He held unwavering faith that even those with distorted views engaging in every kind of violent and wicked deeds against him will invariably all become Buddha. That was what enabled him to venerate everyone. When he approached anyone, he bowed with palms together in veneration.

What if we all made our way through the world like this? It is a concept not readily accepted in today's world. To bow in reverence to every person one encounters with palms together is hard to do, especially if one were told that even evil men must be revered because they, too, will become Buddha. Requiting evil with evil, defending oneself against violence with violence does not leave the world an amicable place. Ultimately, this approach sanctions the view that the best way to ensure one's own safety is to kill everyone else off. Then no one can kill you. As seen in the concept of national defense or the Self Defense Forces, one cannot have faith in others with such misguided thinking. The institution of the state is based on suspicion, the premise that others are there to potentially get you. Here lies the impasse of the modern times. We must turn this around. How? Inherent in the hearts and minds of humans are the ten realms of existence. Anger is found in every person, but so is joy, The only way to create a peaceful world, the ultimate fulfillment of humanity's hope, is to believe in the innate absolute entity of reverence that dwells in the hearts of the people.

昭和三十七年 戊戌 十二月 吉日

日達

昭和三十八年 癸卯 三月廿五日

日達

Opposite top: January 1, 1962. Nichidatsu.

Opposite bottom: March 25, 1963. Nichidatsu.

Above: January 1, 1976. Nichidatsu.

56

THE FOUR STAGES OF FAITH
AND THE FIVE KINDS OF PRACTICE

February 16, 1977
Sri Pada Dōjō, Sri Lanka

THE GOMYŌHAN we just recited is *Four Stages of Faith and Five Kinds of Practices*.[1] Nakayama Hokekyō-ji Temple in Shimousa[2] was once the private residence of Lord Toki Harima,[3] a modest feudal lord. Lord Toki had a very close relationship with Nichiren Daishōnin and offered alms throughout his life. Many issues were addressed and answers provided in Ososhi-sama's letters to Lord Toki. One such issue was the inadequacies of the practitioners in the Era of Declining Dharma. Lord Toki had inquired what was needed in practicing the Buddha Dharma in this era. This letter is a response by Ososhi-sama.

Precepts, contemplation and wisdom[4] are the three objectives to strive for in practicing the Buddha Dharma. First are precepts, the practice of deterring evil and doing good. Second is contemplation or ecstasy,[5] and third, wisdom, seeing the truth of all matters through arriving at a state of tranquility. These are the

---

1 *Shishin-gohon-shō* 四信五品鈔. Written by Nichiren Daishōnin April 10, 1277.
2 下総. Located in Chiba prefecture.
3 Toki Jyōnin 富木常忍 was one of the most influential supporters of Nichiren Daishōnin. He was ordained after the passing of Nichiren Daishōnin and took the name Nichijō 日常 and converted his residence into Hokkeji temple, generally known as Nakayama Hokekyō-ji temple. Nichiren Daishōnin addressed many of his crucial doctrines to Lord Toki, who in turn communicated them to other supporters and followers.
4 *Kai* 戒 precepts, *jō* 定 contemplation, *e* 慧 wisdom. The three types of learning and practice.
5 Reference footnote 3 in *Nipponzan's Mode of Practice*, p. 65.

practices one must go through. As one adheres to the precepts, one can arrive at a special spiritual state of equilibrium called ecstasy. Matters contemplated while residing in the state of ecstasy allow for insight to receive the teachings of Lord Buddha. If the progression through all three of these practices were a requirement applied to all, no one in the Era of Declining Dharma would qualify. It is analogous to loading a small ship with too many heavy stones and cargo that sink it. Asking too much of a practitioner in the Era of Declining Dharma undermines the ability to sustain the Buddha Dharma. The easiest to keep is neither precepts nor contemplation, but Buddha's wisdom. We are to ponder what this wisdom is. Ososhi-sama determined that to be Na Mu Myō Hō Ren Ge Kyō.

In closing, this *Gomyōhan* states, "The five characters of Myō Hō Ren Ge Kyō neither represent the text of the sūtra nor its meaning. They are nothing other than the essence of the Lotus Sūtra." The understanding Ososhi-sama arrived at about the Odaimoku is that it is not the meaning of the sūtra, but nothing other than the heart and spirit of the Lotus Sūtra. The heart and spirit are elusive. They were made into characters to facilitate anyone to readily grasp them.

Chanting the Odaimoku nurtures our aspiration toward enlightenment. Infants feed on milk to grow without knowing what milk is. Feeding on milk is a spontaneous act. Medicine prescribed by a good doctor cures illness without one having to inquire what its compounds are. These are some of the examples cited. We do not approach Na Mu Myō Hō Ren Ge Kyō as a cerebral exercise but simply chant it. That is enough to emancipate us. This is the Buddha Dharma in the Era of Declining Dharma. Na Mu Myō Hō Ren Ge Kyō is essentially the compassion of the Buddha. It was made into a word. It was made into written characters. That is how Nichiren Daishōnin comprehended it. That is how I comprehend it. That is why I chant the Odaimoku with everyone.

57

OSOSHI-SAMA'S CREED

February 17, 1977
Sri Pada Dōjō, Sri Lanka

OSOSHI-SAMA ESTABLISHED the chanting of Na Mu Myō Hō Ren Ge Kyō as his essential teaching in *Reply to Shijō Kingo*:[1] "The singular practice of the seven characters of Na Mu Myō Hō Ren Ge Kyō may seem too narrow." In other words, he teaches that the singular practice of only chanting the seven characters of Na Mu Myō Hō Ren Ge Kyō may appear to be too narrowly focused, yet he continues that it is an exceedingly profound teaching that not even Tendai[2] or Dengyō[3] had spread. This tenet of Nichiren Daihōnin's teachings goes to the very heart of one's appreciation, faith and understanding of the chanting of Na Mu Myō Hō Ren Ge Kyō. He further states that, "The chanting of Na Mu Myō Hō Ren Ge Kyō encompasses the three crucial matters of the essential teaching depicted in *The Duration of the Life of the Tathāgata* chapter of the Lotus Sūtra." This pertains to the core creed[4] of the Nichiren School to be spread in the Era of Declining Dharma. If its components were to be separately identified, they are namely, the Honzon revealed in the essential section of the

1 *Shijō-kingo-dono Gohenji* 四条金吾殿御返事. Written by Nichiren Daishōnin May 2, 1272 at Ichinosawa, Sado Island.
2 Tendai Daishi [天台大師 Great Teacher T'ien-t'ai, 538-597] is another name for Chigi [Chih-i], the third patriarch in the lineage of the Chinese Tendai School [T'ienT'ai]. He lived during the Ch'en and Sui Dynasties.
3 Dengyō Daishi [伝教大師 Great Teacher Dengyō] is a posthumous title given to Saichō [767-822], founder of the Japanese Tendai School.
4 Reference to the Dharma of Three Great Mysteries, *Sandai-hihō* 三大秘法.

Lotus Sūtra,[5] the kaidan of the essential section of the Lotus Sūtra[6] and the Odaimoku of the essential section of the Lotus Sūtra.[7] However, when these three are seen as a whole, they are all together embodied in the single act of chanting Na Mu Myō Hō Ren Ge Kyō. As long as it is chanted, the kaidan spontaneously appears where it takes place. The Honzon of the essential section of the Lotus Sūtra is nothing other than Na Mu Myō Hō Ren Ge Kyō. There may be various other Honzons, but they are not the Honzon determined by Nichiren Daishōnin.

The Honzon of Nichiren Daishōnin, Na Mu Myō Hō Ren Ge Kyō, may seem like the title of the sūtra, but that is not the case. It is called the "the lotus noumenon of Buddha."[8] This all-embracing entity, comprised of the entire universe, including all beings and the physical environment they live in that make up the ten Dharma realms,[9] in other words, living beings and the earth they live upon, such as rivers and mountains, must all be the object of worship. We are but a part of it. Without an understanding of the whole, there is no understanding of its comprising parts. The respective parts of this totality function in their respective ways and, for instance, cause flowers to bloom and the sun to rise. Just as there are workings that result in these phenomena, the most sacred working of the entire universe resulted in Buddha. Buddha Śākyamuni is one such manifestation as are Buddha Amitābha and God, according to Christian faith, although they are called by

---

5 *Honmon-no-honon* 本門本尊. The essential section covers Chapter XV *Bodhisattvas Who Emerge from the Earth* to Chapter XXVIII *The Encouragement of Universal-Sage Bodhisattva*, which is the second half of the Lotus Sūtra wherein Buddha Śākyamuni's true identity as an eternal, primordial entity is revealed. The first half is called *Shakumon* 迹門, the theoretical section. Both the essential and theoretical sections are further divided in to preface, main discourse and epilogue.
6 *Kaidan* 戒壇. Reference Guruji's *Kaidan of Honmon*, p. 293.
7 Reference Guruji's *The Single Great Dharma of Mystery*, p. 240.
8 *Tōtai-renge-no-hotoke* 当体蓮華の仏.
9 *Hokkai* 法界 [*dharma-dhātu*] i) The sphere of ultimate reality; ii) The whole universe; iii) The objects of the mind in general.

different names. This sacred function is called *yū*.[10] *Yū*, the activity and function, work together with us and this is called *kuyū*.[11]

The workings of *kuyū*, the workings of the Buddha, manifest throughout the entire universe including us human beings. This is called *kutai*.[12] Buddha's noumenon is no different from the entire universe. The entire universe is not a separate existence from Buddha's noumenon. Such Buddha, Buddha called Na Mu Myō Hō Ren Ge Kyō, is the Buddha of *kutai-kuyū*, the Honzon. Issues raised by *ita-mandala*[13] and the like are merely side issues. The Buddha of *kutai-kuyū* is nothing like that. When Na Mu Myō Hō Ren Ge Kyō as the Honzon is chanted, dōjōs appear wherein Na Mu Myō Hō Ren Ge Kyō is chanted. Places like temples where people gather to chant the Odaimoku appear. This is what kaidan [the platform for bestowing precepts] is. It exists where there are people who practice the chanting of Odaimoku. It inevitably appears where people come together and practice. I have walked about my whole life chanting the Odaimoku, and hundreds of temples manifested. This is no falsehood. They were not built because I intended to build temples.

Honzon and kaidan manifest in the single act of chanting Na Mu Myō Hō Ren Ge Kyō. Ososhi-sama stated, "It comprises the three crucial matters of the essential teaching depicted in *The Duration of the Life of the Tathāgata* chapter." All three are inclusive in the single act of chanting Na Mu Myō Hō Ren Ge Kyō. That is why nothing is more awesome and wondrous than the chanting of Na Mu Myō Hō Ren Ge Kyō. Not even Tendai or Dengyō had transmitted it. Ososhi-sama says, "That is because it goes a layer deeper than the teachings expounded either by Tendai, Dengyō or others." This is what Ososhi-sama believed. Those who can believe in this are the disciples and followers of Ososhi-sama.

10　用.

11　俱用.

12　俱体.

13　*Ita-mandala*, a mandala represented on a wood board.

We hardly hear voices chanting Na Mu Myō Hō Ren Ge Kyō in temples these days. Its significance is lost even on Nichiren School temples. This would eventually render the Nichiren School itself empty. There is no defining creed of Ososhi-sama's faith other than the chanting of Na Mu Myō Hō Ren Ge Kyō. The Dharma of the Three Great Mysteries revealed in the essential section chapter of *The Duration of the Life of the Tathāgata* is manifested in the chanting of the single phrase of Na Mu Myō Hō Ren Ge Kyō.

58

FASTING

May 5, 1977
Kiyosumi Dōjō, Japan

ALTHOUGH IT WAS ONLY for a handful of days, our practice of fasting was trying. The discomfort we felt was caused by the body, which was inclined toward ill health, trying to respond and restore itself. We tend to undermine our bodies without being conscious of it. The desires we have in our minds are the cause. When led by desire, we find ourselves caught in the perpetual vicious cycle that results in destroying our bodies. Fasting is useful in restoring the state of health of a body compromised by undesirable habits. It serves to drastically regenerate our body's organs and tissues. Our mental mood and sense of well-being are renewed. Our overall health improves as well.

The discomfort of a fast lasts only for a few days. We enjoy health and a sense of invigoration for some time after that. The delusions of the mind and desires of the body are what lead to physical harm. Only through self-control can we temper them. Fasting is precisely that. Not to consume food, which sustains life, is extremely hard for any physical existence. The act of the mind and body to discipline this desire opens up a new way of life. Buddhism that seeks ease and comfort ultimately corrupts and does not serve the world. While asceticism is not the objective, we must put ourselves through strenuous practice. We will face the divide between delusion and enlightenment, darkness and light. We are compelled to face a new way of life different from what we have been accustomed to. We must labor at it to get there. When we embrace these challenges, a world of ease and comfort opens up before us.

59

GREAT ADVERSITY AND COMFORTABLE CONDUCT

May 4, 1977
Kiyosumi Dōjō, Japan

NICHIREN DAISHŌNIN gave discourses on the Lotus
Sūtra for his disciples at Mount Minobu. These sermons are said
to have been orally transcribed and came to be known as *Ongi-kuden.*[1] Nichiren Daishōnin explicated that while the practice of
the Lotus Sūtra in the chapter on *Comfortable Conduct*[2] is meant
to prevent great adversities from befalling [the practitioner of the
Lotus Sūtra], one must "regard the occurrence of great adversity
as comfort."

Without great adversities that confront us, our practice
cannot be that of comfort. This is what it takes to practice the
Lotus Sūtra in the Era of Declining Dharma. To put it differently,
when we, who are deeply shackled with delusions and five desires,[3]
seek to adhere to and keep the right teachings, we must take to
heart that it will not be easy. Practicing with ease and comfort
inevitably results in temptations of the five desires. If we give in,
Buddha Dharma would no longer be viable. When we are working

1 御義口伝. *Record of the Orally Transmitted Teachings.* See footnote 4 in
Ignorant Monks, p. 50.
2 Lotus Sūtra Chapter XIV. *Comfortable Conduct* describes the conduct of the
practitioner in delivering the Lotus Sūtra in the Era of Declining Dharma and how
that conduct would make people more receptive and, with the protection from the
heavens, could work in averting adversities.
3 The five desires that arise in connection with the five senses of form, sound,
smell, taste and touch. Also desire for wealth, sex, food and drink, fame and sleep.

towards cleansing the impurities of the world or pursuing a pure life ourselves, seeking ease and comfort bring depravity. This is why the practice of the Lotus Sūtra is difficult even when called *"Comfortable Conduct."* We must be prepared for the underlying hardship in any circumstances we may face. The validity of everything we do can be judged by the trials we face. We are to know that the adversity we encounter substantiates our practice of the Lotus Sūtra. Schools and denominations that simply engage in easy and comfortable practices are bound to decline.

60

DEBT OF GRATITUDE TO LIVING BEINGS

May 12, 1977
Atami Dōjō, Japan

WHEN BANISHED TO ITŌ, Izu peninsula[1] with his life at risk, Nichiren Daishōnin was rescued by a local fisherman, Yasaburō.[2] It was truly an unexpected, wondrous karmic connection. For just rescuing him could have been done by any passerby, but Yasaburō also came to profess deep faith in the teachings of Nichiren Daishōnin. Since it was a rural area, the local people were extremely fearful of the banished criminal's arrival for they assumed he was a villain. Under such circumstances, Yasaburō and his wife went to great lengths to keep Nichiren Daishōnin alive without the knowledge of others. Nichiren Daishōnin himself wondered how these people came to save his life. Considering their kindliness, he wondered if they might be a reincarnation of his mother and father come to rescue him. He believed he owed his life to the fisherman and his wife and felt deeply indebted to them. Likewise, the sūtra

---

1 Itō 伊東 of the region of Izu 伊豆 is currently Shizuoka prefecture.
2 After presenting the government with *Risshō-ankkoku-ron*, the treatise of remonstration, Nichiren Daishōnin was captured by the government and exiled to Itō in Izu Penninsula [current Shizuoka prefecture] on May 12th of the first year of the Kōchō period [1261]. Nichiren Daishōnin was abandoned at Mana-ita Reef [Butcher's Block], a tiny spur of rock, which was all but submerged by the approaching high tide. Despite a stern decree to the people of Itō not to shelter or look after Nichiren Daishōnin, a fisherman, Yasaburō, approached in a small boat and rescued him. Concerned for the safety of the fisherman and his wife for aiding a criminal, Nichiren Daishōnin declined to stay with them. The couple, with sorrow in their hearts, led Nichiren Daishōnin to a small grotto near the beach and brought him food and water in the secrecy of night to sustain his life for the following months.

says, the Buddha will dispatch men and women of pure faith to make offerings to the practitioner who spreads the Dharma.[3] In light of this passage, Nichiren Daishōnin thought that perhaps *devas* and good protector spirits transformed themselves into the fisherman Yasaburō and saved his life to spare one who spreads the Lotus Sūtra.

In times of adversity, kindness, no matter how small, is keenly felt and appreciated. The teachings of Lord Buddha impart a sense of gratitude towards the whole of creation. This is known as debt of gratitude.[4] With a debt of gratitude, we know to be grateful. Without acknowledging a debt of gratitude, we cannot be grateful. We are indebted to those who save our lives, who aid our aspiration and who join us in faith. This is called *shujō-on*[5] [debt of gratitude to living beings]. We are indebted to all living beings. This indebtedness does not simply come from an offering received today. We were indebted from our previous lives and will be indebted in the future. Toward every one we meet, we must hold this debt of gratitude. This mindset enables us to be grateful to everyone. When our appreciation is felt, they will be impelled to be kind in return. In that, peace is created.

We cannot be grateful when we know no debt of gratitude towards others. Without feeling appreciated, the other party cannot be kind either. Loneliness of isolation results. There is no one but one's self. Being alone is fine when we are well, but once we age or fall ill, it becomes hard if we have no friendly associate because we had failed to acknowledge a debt of gratitude toward anyone. It doesn't end there. We all eventually leave this world, and the next world we head to will invariably become a world of bitterness and enmity instead of a world of gratitude. This is the suffering of transmigration among the six paths.[6] Suffering is

---

3 Lotus Sūtra Chapter X, *The Teacher of the Dharma*.
4 *On* 恩.
5 衆生恩.
6 *Rokudō-rinne* 六道輪廻. A cycle of births and deaths among the six lower states of existence.

created in our own heart and mind. With gratitude, everything is appreciated. A fisherman couple feels like one's own parents. They also could be seen as messengers sent by Buddha. We all live together like this, and if we are likewise thankful to each other, we create a realm of peace. If we cannot be grateful, we turn it into an unpleasant realm, a realm of strife and enmity. This realm of ours should not be such. It must be ever filled with celestial beings. The more there are of us, the more we shall create a realm animated with joy. On the other hand, should we fall into a realm of isolation, we might not have to acknowledge gratitude, but we will not be receiving the kindness of others either.

61

BEGET ARROGANT MINDS

May 19, 1977
Kiyosumi Dōjō, Japan

ARROGANCE IS NOT AROUSED so long as one follows others. Arrogance comes from the desire to lead others. Leading others is fine, but hubris causes one to contrive and command others to walk without walking oneself. Self-indulgence and arrogance beget dissoluteness. One loses introspection and does whatever one pleases, just like a reinless horse that runs wildly about the fields. Where does dissoluteness lead us? It begets attachment to the five desires. The five desires are the desires of the flesh. The life of an ordained is meant to be free from them. An ordained attached to the five desires is far worse than a layperson who is attached to them. Attachment gradually grows starting with things like food, drinks and clothing. Do not think this is someone else's problem. We are all made of flesh. The hurdles of the five desires are different in their form, yet they are no different in that they are all pleasures, desires of the flesh. One is attached to the five desires today, and so is one tomorrow. When one cannot be freed and lives a life of attachment, what happens in the end? One falls into the evil paths. That is what is taught in the *Ojigage*.[1] It is not a good thing.

Water flows. Gentle in its nature, what has already flowed is not overtaken by what will flow. It takes neither command nor

---

1 御自我偈. Reference to the *gāthā* in *The Duration of the Life of the Tathāgata* that starts with "Since I attained Buddhahood" and ends with "And quickly attain the Buddha-body?" Buddha Śākyamuni reveals his eternal nature in this *gāthā*.

instructions for the trailing water to run its course following the exact path as if leading the flow. When we are coalescent, there is no hierarchy in Buddha Dharma—no head, no superior,[2] no rank and file.[3] We are like one body, thereby when those in the front move, so do those coming behind. Things go wrong when those in the front try to make those coming from behind move without themselves moving. Not everything needs be explained with words. When practicing, all that needs to be done by those who come after is to simply follow suit. No explanation is required. When those who go before become Buddha, those who follow will become Buddha. When those who go before fall into evil paths, those who follow will also fall into evil paths. The impasse of Buddhism in Japan comes from this very point. There is no way that those who follow would practice the Buddha Dharma when those who lead do not have faith in it. Buddha Dharma cannot be a living faith that benefits the people where the Dharma is not practiced.

---

2 *Jōrō* 上臈. Monks with seniority in years of practice.
3 *Gerō* 下臈. Junior monks in terms of years of practice.

62

THE BODHISATTVAS WHO EMERGE
FROM THE EARTH—2

May 19, 1977
Kiyosumi Dōjō, Japan

THE BODHISATTVAS Who Emerge From the Earth stay under the ground. That is their abode. Dogs, cats and people tread the ground above them. Without residing under the ground they would not be who they are. At times of grave crisis, they break out from the earth and emerge. The Bodhisattvas Who Emerge From the Earth belong under the earth. Unless we constantly remind ourselves of this, we become arrogant. As monks we read sūtras and writings of Nichiren Daishōnin, and are hence susceptible to fall into thinking that we have acquired some profound theories and become arrogant. Arrogance breeds willfulness, which begets attachment to the five desires.[1] One starts to freely drink and eat meat and is not satisfied without a feast. What awaits after that is falling into the evil path. That is what the sūtra says.[2] Do not think that this has nothing to do with you. It goes to the very heart of how we conduct ourselves throughout our life. Where do we place ourselves? At the bottom of the earth. In times of need we break the earth open and emerge.

The Bodhisattvas Who Emerge From the Earth rarely surface from the ground. These Bodhisattvas emerged when the Lotus Sūtra was being expounded. Never once had they appeared during any other sūtras expounded by the Buddha throughout his

---

1   Reference footnote 3 of *Great Adversity and Comfortable Conduct*, p. 137.
2   Chapter XVI of the Lotus Sūtra, *The Duration of the Life of the Tatāgatha*.

50 years of preaching the Dharma. Their appearance was very brief even during the Lotus Sūtra, and they then concealed themselves once again. They do not show themselves when not needed. They do not appear when others would suffice to do the job. The only time Bodhisattvas Who Emerge From the Earth come forward is at crucial times and places when others do not suffice to do the work. This is why they remain under the earth and strenuously practice the Buddha Way in readiness for the time of need. When the Bodhisattvas Who Emerge From the Earth sprang out [at the time of Lord Buddha's preaching of the Lotus Sūtra], the congregation was incredulous and wondered if they were Lord Buddha's teachers. These Bodhisattvas accumulated virtues under the ground to such an extent that made people initially think that they were like the father and Lord Buddha their son. That is who Bodhisattvas Who Emerge From the Earth are.

63

Hierarchy

June 3, 1977
Kudan Dōjō, Tōkyō

THERE ARE ATTEMPTS to bring hierarchy into Nipponzan. Hierarchy has absolutely no place in the One Vehicle Lotus Sūtra, which is "the teaching of equality, the great wisdom." Buddhism was the antithesis to the discrimination of the class system. Castes exist in India's Hinduism. The highest in hierarchy are the Brāhmans, followed by the Kshatriyas and so forth. This kind of class system is not good. When I was young, the conscription was in place, and I was drafted as a soldier.[1] The military is a complete class system. Japan fought the war with this and was defeated. Hierarchy breeds disunity between those at the top and the rank and file. Those at the top are haughty and those at the bottom are kept subordinate. I don't know how great the people at the top may be, but the very act of imposing restraint under authority is contrary to Buddha Dharma. Not a single Dharma in the Sangha of Buddha Śākyamuni is meant to subordinate others. It is taught that when one is ordained and joins the order, every one becomes equally the child of the Buddha Śākyamuni regardless of which four castes one may come from. Whether a thief, beggar, prince or man of wealth, every person is equal as Buddha Śākyamuni's disciple.

---

1 The Meiji government's policy of *haibutsu-kishaku* [persecution of Buddhism] required the ordained to be included in the national registry system, which imposed conscription.

During his last hours at Ikegami,[2] Nichiren Daishōnin provisionaly appointed six senior bhikshus[3] to guide the devotees and disciples after his passing. However, the recent indiscretions of willfully bestowing upon yourselves the titles of senior bhikshus, elder bhikshus or *jōrō*[4] are arrogant acts destructive to the survival of the order. After the passing of the six elders, people again looked for representatives of the order. People did not volunteer for the position, but through recommendation the status of *chū-rōsō*[5] came into existence. *Chū-rōsō* are not elderly bhikshus,[6] but since they stood above others, the word *chū* [middle] was used to signify their position, which was still a rank below the earlier mentioned six senior bhikshus. These positions do not really mean anything. The position of *chūrō-sō* is no assurance that people with this title practice the Buddha Dharma. What made Nichiren Daishōnin's six senior elder monks *chū-rōsō* and the disciples who they were was the chanting and spreading of the Odaimoku. Once there is *jōrō*, by the very connotation of the word, others are considered *gerō*,[7] creating a situation of subordination whereby those at the top look down on the rest to be less than who they are. *Jōrō* are those who have the mindset of entitlement as leaders of the order. This is arrogance and indeed one of the crimes of slander against the Dharma. Buddha Dharma will be destroyed when monks

---

2 In September 1281, Nichiren Daishōnin left Mount Minobu to recuperate from his illness at a hot spring. En route he arrived at Lord Ikegami Munetaka's residence in Ikegami [currently in Ōta ward, Tōkyō]. His health deteriorated rapidly, and Nichiren Daishōnin, sensing that his death was approaching, gave a discourse on *Risshō-ankoku-ron* for the last time for his disciples and devotees who gathered from throughout Japan. He appointed six elder disciples to serve as bearers of the Dharma light after his passing and entrusted the spreading of the teachings in Kyōto to Kyōichimaru [later called Nichizō]. On October 13, 1282, a great mandala was suspended above his deathbed, and Nichiren Daishōnin passed away amid the prayers of his disciples and followers at the age of 61.
3 *Roku-rōsō* 六老僧.
4 上臈. High monks with years of practice.
5 Intermediate senior bhikshus 中老僧.
6 *Rōsō* 老僧.
7 Junior bhikshus with little experience in practicing the teachings 下臈.

become arrogant.

The Bodhisattvas Who Emerge From the Earth must remain under the ground. Creatures such as cows and horses tread on the earth. We must stoop and keep our heads low, being stepped upon by those who walk the earth. That is why a life of mendicancy—assuming the appearance of humility with a shaved head and wearing a monk's robe—becomes necessary. Equality is listed first and foremost in the teachings of the Buddha. My robe is of the same color and material as yours. The only difference is that ordained men are called *oshōnin-sama* and women *anju-sama*. Titles such as elders or *jōrō* must be revoked. If they were allowed, Nipponzan would fall apart in the future. No one would be willing to serve others but instead constantly seek to move upward. Nipponzan would end up crowded with arrogant people who try to lead others. No one would be willing to be led by such people. Or if they were, it would be a congregation of flatterers and cunning minds. These are not people who would truly build peace in the world. If you want to do good things but are deterred by lack of resources, then stay in that impasse. Nichiren Daishōnin's life at Mount Minobu sets an example for this. The construction of this temple was financially challenging, but I decided to build it. Another temple will be built in Kiyosumi. While building temples and the like could be a detriment if the mind is not in the right place, it is a good thing when we make them the Dharma-work of demonstrating that this *sahā* world is the Pure Land, the Land of Tranquil Light with temples and stately buildings adorned with various treasures as depicted in *The Duration of the Life of the Tathāgata*. To that end, the building of temples must be fundamentally understood as an issue of the mind and heart. Do not think that money is what enables you to build a temple. When money is solicited to build a temple, which includes funds given unwillingly, what happens? Ososhi-sama would not be pleased even if the Buddha hall were completed.

64

CONTRIBUTION

June 13, 1977
Kudan Dōjō, Tōkyō

NO MATTER HOW GRAND the Dharma-work, Nipponzan will absolutely not solicit contributions based on quotas, which is a burden to everyone concerned. We shall get by adhering to this principle. What happens if it does not work? Simply suspend the construction. It would not inconvenience anyone. It becomes intolerable if we were to solicit assigned contributions from our limited number of disciples and supporters each time we take on a succession of major works that other schools cannot undertake. I have no problem encouraging people to chant the Odaimoku. It is a good thing. Soliciting contributions is not. Monks scheming indecent things cause the Buddha Dharma to decline.

The privation Ososhi-sama endured during his eight years at Mount Minobu is hard to fathom. There is a *Gomyōhan* in which he writes that his thin clothing was far from adequate to protect him from the cold, and food had been gone for days; when he thought his life might finally end through starvation, alms of taro and salt arrived unexpectedly. Ososhi-sama wrote that this allowed him to narrowly escape death, and so he might be able to see the correspondent once again.[1] Not a single *Gomyōhan*

---

1 *Haru no Hajime no Goshōsoku* 春初御消息 *Letter on the Inception of Spring.* Written at Mount Minobu to a devotee, Lord Nanjō Tokimitsu, also referred to by Nichiren Daishōnin as Lord Ueno, taken from the name of his fiefdom. The date it was written is uncertain, although some scholars believe it was either in the 1st or 5th year of Kōan [1277 or 1282].

149

among the four hundred writings left by Ososhi-sama asks for contributions to support his life at Mount Minobu. Nipponzan will absolutely not solicit financial quotas. Such dealings involving money with devotees gravely undermine the Buddha Dharma. No contribution is to be solicited. If asked to give, do not comply. As monks, there should be no objection to life in hardship. Manage to get by. If not, you must leave Nipponzan. The teachings of Nipponzan must not be tarnished.

65

GYAKKU-SHŌDAI—2

June 30, 1977
Kiyosumi Dōjō, Japan

EVER SINCE THE ODAIMOKU was handed down from Ososhi-sama, the speed in which it is chanted has gradually increased. Nipponzan's style is to clearly enunciate each and every word of Na Mu Myō Hō Ren Ge Kyō while beating the drum in cadence. Your Odaimoku must be in unison with every one else.

"The chant of the Dharma sound creates music to the ears," according to Venerable Gensei.[1] The rhythm of the drum is Nipponzan's lifeline. If we cannot keep this rhythm harmonious, what else can we possibly expect to keep in unity? Unity cannot be expected with dissonance at the very root of what should unite all sentient beings. "Na, Mu" are short sounds but require two beats with your drumstick. The initial Na, Mu, Myō are three beats. The chanting of Hō Ren Ge Kyō is accompanied with a slower beat of the drum. The three and four beat suits the music. Maintain these beats consistently. When you hit each beat alternately with your hands, you should be able to get seven beats out of the large drum. For those syllables that are short, a lighter touch on the drum would suffice. It can also be quicker. Yet, do not skip a beat just because the syllables are short and only hit twice. Also, do not use a single hand to hit the initial three beats just because they are short, quick beats. The rhythm is lighter but alternate your

---

1 Venerable Sōzan Gensei 草山元政 [1623-1668]. A Nichiren monk of high sanctity and learning, known as author of *Sōzan-shu* 早山集. He is also known as a poet and literary figure in the Edo Era.

151

hands. Try to keep the rhythm. Hitting the beats to your liking creates discordance. Na Mu Myō Hō Ren Ge Kyō is the Odaimoku comprised of seven characters. Likewise, your drumstick must hit seven distinct beats.

66

GREAT DHARMA-WORK

July 8, 1977
Kiyosumi Dōjō, Japan

GREAT DHARMA-WORK is not defined by the scale of construction, amount of contributions or the number of the people who congregate. It is to act according to the right path as taught by Lord Buddha. It takes nothing more than a single person to practice the Lotus Sūtra. "I, Nichiren, alone read it [the Lotus Sūtra] with my life." Ososhi-sama stood alone throughout his life, without relying on anyone else, and practiced this teaching that shall spread throughout the world during the ten thousand years of the Era of Declining Dharma. He had devotees who made offerings to him, but never once did he write letters of solicitation even during the nine years of extreme hardship and destitution at Mount Minobu, where he lived without access to roads, food and clothing, faced with the risk of starvation.

67

OBON

July 23, 1977
Fuji Dōjō, Japan

JULY IS CALLED *bon-tsuki*.[1] There are two major folk festivals observed by the people in Japan. One is the first day of the New Year and the other is the Urabon[2] festival on July 15. Urabon is also referred to as *chūgen*[3] since it marks the beginning of the second half of the year, a time to again reflect and renew one's thoughts on the remaining half of the year. Let us contemplate on the significance of this festival.

We all mourn the passing of those close to us starting with our parents to our ancestors. No one knows where they go after death. Some think it's needless to worry where they go for there is no telling where, still we cannot be unconcerned. This Buddhist commemoration teaches the rite of bringing the ancestors' spirits home. While there is no telling whether they actually come, that is what is taught.

We visit the ancestral grave where the dead are buried to usher them home. This takes place in the evening with a torch called *mukaebi*.[4] "Please come home with us." Upon returning home, the ancestors are welcomed by members of the family.

1　盆月. The month of *bon*, in which the ceremony known either as Obon or Urabon [Japanese transliteration of the Sanskrit *ullambana*] is observed.
2　盂蘭盆.
3　中元.
4　迎え火. A torch lit on the first day of Urabon to welcome back the spirits of ancestors.

"We're happy to have you back." Mortuary tablets are placed on the altar to represent the ancestors who cannot be seen, and a heartfelt feast is offered. Dumplings, pumpkins and eggplants are typically prepared. The ancestors do not actually eat anything, yet this tradition teaches the living to serve the ancestors' spirits by recalling them as if they were actually before their eyes. It is a matter of the heart and mind. On the third day of Obon, fire is lit on hemp stems for *okuribi*,[5] the light to accompany the ancestors back to their graves. Graves, typically located in lonesome places, are brightened up with lanterns placed by the family. Four legs are attached to an eggplant with corn silk forming the horse's tail. This horse is offered for the spirits to ride back to their world. It might sound like nonsense, but this ceremony serves to connect our world with that of the deceased.

Those who respect the tradition of Obon keep their deceased parents close at heart. We don't know whether the spirits of the dead came home or not. We never see them so perhaps they didn't. Nevertheless, we treat them in our minds as if they did and honor them with offerings. It also presents an opportunity each year to impress upon the children by example how parents are to be served. Though the dead may not visit us, the living in this world recall the dead and are happy preparing a feast to be shared. It's a fine tradition. I feel that this tradition greatly serves to create the closely-knit family system of the East. Individualism is embraced in the West. Once one dies it ends there. Sentiments toward others and human relationships that arise from these two views of the East and the West have come to characterize the societies we live in. Western civilization is accentuated by brutality. Eastern civilization is characterized by the peaceful world as shown by the teaching of Urabon.

As a small child, I hollowed out the seeds of an unripe fruit and placed a candle in it, giving it a blue flame. I remember

---

5　送り火. A torch lit on the last day of Urabon to send the spirits of ancestors back to their world.

going around with it. July 15, by the lunar calendar, is a night when the moon casts its bright light. It is just about the time the autumn breeze is felt. The evening landscape provides a delightful backdrop for children to happily play and run about. Mixed into the delight of the children are the procession to the graveyard and other activities that instill awareness towards their ancestors. If we deny the existence of the spirits simply because they are not seen or because they hardly have any communications with the actual world we live in, what happens? We deny not only the spirits of our ancestors, but of our own existence after death. If one were to think that existence ceases with death, one would not be afraid to do any kind of wrong in this world. The Nirvāna Sūtra teaches that concerns about the afterlife inhibit wrongdoing. The thought of retribution in the afterlife makes it more difficult to commit wrong. Without an afterlife, one feels free to commit any wrong believing there are no consequences, and one has no inhibition in conceiving ill thoughts.

68

Modern Religion

September 12, 1977
Kamakura Dōjō, Japan

Japan was the first nation in history to experience the devastation of nuclear weapons. The use of nuclear weapons on Hiroshima and Nagasaki was horrendous, and this continues to be a major issue for world humanity. On the Emperor's [Hirohito] first visit to the United States,[1] he was asked his thoughts on the atomic bombings. The Emperor responded that while he deeply sympathizes with the victims of Hiroshima and Nagasaki, we can only resign ourselves to the fact that it was during a time of war. That might have been the only way he was able to address the issue, but this answer was unacceptable. Given that Japan was the first country where the issue that goes to the very survival of humanity was put to a test, the Emperor, when the opportunity presented itself, should have said, "It was a tragedy for the whole of humanity. It needs to be stopped." Diplomatic reasons may have prevented him from making a statement like that. However, even if the Emperor said it could not have been helped, humanity must not be resigned to it.

If we say that it could not have been helped, the fate of the people of Hiroshima and Nagasaki becomes the future fate of world humanity. Religions engaged in the modern time must stop this from becoming our fate. The next nuclear war will condemn the entire world to death. Even scholars are not hopeful on the

---

1 Emperor Hirohito's first visit to the United States was on September 30, 1975.

prospects for survival. The current peace movement was born when this very issue was taken up as the work of engaged religion. Whether we are clergy or not, for the survival of humanity, the use of nuclear weapons must be prevented at all costs. We must eliminate all nuclear weapons from the face of the earth. This is what modern religion must be about.

PART SIX

A World of Joy

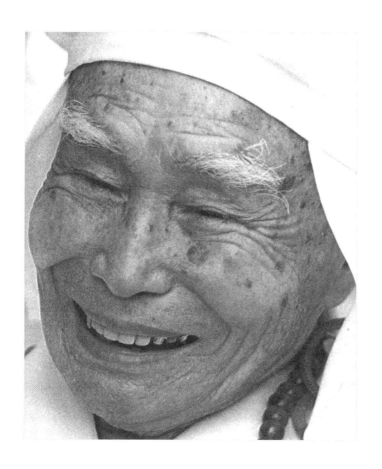

TŌTAIGI-SHŌ

October 4, 1977
Sri Pada Dōjō, Sri Lanka

THE *GOMYŌHAN* of *Tōtaigi-shō*[1] is considered one of Ososhi-sama's important writings. It is primarily a theoretical explication of Na Mu Myō Hō Ren Ge Kyō through philosophical contemplation. Nangaku Daishi[2] mentioned here was Tendai Daishi's master. Despite its brevity, Nangaku Daishi's citation generally gives a complete explication of Myō Hō Ren Ge Kyō.

When we talk about Myō Hō Ren Ge Kyō, it may sound like some kind of theoretical proposition, yet it is not. It is taught that Myō Hō Ren Ge Kyō is the very existence, the entity of all living beings. We live in the realm of humans. The dogs at the front gate belong to the realm of animals, as do the insects. Beneath it is the realm of *asuras*.[3] The national self-defense and security forces and the riot police are somewhat similar to them. Then there is the realm of hungry spirits. They starve to death from deprivation of food. The realm under it is hell. However, the realm of hell can manifest in the realm of humans. Those who witnessed the plights of Hiroshima and Nagasaki all described them as hell. Every one of these realms are said to be the existence of Myō Hō Ren Ge Kyō.

---

1 当体義鈔. *Entity of the Sublime Dharma.*
2 Nan-yüeh, or also known as Hui-ssŭ [515-577], the second patriarch in the lineage of the Chinese Tendai School.
3 Originally in Brahmanism and Hinduism, *asura* is a demigod who fights with the gods headed by Indra. It was introduced into Buddhism and was regarded as a devil fond of fighting by nature.

Myō Hō Ren Ge Kyō is considered sacred and is the religious object of veneration. The very existence of Myō Hō Ren Ge Kyō encompasses every living being in the ten realms from hell to the realm of the Buddha. These are not separate realms, but one and the same. We tend to think that hell is different from where we live; that we are separated from the realm of animals, and, for that matter, that the realm of the Buddha is a totally separate realm. They are separate but are also one and the same. When delusion caused by evil karma occurs within the existences of Myō Hō Ren Ge Kyō noumenon, hell or the realm of hungry spirits manifests. When a pure and undefiled karma is created, it gradually manifests as Buddha. Myō Hō Ren Ge Kyō is the noumenon of our existence; our very existence is Myō Hō Ren Ge Kyō. Therefore, we must strive to become worthy of the sacred Myō Hō Ren Ge Kyō. We chant Na Mu Myō Hō Ren Ge Kyō first and foremost toward that end.

Nangaku Daishi poses the question of, "What are all living beings?" All living beings are the entity of Myō Hō Ren Ge Kyō. He states, "*Myō* because all living beings are *Myō* [ineffable]." What is *Hō*? "*Hō* [Dharma] because all living beings are the Dharma." Living beings and the Dharma are two different things. However, the existence of living beings is the Dharma as in *Myō-hō*, the ineffable, wondrous Dharma. Its wondrous actions could transform into either good or bad. This cosmic dynamic is the Dharma. This dynamic occurs not because of the Dharma, but the Dharma exists because there is this constant dynamic. Living beings in themselves are the Dharma as they are. Living beings themselves are ineffable as they are. They are not a separate existence from the absolute good. Everything is part of the single entity. That is what is expounded here.

70

BLISS OF NIRVĀNA

October 16, 1977
Sri Pada Dōjō, Sri Lanka

IN THE *LETTER FROM SADO*,[1] Ososhi-sama revealed his family's social standing as a son of a fisherman born to a *cāndāla*[2] family, the lowest social class. *Cāndālas* are people who make their living slaughtering living beings. This need not take us aback. No human being is superior to animals. Just like them, we are made of flesh and bones with blood circulating in our body. What separates us from animals is our heart and mind. Our heart and mind are not satisfied with being confined to the animal state, simply preoccupied with eating or drinking *sake*. Instead, our heart and mind aspire for something infinitely lofty. Sometimes the mind may be satisfied with luxury brought about by dishonest conduct. This reflects the state of the mind that is still settled within the physical boundary, the state of animals.

Ososhi-sama states that "while I have professed a bit of faith in the Lotus Sūtra, my body. . ." He says he cherished a bit of faith. Ososhi-sama believed in the absolute sacredness of the Lotus Sūtra. He sought to house the sacred Lotus Sūtra in his heart and mind. The revered Lotus Sūtra came to dwell there

---

1 *Sado-gosho* 佐渡御書. Written on March 20, 1252 by Nichiren Daishōnin at the age of 51 at Tsukahara, Sado. Nichiren Daishōnin's exile caused doubt and turmoil among his disciples and followers. He wrote this letter to ease their doubts and to substantiate his validity as the practitioner of the Lotus Sūtra.
2 旃陀羅. *Sendara, Cāndāla* is the lowest class of people in Hindu India, who are generally considered outcasts or untouchables, below the four traditional social classes. These are people who make a living primarily on hunting or butchery.

because he sought for it. This makes us fearless of even Bonten[3] or Taishaku.[4] When we bear the most sacred in our heart and mind, we are not afraid even of the gods in heaven. We live together with this mind.

Our body is not that different from animals like dogs or cats. Their flesh, once consumed, becomes part of us. Our body might be that of an animal, but our heart and mind seek the absolute sacred, the Buddha. The mind is perturbed when driven by the flesh. When driven by the mind, considerable suffering is imposed on the flesh. It is not a state of contentment, as an animal's existence.

The word "practice" has long been handed down to us. A life of practice is a life of encouraging the flesh to accommodate the mind. That's what we strive for. Our body, which is no different from that of a dog, a cat or a sparrow, must be made to be in concordance with our heart and mind that hold the absolute sacred. Other animals have a mind, but strangely its function is dormant; it is not awakened as much as human beings. Despite the flesh, the mind of human beings is more easily awakened.

The Buddha expounded various teachings, primarily on what humans should do. In terms of numbers, there are also many insects, monkeys or dogs. Although I would not completely deny the possibility, it is extremely rare for the Buddha to appear before them to spread spiritual teachings. The Buddha was born in the human world and delivered his teachings. He left the path to become Buddha in detail. Joy in the world of humans is neither to

---

3   Brahmadeva. i) The highest god according to some Hindus. God as the creator of universe. ii) The first and lowest of the four-dhyāna heavens [shizenten] in the world of form.
4   Śakro devānām indrah, one of the two tutelary gods of Buddhism. He lives in the Palace of Correct Views [Zenken-jō] at the top of Mount Sumeru in the Tusita Heaven [Tosotsu-ten]. He receives reports on the moral conditions of the people of the world from the Four-Quarter Kings [Shitenō] and others, who inspect the world on the eighth, fourteenth and fifteenth days of each month. He transformed into a devil and tested Buddha Śākyamuni on several occasions.

feast nor to possess a villa. We must seek out bliss in the world of the heart and mind. This is called bliss of nirvāna.[5] It is a tranquil joy, free from the flames of delusion.

---

5 *Jakumetsu-no-raku* 寂滅の楽楽. The bliss of *upaśama* [Sk]. Tranquil bliss, having transcended birth and annihilation. A Chinese translation of nirvāna.

71

THE HONZON OF THE DHARMA OF THREE GREAT MYSTERIES

October 18, 1977
Sri Pada Dōjō, Sri Lanka

THE MANDALA[1] HANDED DOWN in the Nichiren School inscribes Na Mu Myō Hō Ren Ge Kyō in the center with Buddha Śākyamuni and Buddha Prabhūtaratna [Buddha Abundant Treasures] attending on each of its sides. Nichiren scholars took this mandala configuration and interpreted the Nichiren School Honzon to be "the Dharma" called "Na Mu Myō Hō Ren Ge Kyō". However, when reading the *Treatise on Seeing the Essential Object of Veneration in the Heart and Mind,*[2] all Honzons have been Buddhas and Bodhisattvas, not the Dharma. The noumenon from which every kind of emancipation for all beings emanates, which is the Honzon, cannot be Buddha Śākyamuni or Buddha Amitābha [Buddha of Infinite Light] because they are perceived to be relative beings. Na Mu Myō Hō Ren Ge Kyō, the Odaimoku, represents the identity of the absolute being rather than the identity of an individual Buddha by name. If that is true, one may wonder if the Odaimoku is Dharma. It is not. It is the mystery of the Tathāgata. It is the Tathāgata.

In *Ongikuden,*[3] Ososhi-sama teaches that, "Na Mu Myō

---

1 A diagrammatic description representing the cosmic nature of Buddhas, Bodhisattvas and other divine beings, which is regarded as a symbol of the universe.
2 Refer to footnote 1 in *Buddha-Nature in All Creation,* p. 125.
3 Refer to footnote 4 in *Ignorant Monks,* p.50.

Hō Ren Ge Kyō is the sacred title of the one and original and never-changing Buddha with triple emanation."[4] However, some scholars still consider that this Honzon cannot be a person since it is called Na Mu Myō Hō Ren Ge Kyō. The *Treatise on Seeing the Essential Object of Veneration in the Heart and Mind* refers to it as the Buddha statue. Ososhi-sama says that this statue of the Buddha appears for the first time in the Era of Declining Dharma with Buddha Śākyamuni and Buddha Prabhūtaratna as attendants. He elucidates that, "...other Buddhas, such as Buddha Amitābha or Mahāvairocana Tathāgata,[5] representing provisional Buddhas in their respective lands, line up on the ground." The two treatises of *Treatise on Seeing the Essential Object of Veneration in the Heart and Mind* and *Requital of Gratitude*[6] provide detailed descriptions of the Honzon of the Dharma of Three Great Mysteries. Both must be carefully perused. *Reply to Lady Nichinyo*[7] is another writing that addresses the issue of the Honzon. As such, Na Mu Myō Hō Ren Ge Kyō is not a Dharma. It is a person.

---

4 *Musa-sanjin* 無作三身 means that the three Buddha bodies embody the original, eternal and never changing Buddha and are all one in the same. The three bodies are *hosshin* 法身 Dharma-body, *hōjin* 報身 Reward-body and *ōjin* 応身 Response-body of the Buddha, i.e., the Buddha who transcends personality; the Buddha body acquired as a result of practice over many kalpas; the Buddha who manifest himself for the benefit of unenlightened sentient beings.
5 Buddha Vaiocana.
6 報恩鈔 *Requital of Gratitude* was written by Nichiren Daishōnin on July 21, 1276 after receiving notice of the death of his master Dōzen-bō.
7 日女御前御返事 *Nichinyo-gozen-gohenji.* Written in 1277, considered to have been sent from Mount Minobu. Lady Nichinyo was one of the female followers of Nichiren Daishōnin. Her identity is not known, but one possibility is said to be the wife of Ikegami Munenaka.

72

Raihai

October 22, 1977
Sri Pada Dōjō, Sri Lanka

There is a phrase *isshin-gasshō sengō-songen*.[1] It means we look up to the noble countenance of Buddha in one mind with palms together. The hands must be placed high at this time. Do not let your hands fall below your face when performing *raihai*[2] [bowing in veneration with palms together] toward Buddha. The hands of those who are perfunctory in performing veneration gradually come down. We must join our palms together and assume the posture of looking up to Buddha as we pay homage. This is the demeanor exemplified by the Bodhisattvas Who Emerge From the Earth in the chapter of *The Divine Transcendental Powers of the Tathāgata*.[3] *Raihai* must be performed with the posture of looking up high at Buddha. Our hands must be in keeping with our eyes and should not be below our face. This is the rite of *raihai* handed down in Buddha Dharma. It is an extremely important rite. Do not take it lightly.

The practice of *raihai* in itself is the practice of Bodhisattva Never Despise. A peaceful world is created wherever *raihai* is practiced respectfully. *Raihai* cannot be performed when quarreling. It should not be done any which way you please. Nothing is more important than *raihai* for Nipponzan. Na Mu Myō Hō Ren Ge Kyō is *raihai* expressed in words. The twenty-

---

1 一心合掌・膽仰尊顔.
2 礼拝.
3 Chapter XXI of the Lotus Sūtra.

168

four-character *gāthā* by Bodhisattva Never Despise teaches the spirit behind *raihai*. "I deeply revere you. I dare not slight you." If one is to take this rite as a mere formality without deep respect in one's heart, one starts to do it the way one pleases and eventually ceases to do it all together. A cursory *raihai* to the Buddha results in taking the Dharma desultorily. If even monks become weary and sloppy in saluting with joined palms, then no one will perform *raihai*. One would no longer salute parents, children, wife and husband, neighbors or laborers with palms together. At Nipponzan the practice of *raihai* takes precedence over reading sūtras.

73

Eighteen Superb Attributes

November 14, 1977
Sri Pada Dōjō, Sri Lanka

Eighteen Superb Attributes[1] was a response by Ososhi-sama to a question raised by a disciple[2] who was previously an Enryaku-ji Temple scholar at Mount Hie. The disciple asked what was meant by "eighteen superb attributes."[3] The Lotus Sūtra provides a congruous solution to everything, hence the disciple inquired into the superior attributes of the Lotus Sūtra from the perspective of various doctrines. This writing expresses Ososhi-sama's ultimate views on this subject. *Tenshin-dokurō*[4] means to transcend mundane cognizance and to clearly perceive phenomena in the natural world, i.e., truth, as existing in one's mind and heart. I would not dismiss *tenshin-dokurō* as a bad thing. It is a good thing. However, this practice does not offer benefit unless it meets the time and the capacity of the recipients. Moreover, not only is it of no benefit but, on the contrary, if it were to be spread just because it is not wrong it can ultimately hinder the teachings that would save the era. Nichiren Daishōnin stated that, "Ultimately, the teaching of *tenshin-dokurō* is of no benefit now that we are in the Era of Declining Dharma." At Nichiren School today, we seem to see more learning for learning's sake rather than for the

---

1 *Jūhachi-enman-shō* 十八円満鈔. Written on Nov. 3, 1280.
2 Sairenbō Nichijō 最蓮房日浄, a former Tendai school scholar who became Nichiren Daishōnin's disciple during his exile in Sado.
3 The chanting of Odaimoku encompasses the eighteen superb attributes.
4 天真独朗.

purpose of bringing emancipation to the people. Nichiren School's university is located in Ōsaki [Risshō University]. It has produced scholars but no sages or monks of high virtue who are vanguards in bringing liberation to the modern time in the Era of Declining Dharma. The teaching of *tenshin-dokurō* is of no benefit now that we are in the Era of Declining Dharma.

In that case, what about reciting the Lotus Sūtra since "every single letter represents Buddha"? It is not a bad thing. It is a good thing, yet sadly, it does not suit the capacity of the times either. Like other Buddhist schools, the Nichiren School still has a tradition of speed-reading. The eight volumes, 69,000 kanji characters of the Lotus Sūtra are recited in two to three hours. In fact, I also recited the Lotus Sūtra numerous times. Until fairly recently, I used to recite all twenty-eight chapters of the Lotus Sūtra at the end of the year. Eventually one knows it by heart making it possible to rapidly recite it in about three hours. When I first went to Manchuria to spread the Dharma, since Manchuria was then a colony, the Japanese were late in rising in the morning. The family that provided me with lodging slept until seven or eight in the morning. I couldn't bear to do that and used to unobtrusively recite the entire Lotus Sūtra. It can be done without raising the voice. However, given the era when emancipation to all is the overarching task at hand, having people merely listen to my recitation of the Lotus Sūtra would not do. Hearing the Lotus Sūtra is certainly not a bad thing. If even listening to the Lotus Sūtra were a good thing, a way allowing everyone to practice it together would be even better.

China's Wise One, Tendai Daishi, and Dengyō Daishi of Japan, who inherited his teachings, practiced the teaching of *kannen*[5] [concentration and insight on truth through contemplation]. This is what is known as the teaching of *tenshin-dokurō*. It is an attempt to discern the true phenomena of the

---

5 観念.

universe through the tools of Buddhism. It is certainly not a bad thing to do. However, while it may be fine for monks who can dedicate themselves to this practice, it is not conducive to lay people who are busy making a living. Precisely for this reason, the Nenbutsu School came into being based on the view that the Lotus Sūtra, despite being a sublime sūtra, cannot emancipate the era.[6] The intention of the Nenbutsu School[7] was not to disparage the Lotus Sūtra. Both Honen[8] and Shinran,[9] representing the Nenbutsu schools, initially practiced at and left Mount Hie. Though they believed that the Lotus Sūtra was superb, yet they did not believe it to suit the capacity of the times. They addressed this issue and gave birth to the faith in the Pure Land. This *sahā* world is defiled, and we cannot but resign ourselves to the inept capacity of human beings to comprehend the Dharma. Therefore, by chanting Na-mu Amida-butsu, we were to receive transmigratory rebirth into the Pure Land and comprehend the Dharma in the next life. This faith gained popularity. This, again, was what the times demanded.

Nichiren Daishōnin then came and stated that the issue is not transmigrating to the Pure Land; rather it is what we do in this *sahā* world we live in. Nichiren Daishōnin closely examined the Lotus Sūtra left for us by Lord Buddha, who appeared in this world. He was of the belief that there is no reason why it would not benefit the Era of Declining Dharma. He determined that the Buddha expounded the Lotus Sūtra specifically to be practiced in the Era of Declining Dharma. If so, how can it be spread?

---

6   Here Guruji refers to the emancipation of the era with the understanding that the era and the people within it are intrinsically connected and cannot be considered separate. An era is characterized by the capacity and disposition of the people within it.

7   The Pure Land schools, such as Jōdo and Jōdoshin schools.

8   Hōnen-bō Genkū 法然房源空 [1133-1212] was the founder of Jōdo School during the Kamakura period that developed the Japanese version of the Pure Land Buddhism with the nenbutsu, or calling on the grace of Amida Buddha.

9   Shinran 親鸞, founder of the Jōdoshin school [1173-1262]. Initially practiced the Tendai method of attaining enlightenment at Mount Hie, he later left and becomes Hōnen's disciple.

Nichiren Daishōnin condensed it into the seven characters of Na Mu Myō Hō Ren Ge Kyō to accommodate the capacity of this era and bestowed it to all. It was not transmitted from Tendai Daishi or Dengyō Daishi. *Eighteen Superb Attributes* states it to be a "bequeathal [to Bodhisattva Superior Practice] that took place inside the stūpa."[10] Above the assembly grounds at the Divine Eagle Peak, the Buddha summoned the Bodhisttva-Mahāsattvas numerous as the sands of sixty thousand Gangā Rivers to the stūpa of treasures of Tathāgata Prabhūtaratna and entrusted the leading Bodhisattva Superior Practice with Na Mu Myō Hō Ren Ge Kyō to be transmitted in the Era of Declining Dharma to cure its grave illness. Although already in the Era of Declining Dharma, Bodhisattva Superior Practice was yet to emerge from beneath the earth. "Since I, Nichiren, have a rough understanding of the Dharma to be transmitted by Bodhisattva Superior Practice, I have been but ceaselessly murmuring it until the advent of Bodhisattva Superior Practice."[11] Ososhi-sama says that although he himself is not Bodhisattva Superior Practice who was designated for its transmission, until such time, he will gently murmur the Odaimoku and spread it.

There are temples even today in the Nichiren School where the Lotus Sūtra is recited numerous times. The Hōonji Temple in Usuki, Ōita Prefecture, where I was ordained, would perform its recitation a hundred times or so during a week in a major ceremony attended by many monks. There is a bronze statue of Nichiren Daishōnin in Hakata, where there is a tradition called *senbue*, a service of reciting the entire Lotus Sūtra a thousand times by a large congregation of monks. Reading the Lotus Sūtra is certainly not a bad thing. However, it offers no benefit in liberating the people in the time we live in. This is why Nichiren Daishōnin taught that the teaching of *tenshin-dokurō* must be employed as auxiliary

---

10 Reference to Chapter XV of the Lotus Sūtra.
11 Citation from *Honzon-mondō-shō* 本尊問答鈔 [*Question and Answers on the Honzon*]. Written at Mount Minobu in September 1278.

practice, not as primary practice. In spite of this, when we go to the morning and evening services at Mount Minobu or adjacent temples, the recitation of the Lotus Sūtra is still the predominant practice. The chanting of the Odaimoku is not established as the primary practice. Reading the Lotus Sūtra is not a bad thing, but it will not save the era we live in.

74

Meditation, Koan, Chanting

December 3, 1977
Sri Pada Dōjō, Sri Lanka

Introductions to Buddhism today usually talk about meditation. Meditation is a very popular word right now. The Zen School was one of the places where I trained.[1] I wouldn't say that contemplation[2] through *zazen*[3] is not helpful, but what appears when one meditates? It's not likely the Buddha. In meditation, the meditator attempts to probe into matters of the mind through discernment, such as innate wisdom, yet in reality does not arrive at much profundity no matter how long he or she may contemplate. Zen master Hakuin[4] wrote that when we meditate, we are likely to think of trivial things, such as getting back the money loaned to a neighbor or the need to go buy groceries for tomorrow. Thinking with eyes closed really doesn't produce much good. The Zen School was in a bind with this. Hakuin Zenji did not feel it to be meaningful to have people sit for hours and conceived of providing kōans[5] for contemplation. Buddha Dharma teaches, "all

---

1 Guruji trained under Zen Master Takeda Mokurai 竹田黙雷 [1854-1930], abbot of Kennin-ji 建仁寺 in Kyōto and one of the most respected Zen Masters of his time.
2 Kanbō 観法. i) Contemplation on an objective thing or a reality principle. ii) A method of contemplation.
3 座禅. Meditation with one's legs crossed.
4 Hakuin Ekaku 白隠慧鶴 [1685-1769] is known to have restored the Rinzai Zen School during the Edo period. Also commonly known as Hakuin Zenji 白隠禅師.
5 公案. In Zen, it is an account of a master's actions or statements, including questions and answers, and is used as an object of meditation for attaining enlightenment.

sentient beings have Buddha-nature." Hence, a question such as "Does a dog have Buddha-nature?" could be asked. Questions like this are provided to replace random thoughts like having to run an errand to buy five cups of rice. This is the Zen kōan. However, whether a dog has Buddha-nature or not is not something we can know for sure through intellectual exercise.

For us to sustain the Lotus Sūtra means to pray in our heart and mind, chant through our mouth and move with our body. All that is required is to say Na Mu Myō Hō Ren Ge Kyō. According to the chapter of *Expedient Means* in the Lotus Sūtra, the very first thing that the Buddha utters in expounding the Lotus Sūtra is, "The wisdom of Buddhas is extremely profound and immeasurable. The gateway to their wisdom is difficult to understand and difficult to enter." We are bestowed with the five and seven characters of Na Mu Myō Hō Ren Ge Kyō imbued with the Lotus Sūtra so that we may hold it. It may appear simple, yet the single phrase of Na Mu Myō Hō Ren Ge Kyō is equipped with the Dharma of Three Great Mysteries revealed in *The Duration of the Life of the Tathāgata* chapter of the essential section of the Lotus Sūtra. It is the master of the Buddhas of the past, present and future. It is the teacher of the Bodhisattvas in the quarters of the ten directions. It contains in it the path to enlightenment for all sentient beings. This was Nichiren Daishōnin's belief in starting to chant the Odaimoku. We chant believing in it.

Votive Lights

December 29, 1977
Sri Pada Dōjō, Sri Lanka

Votive lights on the altar tend to gutter and flow down when the flames are large, and this is wasteful. For this reason, we cut the wick short to control the flame. But while large candles with an incense-like small flame last longer and economize the candle, they lose their significance as votive lights. As suggested by such phrases as "the blazing light created by numerous votive lanterns" or "the luminescence of a single light offered by the destitute," the main purpose of a votive light is to illuminate. Making the light smaller does not take precedence over illumination. If you misunderstand this point, you erroneously think that votive lights serve their purpose so long as there is a faint light that barely goes out and would try to make them as small as possible. Votive lights need to be bright. Yet, at the same time we must prevent wasting candles by their guttering down. These are important considerations when handling votive lights. The world of the Buddha is not in darkness; it is a world of illumination. We are to keep the candles bright to mirror the reflection of the world of the Buddha here. Votive lights must be kept bright. We keep them brighter than usually needed. The world of light we are emulating here needs to be bright. Particularly at the time of major ceremonies, incense-like lights on large candles will not do. Do not forget to keep them bright.

76

A WORLD OF JOY

January 18, 1978
Sri Pada Dōjō, Sri Lanka

DŌJŌS ARE PLACES on earth built to emulate the Pure Land. Here there is neither gain nor loss. I have built dōjōs and stūpas simply out of my desire to create a world of joy. The flowers, altar fittings and drums are all tools prepared to evoke joy in our hearts. The life at a dōjō should be "ever filled with celestial beings."[1] Celestial beings do not come from another world to fill this place. Those who reside here are to enter the world of joy.

The first condition of the Pure Land that can be created in the human world is a world without anger. Gandhiji's effort to free India was not characterized by various arguments or theories, but by his lack of anger. He sat calmly no matter what happened. He quietly excused himself when his opinions were not heard and allowed others to their opinions. In many instances his guidance was solicited when the opinions of others led to a deadlock. The only way to create the Pure Land where a large number of people live together is through the joy of everyone involved. Being right or wrong is secondary.

It is said, "Joyful is the divine, and tranquil is man." Let us first at least try to make this dōjō tranquil, a place without problems, and then strive to elevate a step further and create a world of joy. That is our practice. That is the teaching of Nichiren Daishōnin delivered in the fifth five-hundred-year period after the passing of the Tathāgata. We chant Na Mu Myō Hō Ren Ge Kyō

---

1 Chapter XVI of the Lotus Sūtra, *The Duration of the Life of the Tathāgata*.

with all our hearts so that we may transcend all anger and enmity with a heart of joy. Anger, want, avarice and enmity will all go away when we chant the Odaimoku with a loud voice.

This is the merit of the Odaimoku. The issue does not lie elsewhere. We are to find the Honzon, the sacred entity, within our hearts and minds. When everyone we meet is joyous, this is the Pure Land, a world filled with celestial beings. As the initial step, we must at least create a world of joy in temples, at stūpas and in front of altars.

77

BUDDHA DHARMA OF JAPAN—2

March 15, 1978
Sri Pada Dōjō, Sri Lanka

SHIKAN,[1] WHICH EXPLORES the practice of the Lotus Sūtra within the realm of one's mind, is no longer observed by anyone. Yet, the Lotus Sūtra was not lost because of that. The Buddha left the Lotus Sūtra for the Era of Declining Dharma in the form of the Odaimoku, Na Mu Myō Hō Ren Ge Kyō, to prevent it from being lost. He entrusted its dissemination to Bodhisattva Superior Practice. What I mentioned so far is described in the sūtra. And in reality, Nichiren Daishōnin, born in the Era of Declining Dharma, did start to spread the chanting of Na Mu Myō Hō Ren Ge Kyō. This is the Buddha Dharma that originated in Japan. Being a Buddha Dharma, it neither violates nor conflicts with any of the numerous teachings expounded by Buddha Śākyamuni in his lifetime. Every teaching of Lord Buddha opened the door for dissemination of the single phrase Na Mu Myō Ho Ren Ge Kyō. It is noted that this Buddha Dharma from Japan will be returned to India in the Era of Declining Dharma.

---

1 止観. *Shi* [*śamatha*] and *kan* [*vipaśayana*], which means to discard illusions and attain enlightenment.

PART SEVEN

Faith, Practice and Learning

78

The Spiritual Power of Prayer

June 11, 1978
San Francisco Dōjō

Modern civilization originated in Europe, and its ultimate development is the American civilization. What America now puts all its power and resources behind is, in effect, a scheme to exterminate humanity. The genocide of the Native Americans is but a part of that. Now it is time for this civilization to be expelled from the human world. Modern civilization has placed utmost significance on the physical body, creating machines to serve its convenience and to produce wealth. Wealth and machines have become instruments to annihilate humanity. The appetite for wealth is insatiable no matter how much is acquired. Killing and the production of murderous weapons by the United States are both motivated by the same thing. At the root is not hatred towards others, but blindness induced by the lure of lucre.

The three most dreadful things cited in Buddha Dharma are, first, avarice, second, anger, and third, engaging in sophism. The United States has created a huge government and through greed, anger and ignorance[1] incurs the calamity of obliterating humanity.

What can be done? Transformation must be brought about in the hearts and minds of its people. The path for transformation of the hearts and minds has been handed down from bygone days in the form of religion. America can be saved if the compulsion of

---

1 *Guchi* 愚痴 *moha* [Sk].

183

the American people for material goods is moderated. Humanity will likewise be saved. We must demonstrate the spiritual power of prayer with all we have to bring a halt to America's avariciousness, the root of its wars and murder.

79

The Hour of Death—Chūin

June 25, 1975
San Francisco Dōjō

THE PHENOMENON OF DEATH in Buddhism does not mean that everything vanishes with it. It is the beginning of a transition to another life. Every virtuous and non-virtuous act of the person is weighed before moving on to a new life. There are places where this takes place. One passes through these checkpoints seven times on each seventh day after death. It is said that in most cases, seven times seven, by the forty-ninth day the world into which one transmigrates is generally determined after inquisitions from judge-like figures at each of these checkpoints. The period between one's death and transmigratory rebirth is called *chūin*.[1] We are told that if a decision is not reached during this period, it could at times take as long as a year and up to three years. This is why those who survive the deceased should do good to help him or her move on to a better place. This is the religious teaching that encourages virtuous deeds by the bereaved so that their merits can be sent to those who passed away.

As I just mentioned, the decision on transmigration is made by a number of judges. King Yama[2] is considered to be the

---

1 *Chūin* 中陰 is also called *Chūu* in Japanese. It is one of the four stages of a person's life that includes birth, living, death and *chūin*, the stage of intermediate existence after death and before rebirth.
2 Enma-Daiō 閻魔大王, Yama-rāja [Sk]. King Yama is the fifth of the seven judges of the Buddhist realm of the dead, regarded as the Prince of Hell or the world of hungry spirits.

representative judge. It is an Indian name of the chief judge. A large hanging mirror reflects everything a person did during his or her lifetime. Once the gravity of both right and wrong actions in a person's life are clarified and weighed, and upon the deceased's consent to the decision by King Yama, transmigratory rebirth takes place.

On the other hand, there are times rebirth takes place immediately upon death without the trial that ordinarily ensues. It could be into a good world; it could be into a bad world. Those who transmigrate to a lesser world show suffering at the hour of death. Those who transmigrate into a world of comfort meet death in such a way that reflects the comfort promised in the life to come. It is said that how one appears to be at the time of death is indicative of the life that is to follow.

There are six worlds one can transmigrate into called *rokudō*.[3] The highest of these six worlds is the celestial world, followed by the human, *asura*, animals, hungry spirits and hell. These are all worlds of illusion and not of enlightenment. Each world, both good and bad, is a world of illusion. From the celestial world to the worlds of humans, animals and hell, they are all realms of illusion. Then there are worlds of enlightenment. Buddha Śākyamuni's disciples, such as Śāriputra, Maudagalyāyana, Mahākāśyapa and Ānanda, are referred to as *śrāvaka*.[4] These are people who reach enlightenment by hearing the teachings of the Buddha, acquiring purity of the heart and mind. Next there are those called *pratyekabuddha*[5] who do no wrong. These people do not encounter the teachings of the Buddha, but detach themselves

---

3 六道.

4 *Śrāvaka*. Literally, "one who hears" the voice of the Buddha. Originally, a disciple of the Buddha; later, a follower of Theravāda who contemplates the principle of the fourfold noble truth to attain nirvāna.

5 *Pratyekabuddha*. One who attains enlightenment through completely apprehending the *nidānas*, that is, the twelve-link causal chain [*nidāna*] of existence. Also called "self-apprehended" because the *pratyekabuddha* attains Buddhahood through independent practice, without a teacher.

from illusions of the mind through solitude in places like mountains and through such acts as observing the leaves falling or watching a mountain stream flow by. Above the *pratyekabuddha* is the Bodhisattva. A Bodhisattva is one who aspires to become Buddha. The path of Bodhisattva-hood is extremely long with multiple stages. At the end of the path of Bodhisattva-hood is the Buddha world. This comprises the ten worlds.

The world to which one might transmigrate into varies. We do both good and bad due to the delusions we have. A good place is the celestial world; a reasonable place is the human world; one could possibly even go to the world of animals or *asuras*. What we do in this world is the cause, which brings us to the next world as its consequence. There is no escaping the law of cause and effect.

80

COMMUNICATION OF THE HEART

October 25, 1978
Rajgir Dōjō, India

LEARNING TENDS TO MODULATE what we do within the context of what is learned and impedes us from seeing how we are moved by the Odaimoku. Whether it is learning or language or any kind of skill, reliance on them makes us arrogant. We lose sight of Buddha Dharma. Buddha Dharma requires nothing. It is solely a communication of our heart with Lord Buddha. Nothing more is needed other than to chant Na Mu Myō Hō Ren Ge Kyō. By this we will bring peace to the world. It may not happen. It may happen. We chant believing that it will.

81

Jikihō—1

December 15, 1978
Sri Pada Dōjō, Sri Lanka

I WENT FROM ONE Buddhist school to another to be trained in the teachings of the various schools. The Zen School is the only place where *Jikihō*[1] has been handed down to this day. Apparently it was introduced by Ingen[2] and Mokuan[3] of the Ōbaku School[4] who came to Japan during the Tokugawa Era.[5] "The three virtues and six tastes"[6] is read "*san-te-ru-mi.*" It is neither pronounced according to the ancient *go-on*[7] nor *kan-on,*[8] but rather according

---

1 食法. A *gāthā* from the sūtra offered at meals.
2 Ingen 隠元 [1592-1672]. Born in Fuchien Province 福建省 China, he came to Japan in 1654 and built Manpuku-ji Temple 萬福寺 in Kyōto under the imperial patronage.
3 Mokuan 木庵 [1611-1684]. Chinese monk and disciple of Ingen-zenji 隠元禅師. He came to Japan with his master and succeeded his master's position in 1664 as chief priest of Manpuku-ji. He is the founder of Ōbaku-san Manpuku-ji. 黄檗山萬福寺.
4 One of the three Zen sects introduced to Japan, i.e., Rinzai School 臨済宗, Ōbaku School 黄檗宗 and Sōtō School 曹洞宗.
5 Tokugawa Era spans a period of 260 years, beginning from the time that Tokugawa Ieyasu 徳川家康 united Japan after winning the battle of Sekigahara in 1600 until 1867 when the 15th Shogun, Tokugawa Yoshinobu 徳川慶喜, returned power to the Emperor.
6 三徳六味. The three virtues in reference to food are: light and tender, free of impurities and properly cooked as provided. The six tastes are sourness, saltiness, bitterness, sweetness, spiciness and light flavor.
7 There are several ways that Chinese characters can be pronounced or "read" in the Japanese language. *Go-on* 呉音 is one of the traditional Japanese styles and was used widely for reading Buddhist terms.
8 漢音. One of the Japanese styles of pronouncing Chinese characters that phonetically incorporated standard pronunciation of the Tang Dynasty.

to a more modern[9] pronunciation of Chinese characters. This was how it was pronounced at the Zen monasteries, and I accepted them as they are. "To make offerings equally"[10] is read "*fu-zun-kyū-nyō*." The life of religion is to properly pass down to posterity the exact pronunciation that was handed down to us.

When I was practicing Zen meditation [in 1914] I sat alongside many other fellow monks. These monks said that no other school passed down *Jikihō*, and it was fortunate that at least the Zen School did. Indeed, having heard this, I thought this alone was an achievement. If we truly heed the meaning of each word and phrase contained in the *Gokan-ge*,[11] every single one of them provides an invaluable lesson. Human beings eat to sustain life. Not just once or twice but three times a day. It is a good thing to recite this prayer at every meal. It is an oral practice. Our mind may not always be there, but there are times when it does heed the prayer.

I have spent time here at Sri Pada with many young people. Initially, this was but a small hut. I presently take my meals alone, but back then I ate with everyone else. Among us was an impious young man. He could have at least joined his palms together while the *Gokan-ge* was recited since he wasn't going to join in, but he kept his hands between his thighs. He appeared to be irritated by every one quietly reciting the verse and wore an expression on his face as if he were saying, "What's the big deal. We're going to eat any way. Why don't we get to it?" He looked annoyed throughout the recitation of the *Gokan-ge*. I felt this young man would not be

---

9 Guruji here is referring to the time after the Tang Dynasty by the term modern.
10 普同供養.
11 五観偈. The verse on *Gokan*, the five contemplations at mealtime, is found in the chapter of the *Samantamukha* of Avalokiteśvara. The five kinds of remembrances to be held by a monk before meals are: i) reflection on the labor required to obtain food and on the indebtedness to those who provide the food; ii) reflection on whether one deserves to receive the food; iii) self-restraint to take food in moderation; iv) to regard food as medicine that cures thirst and hunger; v) to regard food as taken for the sake of practicing the Dharma, and not merely for sustaining life.

able to live a life of Buddhist faith now or in the future. I will not accept anyone to be ordained at Nipponzan or allow anyone to stay who appears to think that, "Food is something that is bought with money. Why bother reciting a lengthy *gāthā* from a sūtra? Let's just chow it down. It's just food." If you also come to think when you are busy that "It's meaningless to recite a lengthy sūtra. It's just food after all," you cannot embrace the *Gokan-ge*.

We are all sustained by food, but I know of no other religion in the world that teaches such a noble and pure approach towards food. The Christian faith likewise offers a brief grace before meals in gratitude to God for the food given. It is certainly a good thing, but not as thorough and complete as the *Gokan-ge*. Eating is an act that no one can be free from. Buddha Dharma teaches the truth behind it, what to contemplate on before and after food is taken, as we are just about to do now. The fact that we are able to eat is not simply owed to the purchase of food or offerings by others. The Lotus Sūtra states, "Then all gods and humans shall make offerings to them."[12] When we believe that all beings make offerings to us in accordance with the mandate of Lord Buddha, our perception towards food cannot remain superficial. Do not consider food as mere material objects such as vegetable or meat. It is much more than that. Whatever food it is, it is what allows us to sustain our life, and we are grateful for Lord Buddha's mandate that keeps us alive.

Merely reciting the letters of the sūtra is no different than looking at food as nothing more than objects to be consumed. It causes us to lose sight of the path to spiritual life. We then are no longer people of faith, not qualified as people of faith. The *Gokan-ge* cannot be kept with the mind that sees the recitation of a lengthy sūtra as pointless. We must learn from the *Gokan-ge*. We must learn the Buddha Dharma at each and every meal we

---

12 "Them" refers to those who practice the Lotus Sūtra in the Era of Declining Dharma. Chapter XI of the Lotus Sūtra, *Beholding the Stūpa of Treasures*.

take. The meals we take may be unsavory or meager from a frank perspective of those living in the ordinary world. However, when we recite the *Gokan-ge*, we learn that we are leading a revered life. Take these words to heart as you recite them. Lord Buddha bestows on us a precious lesson each time we take food. *Gokan-ge* is not a fabrication by those who came after the Buddha, but a teaching handed down to us from the days of Lord Buddha.

82

BUILDING STŪPAS

April 16, 1979
Yoshino-yama Dōjō, Japan

OUR EFFORTS IN BUILDING stūpas for peace are no longer limited to Buddhist countries. The first such stūpa appeared in the peace city of Milton Keynes in England. I understand that the vision behind the newly developed Milton Keynes, as a city of peace in England, was to build a model city to be emulated by the world in the 21st century. A stūpa emerged there. It was not by my asking. It was a spontaneous development. As this illustrates, I urge you to do what is right with faith in the inexplicable workings of the worlds we cannot see. It may sound like an extremely difficult thing to do, but it simply boils down to not taking the life of others and not stealing from others. Arms build-up is another word for killing. Trade is another word for stealing. Frivolous and cunning sophism is used to cheat others of their possessions or to openly scheme to kill others. Correcting these fallacies of the world, of the governments and their leaders, is likewise a matter of the heart and mind that we cannot see. The human heart and mind are the agents driving the transmission of the teachings of Lord Buddha. Fortunately, there are prospects for still more stūpas to be built in Japan as well. Over 1,400 years ago, Emperor Shōmu[1] created

---

1 Emperor Shōmu 聖武天皇 [701-705], 45th Imperial ruler of Japan reigned between 724-749. He is best known for commissioning the 16-meter high statue of Buddha Vairocana in the Tōdaiji Temple in Nara as well as establishing the provincial temple system [Kokubun-ji 国分寺 for monks and Kokubuni-ji 国分尼寺 for nuns] in each province in Japan.

the foundation of peace in our nation by building major Buddhist temples in 66 provinces, spreading the teachings of peace. I, also, shall build 84,000[2] stūpas throughout the world to create peace.

---

2 Eighty-four thousand is a representation of an extremely large number according to Indian tradition. It is said the Buddha Śākyamuni expounded 84,000 teachings, and Emperor Ashoka built 84,000 stūpas.

83

THE ECONOMY OF BUDDHA DHARMA

May 6, 1979
Kanazawa Dōjō, Japan

THE CURRENT ECONOMY needs to be converted to an offering economy of generosity. Western economy developed through the industrial revolution, focusing on how to efficiently produce, distribute and store goods. The economy of Buddha Dharma of Japan teaches nothing about considering whether one has enough money to spare or to save. If there are people who are hungry, thirsty or cold, the acts of offering, be it food, water or clothing, are themselves the practice of Buddha Dharma. It is not only out of concern for the recipients, but these acts are actually the practice of the Buddha Dharma to the benefit of the one who gives. This traditional offering economy will be restored from Asia. There is no other way to correct the misguided economic system of the West.

One must be willing to have less when giving to others. If the whole purpose of our life becomes to amass as much as we can while willfully spending on ourselves alone, we will come to the same dead end as the West. Asia has what it takes to save the modern civilization. The core of the Asian civilization is the spiritual civilization; it is not the civilization of science. Venerating the Buddha, building stūpas and temples are the kinds of things that make up the spiritual civilization.

84

THE RIGHT PATH

April 7, 1979
Atami Dōjō, Japan

SOME IN NIPPONZAN lead an easy life, making a living out of monkhood. Yet, there are always others who place themselves in the most arduous and challenging circumstances in the world as far as monks today are concerned. This handful of people will bring the spirit of Buddha to the world. Nipponzan owes its existence and survival to this day to these people who toil to spread the Lotus Sūtra through adversity. If there are prospects for Nipponzan to make advancement in spreading the Dharma, it is not because we are many in number, but because there are monks who diligently practice the right path. The right path must be adhered to. It has nothing to do with producing happiness through avarice or to cure an illness.[1] It is to chant and spread the Odaimoku to benefit all sentient beings. The effort of spreading the Odaimoku does not yield monetary offerings or acclaim. People who live abroad do not know what it is, nonetheless they chant, walking around with the monks. This is the reason Nipponzan has spread throughout the world. When monks who chant the Odaimoku lead an idle life, others will follow suit. This becomes the greatest cause for the order to collapse from within.

---

1 Reference to the chanting of Na Mu Myō Hō Ren Ge Kyō for material gain or curing illness.

85

REBUKING THE KWANTUNG ARMY[1]

July 16, 1979
Tama Dōjō, Tōkyō

LAST EVENING I WAS INVITED to a celebration of the 57th anniversary of the Communist Party of Japan held at the Tsubakiyama Hotel. I attended the function, although I am not a member of the Communist Party. While I was seated and resting, many people came up to greet me. Among them was Mr. Kuroda, who served two terms as the Governor of Osaka. I believe he was a police officer when he was initially in Manchuria. He stood in front of me and said, "I remember you at a gathering when you were invited to speak to the major officers of the Kwantung Army 40 years ago in Xinjing, China. I was terrified when you started to rebuke the Kantō Army." It was just about the time I was going here and there after my return from India. I hardly knew anyone with the Kwantung Army, but a lieutenant general by the name Ninomiya, who was previously an assistant chief of staff, introduced me, and I was asked to address the officers of the Kwantung Army.

I initiated the spreading of the Dharma in Manchuria quite some time ago, and by that time there were 10 temples. It gave me frequent opportunities to come in contact with the people. The

---

1 Also known as the Kantō-gun or Guandong Army, the Kwantung Army was a unit of the Imperial Japanese Army. Headquartered in Xinjing. It became the largest and most prestigious command in the Imperial army. Many of its personnel, such as Hideki Tojo, the Chief of Staff of the Kwantung Army, were promoted to high positions in the military and the government.

197

ordained members of the Manchurian temples and ordinary people from farmers to construction laborers all had close association with our temples, so I was able to directly hear their voices. It was clear that the people were not happy with the politics of the Japanese Army. Based on that understanding, I addressed the officers. "Although the Kwantung Army is governing Manchuria now, before long it will be unable to maintain its rule. You do not have the support of the people. There are two courses of actions available to the Kwantung Army at this juncture. If you wish to permanently keep your presence in Manchuria, you could kill every Manchurian. Then there will be no one to hate you. That is not an option. In this case, there is another option. Withdraw now and return to Japan. The Manchurians would be happy, and you can also all go home unhurt."

There was no way the Kwantung Army could have accepted my advice. They felt it was unpardonable for me to suggest relinquishing their rule of Manchuria, which they claimed to have built with great effort in the interest of Japan. However, they had to save the face of the organizer who arranged this meeting, and nothing happened to me on that occasion. The military greatly resented my presence in Manchuria and ordered the mandalas I inscribed that were enshrined at the different regional branches of the Concordia Association to be taken down. The fabric mounting of the mandalas was completely torn off, and only the Odaimoku was sent back to me. The then-superintendent Kuroda, who was present as a police officer, told me, "I was terrified when you rebuked the Kwantung army 40 years ago. I was shuddering, not knowing what might happen to you."

86

ORDAINED LIFE

October 22, 1979
Delhi, India

THE ORDAINED PERSON must lead a life of service to the world. The purpose of becoming ordained is not in leading a life of comfort, simply getting by and doing nothing more than eating, making monkhood into a livelihood. Our momentous objective is to spread the Odaimoku by chanting it. Everything else falls apart if this is neglected.

Buddhism eventually disappeared from India because it grew to place greater importance on theorizing, thus neglecting the observance of precepts. Buddha Śākyamuni's last words are known as *furitsu-danjō*.[1] It means to uphold and abide by the precepts to sustain the eternal life of the unchangeable Buddha Dharma and continue to practice with the same mind as if Buddha were with us. He admonished his disciples to practice the Buddha Dharma and abide by the precepts as a way of continuing to serve him after his passing. However, Buddhism went against it. In recent years, even among the Nichiren School, we see monks leading a life of secular Buddhism,[2] with the misconception that simply giving discourses on the teachings of Ososhi-sama makes them legitimate practitioners of the Buddha Dharma. Lay Buddhism

---

1   扶律談常.
2   A view that denies or makes light of the clergy, which is an important component that comprises the Triple Jewel [the Buddha, the Dharma and the Sangha] or Buddhist monks who marry and lead a life of a lay person while being ordained in a Buddhist order.

will inevitably decline on its own by virtue of delusions and the five desires that are inherent in the life of the non-ordained. If the life of the ordained is no different than that of the laity, it is no longer religion.

Ososhi-sama also upheld the tradition of monastic life despite the turbulent times he lived in. The Era of Declining Dharma does not make ordained life unnecessary. There is no room for that kind of interpretation. At the time of his death, Ososhi-sama went so far as to designate the ordained disciples who were to guide the people to the Buddha Dharma on his behalf after his demise. Monastic life, the life of *dōshi*,[3] needs to be preserved. Without it there is incongruity. There will be those who misconstrue, giving self-justifying lectures as Buddha Dharma or who think that disparaging others is *shakubuku*. They will not serve the transmission of Buddha Dharma because it goes against the desires of the Buddha; it goes against the desires of Ososhi-sama.

---

3 導師 *Dōshi* [*nāyaka, netr*]. A leading teacher, spiritual leader. One who leads others to the true Dharma, a title generally applied to the Buddha or Bodhisattva. Here it is the spiritual leader who leads others in the Era of Declining Dharma as the messenger of Buddha to bring salvation to living beings by walking about and practicing in the world as taught in Chapter XXI of the Lotus Sūtra, *The Transcendental Power of the Tathāgata*.

87

THE BLISS OF NIRVĀNA—SADO ISLAND

October 28, 1979
Milton Keynes Dōjō, England

PRACTICING THE BUDDHA DHARMA inevitably involves hardship. This is a path all people of religion have experienced and walked. Nipponzan must also endure whatever tribulation confronts us, even at the risk of our lives. That is when our resolve is tested. That is when our mission becomes evident. We will be able to finally arrive at eternal life after rising above these adversities. The imperishable work of our lifetime then appears before us. Ososhi-sama's life at Sado Island started on October 28. Upon arrival at this land of privation, Ososhi-sama exclaimed, "Oh, What a joy!" Let us be mindful so that we too can say the same when faced with hardship. When we do the right thing, when we engage in revered work, difficulties will befall us. We must be able to meet them with joy. Those who are able to relish successions of hardships, in essence, experience the bliss of nirvāna [*jakumetsu-no-raku*]. *Jaku* is nothingness. We neither gain nor lose. Yet, we are joyous. The bliss of nirvāna is joy that cannot be bought with money or materials. Ososhi-sama was joyful being at Sado Island. It was bliss of nirvāna, a tranquil bliss.

People of faith rejoice in tranquil bliss. There is a state where one derives joy out of nothingness, even if no one else would perceive it as joyous. This is the sacred state that exists in the world of human beings. Teachings expounded from that place have moral authority. We shall lead the world relishing bliss of nirvāna in the midst of life in hardship. People of faith find joy in such things. Joy of the heart and mind is a completely awakened joy. It is a world of void where there is no gain or loss. Joy is the one thing that arises there; simply, that we did the right thing.

88

Faith, Practice and Learning

November 24, 1979
Milton Keynes Dōjō, England

In the *Shohō-jissō-shō*[1] [*The True Aspect of Existence*], Ososhi-sama writes, "Be undaunted, be undaunted, and forge your faith strong so as to be afforded the protection of the three groups of Buddhas."[2] As such, we must be firm in believing in the presence of the Buddhas. For those who do, spiritual strength is afforded by faith in the Buddhas' protection. It is the merit of the faithful. Without faith one will never know this protection no matter how much the Buddhas offer. It is analogous to an unfilial child who is oblivious to the debt of gratitude towards his or her parents. A filial child is grateful towards the parents and holds no grudges even if, at times, parents seem unreasonable. It is a matter of one's heart and mind.

Following the earlier phrase, Ososhi-sama writes, "Exert yourselves in the dual paths of *gyō-gaku*." *Gyō* is practice. *Gaku*, learning, starts with reading and writing. We must exert ourselves in these two paths. "Without practice and learning, Buddha Dharma cannot be sustained." Decline in Buddha Dharma today is a result of monks failing to practice while they pursue learning.

---

1 諸法実相鈔. Written by Nichiren Daishōnin on May 17, 1273 addressed to Sairen-bō from Sado Island.
2 The three groups of Buddhas described in Chapter XI of the Lotus Sūtra, *Beholding the Precious Stūpa*, i.e., Buddha Śākyamuni, Buddha Prabhūtaratna and the Buddhas of the ten directions emanated from Buddha Śākyamuni.

I can still hear the words of the Chief Abbot[3] of Hōryūji[4] temple who lamented, "It is a shame that young people these days are eager to study, but do not exert themselves in practice."

Nipponzan does not teach anything aside from practice without remission. Construction work, kitchen duty, cleaning and the like are all part of it. I encourage any practice that physically involves your bodies. This is what helps sustain Nipponzan. "Buddha Dharma cannot be sustained without practice and learning."[5] Without these two, Buddha Dharma ceases to exist and we become no different from the laity. The laity study and learn as well. Yet, a layperson cannot freely practice the Buddha Dharma. The life of a monastic allows the freedom to practice without any restriction. The Buddha Dharma will perish when monks no longer practice. "Buddha Dharma cannot be sustained without practice and learning. Preserve them yourself and guide others to do the same." We are to practice ourselves and likewise encourage others to practice. The same is true with learning. Fellow monastics must study by encouraging one another. However, both practice and learning "arise from faith." Deep faith motivates one not to be indolent but to be diligent in both practice and study. Faith is of utmost importance and comes before any practice or learning. "Be undaunted, be undaunted, and forge your faith strong." Be assiduous in your faith. This is the epilogue of *Shohō-jissō-shō*. This essential phrase has always inspired me since the time I was ordained, and I have constantly recited it to myself. It is a brief phrase, which you, too, can learn by heart to remind yourselves to be undaunted, be undaunted and be resolute in your faith.

---

3 Saeki Jōin 佐伯定胤 [1867-1952], 103rd chief abbot of Hōryū-ji.
4 The Hōryu-ji Temple 法隆寺, the principle temple of the Shōtoku School 聖徳宗, is the oldest completely preserved temple complex in Japan. Yomei-tennō 用明天皇, the first Buddhist Emperor of Japan, was overtaken in 586 by a serious illness and ordered a statue of the Healing Buddha [薬師如来 Yakushi-Nyorai] to be made, but died before it was completed. To fulfill his wish, Shōtoku-taishi 聖徳太子, the Emperor's son, caused the Hōryu-ji Temple to be built in 607. UNESCO designated it as one of the world's most important cultural heritages in 1993.
5 諸法実相鈔 *Shohō-jissō-shō*.

89

Hokke-Shoshin-Jōbutsu-Shō

November 28, 1979
Milton Keynes Dōjō, England

Hokke-shoshin-jōbutsu-shō[1] [*On Buddhahood to be Attained Through the Lotus Sūtra by Even the Newly Initiated*] contains the passage, "This is what is meant by Buddha." There are six stages on the way to enlightenment.[2] The first of the six is *ri-soku*.[3] It is our identity connected with the Buddha as part of the principle of reality. Every person, whether virtuous or not, is inherently endowed with the connection to become Buddha. This is *ri-soku*. Having said that, the Buddha is yet to manifest during this stage. The next stage is *myōji-soku* [verbal identity].[4] When we chant the Odaimoku, Na Mu Myō Hō Ren Ge Kyō, we are verbally connected with the Buddha in name. That is *myōji-soku*. Our stage to enlightenment is a step beyond *ri-soku*, yet is still at

---

1 法華初心成仏鈔. Written by Nichiren Daishōnin in 1277.
2 *Roku-soku* 六即, six identities, is a T'ien-T'ai interpretation of the interpenetration and identity of the 52 stages leading to Buddhahood.
3 *Ri-soku* 理即, [Identity in the Principle of Reality]. All things are inherently endowed with Buddha-nature and the integrated, underlying unity of the nature reality. This is shared by all sentient-beings, even those who have not heard the Buddha Dharma. This is the stage at which an ordinary person is ignorant of one's identity with Buddha, i.e., the Buddha nature. A stage of an ordinary human being in which one cannot escape from transmigration without being aware of the inherent True Thusness of Buddha nature.
4 *Myōji-soku* 名字即 [Verbal Identity], the stage of coming to an understanding that one has Buddha-nature and is connected through hearing the name and truth. *Myōji-soku* is followed by *kangyō-soku* 観行即 [Identity in Contemplative Practice]; *sōji-soku* 相似即 [Identity in Outer Appearance]; *bunshin-soku* 分真即 [Identity of Partial Realization] ; and *kukkyō-soku* 究竟即 [Ultimate Identity].

the level of *myōji-soku*, the second stage of *roku-soku*. The Buddha in this stage is described in *Hokke-shoshin-jōbutsu-shō* as, "...the invocation by and manifestation in response [to the chanting of the Odaimoku] is what is meant by Buddha."

At the end of this *Gomyōhan* it states, ". . . on the path of attaining Buddhahood, [chant Na Mu Myō Hō Ren Ge Kyō] without arrogance or obstinacy to distorted views." Ososhi-sama points out there are two hindrances to the path of Buddhahood even when chanting the Odaimoku that makes us Buddha. One is arrogance arising from distorted views,[5] and the other obstinacy.[6] Obstinacy is attachment to one's views. Despite Nichiren Daishōnin's grave concern about arrogance and obstinacy, there is no denomination other than the Nichiren School where arrogance and obstinacy are so prevalent. Arrogance puts oneself far above others. This is described as "drinking poison and losing their senses" in the *Juryō* chapter [*The Duration of the Life of the Tathāgata*]. The most poisonous of all illusions that affect human beings are called the three poisons, which are covetousness, anger and ignorance. All hostilities today are caused by greed. Anger is the source of struggle and hostilities. The ordained are not to be angry, yet can become indignant by an insult or when subjected to violence. When we lose our temper, we are allowing ourselves to be exposed to illusions of the three poisons. We will not be provoked if we clad ourselves with the armor of perseverance.

> Evil spirits will possess them,
> To curse and revile us.
> But revering and believing in the Buddha,
> We will wear the armor of perseverance.[7]

When humiliated, we are offended knowing that what is done to us is unreasonable. However, we are creating an illusion by being

---

5 *Gaman* 我慢.
6 *Henshū* 偏執.
7 Chapter XIII of the Lotus Sūtra, *Exhortation to Hold Firm*.

indignant. The last of the three poisons is ignorance.[8] We can be caught up in senseless thoughts. We worry about things we don't need to worry about or think of things we need not think of. This is all ignorance. As such, the three poisons are greed, anger and ignorance,[9] the most fundamental enemies of Buddha-nature. Buddha-nature cannot rise to the surface while we hold the three poisons in our hearts and minds.

After the three poisons of greed, anger and ignorance, there are the five major illusions. In addition to covetousness, anger and ignorance, arrogance is listed as one of the five major illusions. Ososhi-sama warned against arrogance even more strongly than against covetousness, anger or ignorance. Arrogance comes in different forms. *Zōjōman*,[10] [self-conceit, arrogance based on the misconception that one has attained the truth] is one such example. *Jiman*[11] or *gaman*[12] is another. *Jiman* or *gaman* is the mind that deems oneself to be much greater than one really is. When one is pompous, others are looked down on. One does not feel superior without looking down on others. One becomes attached to this thought, which is *henshū*, and thinks no one is more right than oneself. Sōka Gakkai is a good example. It claims that no other Honzon is acceptable but theirs. The Buddha Dharma is used as a tool of *gaman* and *henshū*. Perhaps Sōka Gakkai is affected by a more serious case of *henshū* than Nipponzan. On the other hand, Nipponzan is deeply affected by *gaman*. We would be able to do much more if we were not affected by it. The sense of self-importance by those who lead hinders Nipponzan's work. No one would care to follow those who are pompous. I, for one, cannot follow them. The *Gomyōhan* says, "Chant Na Mu Myō Hō Ren Ge Kyō without arrogance or obstinacy to one's views." Arrogance is one of the five major illusions.

---

8 *Guchi* 愚痴.
9 *Ton, jin, chi* 貪. 瞋. 痴.
10 *Zōjōman* 増上慢.
11 自慢.
12 我慢.

Another impediment to progress in pursuit of the Buddha Dharma is doubt. There are two kinds of doubt; one is self-doubt, the doubt in your ability to accomplish something. Then there is doubt of others, doubting the worth of one's teacher or those who lead the way. Thoughts like "I'm not getting anywhere by training under a monk like this" runs through one's mind. There is a book entitled *Sōzan-yōro*.[13] It emphasizes first and foremost the importance of invoking faith, and second, eliminating doubt. Should we doubt our teacher and ourselves, our path of attaining the Buddha Way cannot be realized. Ososhi-sama exhorts us to "chant Na Mu Myō Hō Ren Ge Kyō on the path to attaining Buddhahood without arrogance or obstinacy to distorted views." This is enlightenment of *myōji-soku*. This is the level of enlightenment that is possible for us to attain. Arrogance and attachment to one's views prevent us. Ososhi-sama specifically cautioned against these two. The path for us to attain Buddhahood is through eliminating arrogance and obstinacy. This is the very first step for us newly initiated to attain Buddhahood described in *Hokke-shoshin-jō butsu-shō*.

---

13 草山要路. Written by Reverend Gensei [1623-1668], a representative scholar of Nichiren School in the early Edo period. He is also known as Gensei of Fukakusa since he lived in Fukakusa, Kyōto.

90

LIFE OF A MONK

December 3, 1979
Milton Keynes Dōjō, England

A PASSAGE IN *Devadatta*[1] says:

I diligently sought the Great Dharma,
Not for my own sake,
Nor for the pleasure of the five desires.

If Lord Buddha wanted to make a living, he could have kept the throne and remained in his palace instead of entering the life of Buddha Dharma. On his own accord, Lord Buddha left the palace, abdicated the throne, became a monk and sought to practice asceticism. What for? To protect the Dharma, to protect the Right Path, he trained and prepared his body for that purpose. Our practice of *rōhachi-sesshin*[2] is performed for the same reason. Once we complete the practice to ready ourselves to protect the Dharma, we must avail ourselves in serving the people. If by "the people" you think of those in faraway places, your focus becomes blurred. Start with those close to us, such as parents, children or siblings. We must make sacrifices for those whom we share our life with. A model for this is set in the chapter of *Devadatta*. King

---

1 Chapter XII of the Lotus Sūtra, *Devadatta*. Devadatta was one of Śākyamuni's cousins who initially followed him but later turned against him and tried to have him killed. In this chapter, the Buddha predicts that Devadatta would become a Buddha. He discloses that he was the King who served the sage Asita in his previous life, and Devadatta was the sage.
2 *Rōhachi-sesshin* is a week of fasting commemorating the practice of the Buddha under the bodhi tree before attaining enlightenment.

Charity is described as having waited on Asita,[3] "providing for his need, gathering fuel, fruit," and serving him "for a millennium, ...keeping the Sublime Dharma in my heart; hence my body and mind were unwearied." For him, there was nothing tedious about it. When a society where people serve others is brought to fruition, the impasse of the modern world marked by individualism will be transformed. We shall set examples of this transformation at the dōjōs.

Monks are to first and foremost lead a life of harmony. The term monk denotes harmony. Monks or Sangha is a name given to a group of people who are in harmony. One person cannot achieve harmony alone. Three or more monks constitute a Sangha. A place that houses a large number of monks is called sōrin[4] [forest of monks, i.e., a large monastery with many monks likened to a forest]. A single tree does not make up a forest. Trees growing in multitude constitute a forest. Just like now, I live with many people wherever I go. Many exert themselves for me while I am unable of doing anything in return. This way of life needs be extended into the actual society. People who work for the sake of others are a rarity these days.

People take on various jobs in society, but they work for their own sake. Everyone in society works for his or her own good. A radical transformation must be brought about in livelihood and the economy to create a society where people work for the sake of others. Religion introduced this perspective to society. Things done solely in one's own interest lead to narrow, distorted views and arrogance. Self-centered, narrow views benefit no one.

Hair growing on one's head does not really serve any purpose either. It just grows. Beards and mustaches also grow without a useful purpose. They are the prime causes of arrogance. The reason ordained shave their heads is to assume the form of

---

3 When the Buddha was born, Asita came to see him and foretold that he would become a great saint or king.
4 僧林.

relinquishing arrogance. Lord Buddha said that mendicancy and shaving one's hair are the hardest practices. Despite serving no particular useful purpose, hair takes much more attending to than our hands, feet or any other part of our body. Women used to spend almost half a day to have their hair done. On top of that, they go to professionals to have it coiffured. Then they must pay for it. Nevertheless, they feel it's worth it. They have their hair done every day. Men grow beards and mustaches. Are they useful for anything? They are not. But because they grow in places others can see, men go through a lot of trouble trimming them. They probably don't give it much thought other than assuming it better to be groomed than not. We shave hair on our head and face because the absence of hair creates no problems. We suffer no loss.

However, attachments and arrogance make shaving the head and beards difficult. Hair and beards cause arrogance and indolence. There is nothing good about them. We must let go of arrogance. Lord Buddha said that shaving the head and beard are most difficult because they are manifestations of arrogance. The external appearance assumed by the ordained signifies relinquishment of arrogance. However, that is not enough to be free from arrogance in our minds. Even without hair or beards, one could still feel superior. One would boast of one's importance. That makes us no different than having hair on our heads. Greed and ulterior motives are held even while engaging in spiritual practices. Let us not be captive to desire.

Having said that, the desire to sustain our life is a major issue. Becoming monks doesn't mean that it's all right to die. Lord Buddha showed the way to sustain our life, which was to seek sustenance from the leftovers of others. The *Jikihō* [the *gāthā* recited before meals] starts with the words "May all the misfortunes of almsgivers in the ten direction be eliminated." Our life shall be sustained by the alms of someone. We do not know who this will be. However, we would not go wrong when considering everyone as our benefactor. In return for the food received, monks pray that any misfortune that befalls the people in the ten directions who sustain our life may dissipate. This allows us to lead a life of gratitude towards the people in the ten directions. We are not only thankful to those who feed us today. There will be others who feed us tomorrow. We are also grateful to them.

91

Rōhachi -Sesshin

December 6, 1979
Milton Keynes Dōjō, England

People have asked whether the practice of *rōhachi-sesshin*[1] observed at every Nipponzan Myōhōji dōjō throughout the world is referenced in any sūtra or whether Nichiren Daishōnin himself observed it. None of the writings left by Nichiren Daishōnin mentions it. I learned of it when I was practicing with the Zen School and took the liberty of incorporating it into Nipponzan's practice. The Zen School observes the *Jōdōe*[2] ceremony marking Buddha Śākyamuni's Enlightenment, which takes place on December 8th every year. *Jōdōe* in India and Sri Lanka is called *Wesak*, although it is not commemorated on December 8th. I felt that the spirit of celebrating and honoring the Enlightenment of Lord Buddha needed to be incorporated in our practice.

The Nichiren School has no tradition to observe this day. In that case, some might think it better to incorporate *Wesak* celebrated in India and Sri Lanka, but not necessarily. *Jōdō* is a practice to open the path to enlightenment. December is the most appropriate season for this practice in Japan. That is why Nipponzan came to observe it on December 8th. We emulate Lord Buddha's practice to enlightenment by fasting for eight days starting December 1st to *Jōdōe* on December 8th. It is possible that the Zen School had not yet started the *rōhachi* practice

---

1 *Rōhachi-sesshin* 臘八摂心, practiced at Nipponzan Myōhōji, is a week of fasting without water or food, chanting the Odaimoku from daybreak to dusk.
2 成道会, celebration of *jōdō*, Buddha Śākyamuni's Enlightenment.

during Nichiren Daishōnin's days. Eisai[3] and Dōgen[4] traveled to China, but there is no indication that they practiced *rōhachi*. It might be that this practice was taken up after their time. That's all right. As his disciples, we observe it to celebrate Lord Buddha's Enlightenment.

---

3 Eisai [1141-1215] is a priest of the Rinzai School, ordained at the age of thirteen at Mount Hie. He went to China in 1168 for six months and returned to Japan with the new Tendai works. He went to China again in 1187 and studied under Huai-ch'ang of Mount T'ien-t'ai. In 1191 he returned to Japan and founded the Shōfukuji temple at Hakata. This is considered to be the first Zen temple in Japan.

4 Dōgen [1200-1253] is the founder of the Sōtō School in Japan. He was ordained at Mount Hiei at the age of twelve and became a disciple of Eisai thereafter. In 1223, he went to China and studied under Ju-ching [Nyōjō] for four years.

PART EIGHT

Our Mission

92

When the Sublime Dharma Alone Burgeons

January 1, 1980
Milton Keynes Dōjō, England

OUT OF THE ENTIRE Buddhist canon, Nichiren Daishōnin deduced from explicit words in four sūtras[1] that the world and all its inhabitants, without exception, were to be subjected to misfortune and suffering. He therefore beseeched "all the people of the world to take up the Single Vehicle of Buddhahood,"[2] since the entire world would be facing the same affliction, sorrow and downfall, without exception. He called upon the various religions to become one. Those with a jaundiced view took his call as an attempt to force his religion on others. However, religion is not an arbitrary pastime. It is the last stronghold that determines the rise or fall of humanity. When this stronghold suffers from disunity, it cannot serve its purpose. Karl Marx's success in creating Communism owes not to the brilliance of his theory, but to the single phrase, "Workers of the world unite."

In order to solve the most crucial and noble spiritual issue of humanity, the various vehicles should not exist separate from each other but must become the single Buddha vehicle. The search for a path of emancipation must bring us to the ultimate

---

1 The Golden Splendor Sūtra [金光明経 Konkōmyō-kyō, Suvarna-prabhāsa Sūtra], The Great Collection Sūtra [大集経 Daishū-kyō, Mahāsannipāta Sūtra], The Benevolent Kings Sūtra [Ninno-kyō 仁王経] and Medicine Master Sūtra [薬師経 Yakushi-kyō, Bhagavān-bhaisajya-guru-vaidūrya-prabhāsa-pūrvapranidhāna-viśesa-vistara].
2 Citation from the *Nyosetsu-Shugyō-shō* 如説修行鈔 written by Nichiren Daishōnin in Sado Island on May 17, 1273.

single path. When "all the people of the world," in other words, all of humanity, rise unarmed opposing the use of nuclear weapons, such weapons cannot possibly be detonated. This is the tenet of Ososhi-sama's teaching described by the words, "When all the people of the world forgo the various vehicles for the Single Vehicle of Buddhahood with the Sublime Dharma alone burgeoning throughout the land."

93

SECESSION FROM NICHIREN SCHOOL

April 9, 1980
Yoshino-yama Dōjō, Japan

AT THE TIME EMPEROR TAISHŌ was convalescing at the Imperial villa in Hayama, we prayed beating the drum.[1] We were told that our voices were too loud and to temper the drum beat. Instead of detaining us at the police station in Hayama, we were sent to one in Kamakura. The police, knowing that we would immediately return to beating the drum if we were released, seemingly decided to hold us in custody indefinitely. I had no plans to stay in detention indefinitely. Together with the disciples, I started to fast. The disciples and devotees who learned of the development were concerned that it may cost us our lives and called for our release. The situation became tense. [One of the devotees] at that time, Commander Iwao Matsuya of the Shizuoka regiment, who later became ordained in the order,[2] was assigned to security at the Imperial villa. He had soldiers load their guns and went to see the person in charge at the police station. He indicated that there would be bloodshed unless his teacher was pardoned. The police backed down and transferred us to Echi[3] and then released us.

When the Emperor passed away,[4] the funeral rite took

---

1 November 1926.
2 After WWII, he was ordained as Guruji's disciple and was named Gyōjōin Nichiun 行浄院日運.
3 The location where Nichiren Daishōnin was held after the unsuccessful execution at Tatsunokuchi before being exiled to Sado Island
4 December 25, 1926.

place. Religious representatives, including chief abbots of different schools and denominations, were to quietly accompany His Majesty's hearse to the Imperial mausoleum at Tama. Since I would be sending the Emperor off beating the drum, I went to discuss the matter with the Metropolitan Police Department. Permission was denied. Nevertheless, I informed them that I would be sending the Emperor off by beating the drum and left without coming to an agreement. The metropolitan police said that since I belonged to the Nichiren School, the chief abbot would be punished. The last thing I wanted was for the chief abbot to be denied from partaking in the funeral procession. I went to the Nichiren School headquarters and announced that I would secede from the order to work on my own since my presence would cause trouble to the Nichiren School. I requested that if any actions of mine brought problems to the Nichiren School, it should be flatly stated that I am longer with the school. I made my own decision and founded Nipponzan Myōhōji separate from the Nichiren School. It was not because there were any irreconcilable differences between us. I simply avoided becoming a problem to the Nichiren School as a whole.

My ordination master in Usuki, Ōita prefecture, was still alive then. The police went to him and complained that something needed to be done since his disciple was acting disorderly and was too much for them to handle. My master responded that I seemed to have lost my mind and was banished from the temple, that he had nothing to do with me any longer. Officially, my connection with my master was cut off. With no other affiliations but the disciples and myself, we were free to practice without reserve. That is how Nipponzan came about. It made me happy. Without any interference from the Nichiren School, we were free to go to any country we pleased to spread the Buddha Dharma. Despite various hardships and persecutions we suffered, we were no longer any cause for trouble for the Nichiren School.

94

INDIA'S STRUGGLE OF NONVIOLENCE

July 25, 1980
From *Buddhism for World Peace*

MAHATMA GANDHI of India set a precedent in putting nonviolence into practice. On March 12, 1930, he launched a nationwide civil disobedience movement against British rule, calling for complete Indian independence. A small town called Dandi, located at the mouth of the Gulf of Cambay, was to be the stage to demonstrate their aspiration for freedom. Gandhi initiated a march to Dandi from the ashram in Ahmedabad together with 78 ashram members. On March 11, the eve of the march, Gandhi spoke at the evening prayer meeting. Let me cite from his speech given that night:

> From what I have seen and heard during the last fortnight, I am inclined to believe that the stream of civil resisters will flow unbroken. But let there be not a semblance of breach of peace even after all of us have been arrested. We have resolved to utilize all our resources in the pursuit of an exclusively nonviolent struggle. Let no one commit a wrong in anger. This is my hope and prayer. I wish these words of mine reached every nook and corner of the land.

Gandhi was more than sixty years old at that time. After walking 12 miles a day for 24 days, they arrived at their destination. Flowers were strewn on the path in villages along the way, and villagers sprinkled water to keep the dust from rising as they walked. I saw a picture carried in a Japanese newspaper of

Gandhi and fellow marchers with broad smiles responding to the reception by the people. At the end of the walk, Gandhi made salt out of seawater and sold it. Thousands upon thousands followed suit on the seacoast of India. Madame Sarojini Naidu, Manilal Gandhi and 2,500 volunteers later headed to the Dharasana Salt Works located near Dandi.

According to a report filed by a [American] foreign correspondent:[1]

> In complete silence, the Gandhi men drew up and halted a hundred yards from the stockade . . . A picket column advanced from the crowd, waded the ditches and approached the barbed-wire stockade . . . Suddenly, at a word of command, scores of native policemen rushed upon the advancing marchers and rained blows on their heads with their steel-shod lathis. Not one of the marchers even raised an arm to fend off the blows . . . The waiting crowd of marchers groaned and sucked in their breath in sympathetic pain at every blow. Those struck down fell sprawling, unconscious or writhing with fractured skulls or broken shoulders . . . The survivors, without breaking ranks, silently and doggedly marched on until struck down . . .

> They marched steadily, with heads up, without the encouragement of music or cheering or any possibility that they might escape serious injury or death. The police rushed out and methodically and mechanically beat down the second column. There was no fight, no struggle; the marchers simply walked forward till struck down . . . If they were unable to break the skulls of all the protesters,

---

1 Webster [Webb] Miller was the European News Manager for United Press news service when he went to India in 1930 to report on the civil disobedience campaign. His eloquent description of the horrific beatings, which belied official accounts from the Bristish colonial government, ran in hundreds of newspapers and contributed to the growing international support for the independence movement.

they now set about kicking and aiming their blows at the genitals of the helpless on the ground. For hour upon hour, endless numbers of motionless, bloody bodies were carried away on stretchers.

The high standard of the paragon of the struggle of nonviolence was hoisted. Those who speak of nonviolence should never in all eternity cloud this shining mirror of the nonviolent struggle that challenged the law preventing Indians from making salt at Dandi. What did the practitioners of nonviolence gain at the time? They were not able to effect a total revision of the Salt Laws nor did they take over the salt works. Gandhiji, who was staying near Dandi, was arrested on May 4th. More than 50,000 practitioners of nonviolence were arrested for breaking the Salt Laws, starting with Jawaharlal Nehru. Nevertheless, the movement of nonviolence was not defeated. This incident proved to the world that the Indian people were able to execute a flawless, peaceful campaign in an unprecedented struggle of nonviolence, achieving a monumental political revolution in human history. International media gathered, and the world started to awaken to the tremendous power of nonviolence. This is when the victory of nonviolence manifested. Gandhiji's Salt March was one of the major reasons why I came to beat the Dharma drum in *Saiten* [Western Heavens] India.

The British Empire later accepted India's complete independence. Jawaharlal Nehru visited Gandhiji at his ashram in Wardha carrying with him the official document of independence. I saw a picture of the two laughing in sheer delight as they opened the document before them. Gandhiji said while he thought it was India that practiced nonviolence, on that day it was Britain that was nonviolent. Thus, India's complete independence was the fruit of nonviolence.

95

TREASURE

October 8, 1980
Milton Keynes Dōjō, England

AMONG THE SEVEN TREASURES—gold, silver, lapis lazuli, shell, agate, pearl and ruby—that adorn the stūpa cited in Chapter XI of the Lotus Sūtra, *Beholding the Precious Stūpa*, shell and pearl are produced from shellfish of the sea. They are considered precious articles.

The kanji character for shell is represented in the character for treasure. From ancient times, shellfish dwelling in the waters, seemingly isolated from life on shore, have become treasures for those living ashore. Treasures of the land are stones produced from the mountains, such as gold and silver. Lapis lazuli is also a stone. Stones from mountains and shells of sea creatures have become treasures that gracefully adorn the human world.

The ornaments that grace the neck of Lord Buddha's image as well as my own are made of shells from the sea. There is an old saying that "a tiger leaves his fur behind," which describes how one's remains can be of service to others even after one's passing. Shellfish that dwell in the ocean were taken ashore and became food and at the same time their shells became treasures on land.

We, who are alive, will eventually pass away. I hope that we leave behind something beautiful that will become a treasure to the world. Lord Buddha, as represented by these Buddha images, is an example. After more than 2,500 years, he remains the unsurpassed treasure in the human world. He is beautifully represented in gold, silver or wood, be it in a drawing, sculpture or statue, because he taught the right path, which benefited the people.

Our life in this world is fleeting, yet we must leave something beautiful behind for posterity. We may not be able to become Buddha, but we can work on behalf of Lord Buddha, which is the best way of leaving a lasting treasure for those to come. When our work on behalf of Lord Buddha spreads, the human legacy we leave behind will be handed down in the human world. Herein lies the noble mission of people of faith. Just like shells, we can adorn the world after we are gone.

96

OUR MISSION

October 23, 1980
Milton Keynes Dōjō, England

OSOSHI-SAMA SAYS, "The time has come." Great significance was placed on time. There is a writing titled *Discerning the Opportune Time*.[1] The Dharma that meets the needs of the time is revealed. What is the time? "The fifth of the five-hundred-year period after the Parinirvāna of the Tathāgata" [2,500 years later] is the era of greatest darkness following the Tathāgata's demise. Buddha Śākyamuni foretold that during this era the Lotus Sūtra will wondrously "spread far and wide throughout the entire world."[2] Ososhi-sama says it must be spread because the time has come. He stressed the importance of time. We beat the drum and chant the Odaimoku. For one, it suits the capacity of the people of the time we live in, a concept Hōnen also emphasized. It is a practice that can be performed by anyone. Children, women, foreign nationals or anyone else can easily emulate the chanting of Na Mu Myō Hō Ren Ge Kyō. Even children can beat the drum. It suits the capacity. Yet Ososhi-sama's point is we must beat the drum not necessarily because we enjoy it, but because the time has come. What time has come?

It is an era rife in conflict,[3] a time of war. The time has come

---

1 *Senji-shō* 撰時鈔. Written by Nichiren Daishōnin in 1275.
2 *Ichi-enbudai* or *Enbudai* 一閻浮堤、閻浮提 is the phonetically transplanted Japanese term of the Sanskrit *Jambudvīpa*, the world of human beings.
3 Citation from 大集経 The Great Collection Sūtra [Mahāsannipāta Sūtra]. The phrase used here is *tojō-kengo* 鬪諍堅固.

226

when humanity is about to be consumed by a great conflagration. Ososhi-sama explicated that the teaching to bring emancipation to this time is the quintessence of the Lotus Sūtra, Na Mu Myō Hō Ren Ge Kyō. We are now in such a time. As the sign of its impending dissemination, it is taught that there will be a war that engulfs the entire world, wreaking turmoil. Na Mu Myō Hō Ren Ge Kyō is the teaching left by the Buddha specifically to quell the conflagration. This is why we must spread it. This war is already in the making. That makes it incumbent upon us to spread it whether we want to or not. To that end, whether one is ordained and adheres to precepts or not, whether a person of wisdom or not, in other words, whether one is a learned scholar or not, smart or foolish, none of this is relevant. Whoever we are, whatever we are, everyone must in unison chant Na Mu Myō Hō Ren Ge Kyō. The time demands that of us. This is the essence of Ososhi-sama's teaching. Nipponzan believes in this and has continued to chant it to this day. It now appears that the people of the world are truly searching for a way and are ready to accept it regardless of faith or denomination. This again is brought about by the time. It will become true because the time has come. We must believe in it and take it upon ourselves as our mission to make it happen.

97

THE FUNERAL RITES OF EMPEROR TAISHŌ

October 30, 1980
Washington, D.C., Dōjō

EMPEROR TAISHŌ upon his passing[1] was buried in the Imperial mausoleum in Tama. At the time of the burial, representatives from the various schools of Buddhism, mostly chief abbots, were to accompany the Emperor in the burial procession. They were to walk quietly behind the hearse, hardly uttering a word. I did not believe this was the right thing to do. I went to the Chief Commissioner of the Metropolitan Police and conveyed my intent to beat the drum and chant the Odaimoku in sending the Emperor off. The Chief Commissioner responded that it would not be allowed; if he did allow it, it could encourage others to come up with something else and the grand funeral rite could descend into chaos. I maintained that if my prayers were not allowed, His Highness's journey to the nether world would be in darkness, and that I was resolved to beat my drum and chant the Odaimoku. No agreement was reached, and the Metropolitan Police Department threw me in the Sugamo Prison. In the meantime, my disciples were starting to gather from all over the country. They were all arrested at the train stations and sent to the Sugamo Prison. As I was chanting together with my disciples in jail, police officers came in and beat us. I did not want to make a huge commotion, so we sat there in silence.

A moment of silent prayer was to be observed by the

---

1 December 25, 1926.

nation at the time the Emperor's hearse leaves the Imperial Palace. Those in jail were no exception. The time was upon us. Everyone, including police officers, bowed their heads in silence. I seized that moment to recite a passage from *Letter to Lady Oto*.[2] "The people of Japan have become foes of the Lotus Sūtra, which will bring ruin on themselves and the nation." This passage was the *indō*[3] I imparted to the Emperor; the current course taken by Japan as a nation is misguided, which does not bode well for the Emperor, whose journey to the other world would be cast in shadow. The police officers could not rise from where they were since it was during the silent tribute. I overcame the circumstances and managed to offer my guidance to the soul of the Emperor.

After daybreak, this time when the warden summoned me to his office, he told me that I was crazy and would be sent to the Matsuzawa Hospital [a psychiatric hospital]. He referred to my chanting of Na Mu Myō Hō Ren Ge Kyō and asked me if I knew any sūtras. His question was indicative of his apparent confusion in matters of importance. It insinuated that my chanting of Na Mu Myō Hō Ren Ge Kyō came from not knowing any sūtras to recite. This is a point of misconception not only by the police but also by some in Nipponzan. The Odaimoku comprised of the five or seven characters of Na Mu Myō Hō Ren Ge Kyō is the very teaching of Nichiren Daishōnin, the Dharma of liberation left by Buddha Śākyamuni for the Era of Declining Dharma.

---

2 *Otogozen-gosho* 乙御前御書. A letter written by Nichiren Daishōnin on the fourth day of the eighth month of 1275 to Lady Oto from Mount Minobu.
3 引導. The last words offered by the presiding monk of the funeral rite that shows the way to liberate the departed soul from delusions.

98

Nipponzan's Calling

November 17, 1980
Kudan Dōjō, Tōkyō

THE POWER OF NONVIOLENCE is the divine power of the Buddhas that we cannot see. We are powerless; yet we refuse to stop beating our drums even if we are ordered to stop. We will accept the consequences and go to jail. This very situation is the practice of the teaching of *ichinen-sanzen*.[1] We cannot save the nation by performing memorial services for the dead. If that could save the country, Nichiren Daishōnin would not have brought himself in front of the shogunate to remonstrate the government. Once temples and followers appear, even some in Nipponzan have come to think that a monk's job is to do things like holding memorial services on the death anniversary of Nichiren Daishōnin or rituals during Obon[2] to console the souls of the dead. This is not Nipponzan's calling.

Nipponzan does not perform memorial services for the dead. At a time when the fall of humanity is impending, monks

---

1 一念三千. The doctrine of three thousand realms contained in one thought. All phenomena in this world [三千 *sanzen*, three thousand worlds] are encompassed in a single thought [一念 *ichinen*] of human beings. Here the practice for attaining Buddhahood of the *ichinen-sanzen* is the chanting of the Odaimoku in prison [remonstration of the sovereign] for enlightenment of all three realms of *shujō-seken* [realm of sentient beings], *kokudo-seken* [non-sentient natural environment that surrounds the realm of sentient beings] and *go-un-seken* [五蘊世間 the five aggregates of matter, perception, mental conceptions, volition and consciousness of the mind that constitute the aforementioned two realms]. The three realms, ten worlds and ten aspects of existence comprise the three thousand worlds in one thought.

2 A Japanese festival to honor the ancestors.

who fail to stand in the vanguard of the movement to prevent it should not stay in Nipponzan. I will set the principles while I am still with you, but what will happen to Nipponzan when I am gone? This is my great concern.

99

GANDHIJI'S WISDOM

January 21, 1981
Rajgir Dōjō, India

PERHAPS GANDHIJI WAS the only Indian person who truly had trust in me. His trust in me was sincere. I left the ashram in his absence to build a temple. This troubled him and he said, "You should not go. Stay at the ashram until the very end." However, I was excited with the prospect of a temple appearing, and I went ahead to build it in Calcutta. It would have been better had I stayed at the ashram until independence was won. I have been careful not to make too many mistakes in my life, but now that India attained her independence, in hindsight, I would say that I was amiss to have left the ashram to build a temple. I wish I had not. It would have been best had I been able to greet India's independence at the ashram.

My misjudgment came from the perception that politics and religion are not quite in accord. Being a monk, I took delight in building the temple. I was more taken by it than by India's independence. That was where I went wrong. Everything I do should be for the purpose of *Risshō-ankoku*. "When the nation is destroyed and her people perishing, who will revere the Buddha, who will have faith in the Dharma?"[1] I left the ashram just when peace was about to be brought to the nation. It was the greatest mistake of my life. Gandhiji had greater wisdom.

---

1   Quote from *Risshō-Ankoku-Ron.*

100

Setsubun: The Last Day of Winter

February 3, 1981
Rajgir Dōjō, India

TODAY IS *SETSUBUN*[1] in Japan, a day of turning of the seasons. *Shōkan*[2] and *daikan*[3] with their abundant snowfalls have now passed, bringing us to the beginning of a warmer season. Although today marks the arrival of a new season, it is not noticeably warmer than yesterday. We can barely tell the difference between today and yesterday, today and tomorrow, yet spring unnoticed, comes seamlessly.

Our Bodhisattva practice is very much like this. We cannot always do exemplary things in ways that set us apart from others. In all aspects, we are not that different today compared to yesterday or for that matter tomorrow from today. However, with the arrival of spring, warmth increases without us realizing it. When Buddha-nature awakens, small seeds of good eventually grow into great good. The reverse is true when the weather gets cold. By the same token, one who is good with initially a hint of misdoing could eventually fall to grave evil, not only bringing error to one's own life but also causing problems for others. That single step we take can have monumental ramifications.

---

1 節分. The last day of winter.
2 *Shōkan* 小寒 is one of the twenty-four divisions of the four seasons [around January 5 according to the solar calendar]. It is the period of the second most severe cold in midwinter [the 15-day period starting on that day to the day of *daikan* 大寒].
3 *Daikan* is around January 20 according to the solar calendar. The 15-day period starting this day to the first day of spring is the height of winter in Japan.

233

There is an age-old Buddhist tradition called *tsuina*[4] performed on *setsubun*. When ogres show themselves, they are chased away with peas, although I don't think it was meant to be a violent thing. Many years ago when I was still studying at Hōryū-ji Temple and elsewhere, I attended a *tsuina* ceremony held at Hōryū-ji to expel ogres. *Tsuina* comes from the term "expelling hardship." The Japanese were more averse to cold than heat since everything in sight withers with the coming of the cold weather. Heat, no matter how hot it is, still allows things to grow; trees are lush with foliage and plants luxuriant. As cold intensifies, trees lose their foliage and plant life withers. The rigor of winter eases away at just about the time of *setsubun*. A tangible representation of this is the chasing of ogres, the expelling of misfortune. This is the ceremony of *tsuina*.[5]

Tonight we will be observing the *tsuina* ceremony, which purports to chases the ogres away. Instead of bullets or stones, dried beans are used to expel them. We have sweets prepared in addition to beans. Perhaps when these beans and sweets strike the ogres, instead of dying they might be tempted to pick them up and try them. That's fine, too. This tradition is an expedient for nurturing.[6] Shall we turn the lights out then?[7] Na Mu Myō Hō Ren Ge Kyō. "In with good luck, out with the ogres."

---

4 追儺. A ceremony for driving out evil spirits.
5 追儺会 *tsuina-e.*
6 In addition to dried beans, sweets were prepared for the children to scatter along with the beans so that they may enjoy them later. The scattering of the beans and sweets is an expedient to nurture joy in the children.
7 The lights are turned out when the phrase, "In with good luck, out with the ogres [鬼 *oni*]" is chanted as the beans are scattered to expel misfortune.

PART NINE

A Religion for Universal Emancipation

101

The Secret of the Tathāgata

June 8, 1981
Atami Dōjō, Japan

BUILDING STŪPAS as a means of realizing *Risshō-ankoku* in the immediate present shall show the way to a peaceful world. The building of stūpas is the concretization of a spiritual movement to emancipate the modern world. It is emitting a ray of light that illuminates the way for many Japanese, who are uncertain and at a loss about what can be done.

The *chūson*[1] of the Honzon identified by Ososhi-sama is Na Mu Myō Hō Ren Ge Kyō. A representation of this Honzon made by *busshi* [sculptors of Buddhist images] on a wooden plank is still made available and it is known as *ita-honzon*, a wooden plank inscribed with the Honzon [in Japanese calligraphy]. According to the *Treatise on Seeing the Essential Object of Veneration in the Heart and Mind*, "The visual, sacred appearance of this Honzon is a stūpa of treasures suspended in midair above the *sahā* world of the Eternal Buddha Śākyamuni..."[2] It is the Stūpa of Treasures. Nevertheless, it is absent from the Nichiren School Honzon. "On both sides of the Myō Hō Ren Ge Kyō[3] within the stūpa are

---

1 中尊. The representation of the sacred entity in the center of the Honzon. It is also generally referred to as Honzon. The two Buddha images on both sides of the *chūson* are called *kyōji* 脇士, attendants to the *chūson*, who support the *chūson* in providing guidance to the Dharma.

2 本時の娑婆. *Honji-no-shaba* is the world of the Eternal Buddha Śākyamuni, which is also the world we live in.

3 Odaimoku, Na Mu Myō Hō Ren Ge Kyō, is the Eternal Buddha who is also the historical Buddha Śākyamuni.

Buddha Śākyamuni and Buddha Prabhūtaratna. They are in turn flanked by Buddha Śākyamuni's four attending Bodhisattvas,[4] starting with Bodhisattva Superior Practice." This is the visual arrangement. Buddha Śākyamuni preached the essential section of the Lotus Sūtra, which reveals *The Duration of the Life of the Tathāgata* [5] from within the stūpa, not outside the stūpa. In spite of this, the stūpa is not represented.[6] This goes to show Nichiren School's confusion on the Honzon. When you read *Treatise On Seeing the Essential Object of Veneration in the Heart And Mind*, it clearly states, "The sacred visual appearance of this Honzon is a stūpa of treasures suspended in midair above the *sahā* world of the Eternal Buddha Śākyamuni."[7] The eight chapters, including *The Duration of the Life of the Tathāgata*, were expounded from within the Stūpa of Treasures, in particular, *ippon-ni-han*[8] and *Ojigage*,[9] which is the very core of *ippon-ni-han*.

The Buddha's life is immeasurable, infinite, spanning over numberless and countless[10] kalpas. He is forever existing and immortal. This revelation by Buddha Śākyamuni all took place inside the Stūpa of Treasures. None of the teachings delivered

---

4 Superior Practice, Boundless Practice, Pure Practice and Steadfast Practice, are the four major leaders heading the host of Bodhisattvas Who Emerge From the Earth.

5 Honzon of Honmon *Juryō-hon* 本門寿量品. Chapter XVI of the Lotus Sūtra.

6 Myō Hō Ren Ge Kyō is placed in the center of the Nichiren School Honzon as *chūson*, yet there is no stūpa over which the Na Mu Myō Hō Ren Ge Kyō can be suspended.

7 The Eternal Buddha is represented by Na Mu Myō Hō Ren Ge Kyō in the Honzon.

8 一品二半 [One chapter and two half chapters]. *The Duration of the Life of the Tathāgata*, the second half of *Bodhisattvas Who Emerge From the Earth* and the first half of *Discrimination of Merits* constitute *ippon-ni-han*, containing the main discourse of the essential section. *Ojigage* is the core of the main discourse.

9 御自我偈. Reference to the *gāthā* in the *Duration of the life of the Tathāgata* that starts with "Since I attained Buddhahood" and ends with "And speedily accomplish their Buddhahood?" Buddha Śākyamuni reveals his eternal nature in this *gāthā*.

10 *Asōgi* 阿僧祇 *asamkhyeya* [Sk]. The fifty-second unit of decimal numeration according to volume 12 of Abbidharma-kośa.

outside the stūpa by Buddha Śākyamuni throughout his life revealed the eternal nature of the Tathāgata. Nevertheless, that very stūpa is missing [from the Honzon]. Raising money does not build stūpas. They are built spontaneously when the wondrous power of the Buddha is evinced, capturing the people's hearts and minds. This is the "secret of the Tathāgata." Without this power we cannot liberate the world.

102

THE SINGLE GREAT DHARMA OF MYSTERY

September 20, 1981
Milton Keynes Dōjō, England

THE MOST IMPORTANT writings of Nichiren Daishōnin that address the issue of Honzon are *Treatise on Seeing the Essential Object of Veneration in the Heart and Mind, Requital of Gratitude*[1] and *Reply to Lady Nichinyo*.[2] *Questions and Answers on Honzon*[3] and *The Chanting of the Daimoku of the Lotus*[4] also address the issue of Honzon, but merely peripherally. The most complete account on the Honzon of The Dharma of Three Great Mysteries[5] is *Treatise on Seeing the Essential Object of Veneration in the Heart and Mind*, then secondly, *Requital of Gratitude* and thirdly, *Reply to Lady Nichinyo*.

Odaimoku is cited as one aspect of the Dharma of Three Great Mysteries. However, the single act of chanting the Odaimoku encompasses the whole of the Dharma of the Three Great Mysteries. The Dharma of the Three Great Mysteries is explained in three facets, yet it is none other than the chanting of Na Mu Myō Hō Ren Ge Kyō. Peace is said to prevail in the country

---

1 Refer to footnote 6 in *The Honzon of the Dharma of Three Great Mysteries*, p. 167.

2 Refer to footnote 7 in *The Honzon of the Dharma of Three Great Mysteries*, p. 167.

3 *Honzon-mondō-shō* 本尊問答鈔. Written in September 1278.

4 *Shō-hokke-daimoku-shō* 唱法華題目鈔. Written on May 28, 1260, about the same time as the *Risshō-ankoku-ron*.

5 *Sandai-hihō* 三大秘法. Honzon 本尊 [principle object of veneration], Kaidan 戒壇 [platform where precepts are bestowed]and the Daimoku 題目 [Na Mu Myō Hō Ren Ge Kyō] comprise the Dharma of Three Great Mysteries.

when "all the people of the nation forgo the various vehicles for the Single Vehicle of Buddhahood with the Sublime Dharma alone burgeoning throughout the land; and when the entire nation at that time comes to chant Na Mu Myō Hō Ren Ge Kyō in one voice."[6] The Dharma of the Three Great Mysteries is embodied right there. It is singly in the chanting of Na Mu Myō Hō Ren Ge Kyō; the Dharma of Three Great Mysteries is, in essence, the Dharma of the Single Great Mystery.[7] The Dharma of Three Great Mysteries elucidates the three facets of the Single Great Mystery, the Odaimoku.

Ososhi-sama's life substantiates this. He wrote, "I, Nichiren, born in the Era of Declining Dharma, am thus persecuted for spreading the five characters of the Sublime Dharma [Odaimoku]." All he did was to spread the Odaimoku wherever he went. He did not focus on issues of Honzon or Kaidan. They are not as consequential an issue. The tenet of Ososhi-sama boils down to the dedicated chanting of the Odaimoku, and the rest is of little consequence. Nipponzan must have an accurate appreciation of this very point. Without a clear understanding of Ososhi-sama's true intention, we lose sight of the significance of the Lotus Sūtra as a whole from the perspective of Ososhi-sama's creed. It would then become the Lotus Sūtra as spread by Tendai[8] and Myōraku.[9] Accordingly, a firm determination to practice the singular chanting of the Odaimoku is required. The daily prayer services, peace walks and chanting on the streets are where we put this into practice. Our one and only focus is to be walking about chanting the Odaimoku to disseminate it. Building stūpas, temples or gardens are merely manifestations that arise from this practice.

---

6 Citation from Nichiren Daishōnin's *Nyosetsu-shugyō-shō* 如説修行鈔 [*Thusly Practice the Teachings Preached by the Buddha*].
7 *Ichidai-hihō* 一大秘法.
8 Refer to footnote 3 in *Tathagata Na Mu Myō Hō Ren Ge Kyō*, p. 109.
9 Miao-lê-ta-shih [Myōraku-taishi 妙楽大師], also known as Chan-jan of the T'ang Dynasty, who revived the Chinese Tendai School.

103

Ososhi-sama's Religion

December 7, 1981
Tama Dōjō, Tōkyō

Ososhi-sama's religion is the movement of *Risshō-ankoku* to set politics aright—the movement to usher political power in the right direction without being taken in by power. There are but a few of us. Just a handful of Nipponzan's young monks and nuns are undertaking this mission. What a marvel should we succeed! This movement is worlds apart from something like building a temple or a stūpa. It is the materialization of Ososhi-sama's *Risshō-ankoku-ron.* "Then the triple world[1] will become the Buddha Realm. How can the Buddha Realm ever decline? All the worlds in the ten directions shall transform into the Pure Land. How can the Pure Land ever be destroyed?"[2] This is the magnitude of the outcome. This is Ososhi-sama's prophecy that will illuminate the darkness veiling this fifth five-hundred-year period of the Era of Declining Dharma. This is what we must materialize.

---

1 *Trayo dhātavah.* The three worlds of unenlightened people: the world of desire, the world of form and the world of non-form.
2 Citation from *Risshō-ankoku-ron.*

104

Jikihō—2

January 13, 1982
Ōsaka Dōjō, Japan

Jikihō[1] is recited at Nipponzan. It starts with the phrase, "May the adversities and miseries of the almsgivers in the ten directions be removed."[2] Before taking our food, we offer a prayer that no misfortunes may befall our almsgivers in the worlds in the ten directions and that "they may be blessed with happiness."[3] Anywhere in the worlds in the ten directions there are people who could be our benefactors, but we do not know who they may be. When we behold everyone living in the worlds in the ten directions to be those who would eventually make offerings, it is safe to say that everyone is our almsgiver. When this is believed to be true, we cannot be upset or in conflict with anyone in any direction in this world. Someone in the worlds in the ten directions is an almsgiver today; someone else will make offerings to us tomorrow. We are equally thankful to all of them. This becomes the source of creating peace in the world. No matter where we go, we can never be in discord with anyone if we believe that the people in the ten directions are our almsgivers.

---

1 Recitations from the Lotus Sūtra and other prayers chanted before a meal.
2 *Jippō-seshu-saishō-shōjō* 十方施主災障消除.
3 *Fukue-zōchō* 福慧増長.

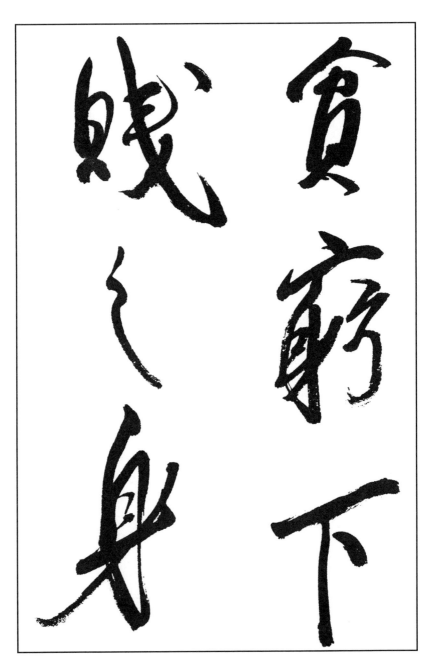

Bingū/ Gesen/ no mi [Destitute/ A pariah/ This is what I am]

105

Learn From Poverty

January 16, 1982
Ōsaka Dōjō, Japan

Nipponzan has been well and alive so far because we are poor. Nipponzan will cease to exist if we start to indulge ourselves. We would err on our path if our thinking starts to deviate from the teachings of Lord Buddha. One would come to expect a nice meal and become a good-for-nothing. Those who are successful at Nipponzan are those who do not mind life in poverty, to whom food is not an issue. Those who are not frugal with food will not be successful. Monks who are accustomed to a life of comfort and luxury cannot achieve the Dharma-work that Nipponzan engages in. Let us all be mindful to avoid lavishness. It starts with me since everyone else will follow suit if I were to be extravagant. Please take this to heart; otherwise we are no longer practicing Buddha Dharma. The stalemate at Sōka Gakkai is likewise caused by their thriftlessness. Having too much money will cause their decline. Nipponzan will not decline because we have no money. We will somehow be able to do our job. The inability of institutional religion to do any useful work comes from a guaranteed livelihood. If there is no offering of food for the day without walking around the streets drumming, naturally, this knowledge motivates us to be more assiduous in our practice. Nipponzan's achievements in Dharma-work come from our poverty. My disciples who lived like spendthrifts all fell. Providence does not tolerate it. Indolent or thriftless disciples left Nipponzan one after another. They would not have been able to achieve anything even if they had stayed.

106

OHIGAN/EQUINOX

March 18, 1982
Tama Dōjō, Tōkyō

THE SPRING EQUINOX is finally here. I encourage you all to read Ososhi-sama's *Higan-shō*[1] written about the equinox. The week of the equinox is a pleasant time of year, neither hot nor cold. Both the spring and autumn equinoxes are delightful times of the year. Ososhi-sama teaches us to do good on the equinox, no matter how small a good it may be. The term *higan* [equinox] signifies "the other shore." We are on this side of the shore that is separated by the river of suffering. We cross this river to arrive at the other shore.[2] It provides us with a goal to work towards in our lives. [Ososhi-sama] seized on the transition of the seasons to teach us how to conduct ourselves as human beings.

Seeds sown at the spring equinox bear fruit by the autumn equinox. This example teaches us the law of cause and effect. A small good planted at the spring equinox grows into the root of great goodness.[3] By the same token, small misdeeds grow into major misdoings. The turning of the seasons presents an opportunity to show us the truth of cause and effect. Be it good or bad, the seed sowed must eventually be reaped. Ososhi-sama taught us to sow seeds of good, not of harm.

---

1 彼岸鈔.
2 The Odaimoku or good deeds serve as means to cross the river to arrive at the other shore.
3 *Zenkon* 善根, *kuśala-mūla* [Sk], "Root of goodness;" a meritorious, good act. "Root" because of the firmness of the good acts, and because they produce good fruit.

107

ODAIMOKU—3

March 18, 1982
Tama Dōjō, Tokyo

I CANNOT BUT URGE YOU to believe in the blessings of the Odaimoku and to uphold it. When all is said and done, we must set aside every thing else and constantly chant Na Mu Myō Hō Ren Ge Kyō every second with every thought throughout our life. Never relinquish it, even at the cost of our lives if we are forced to stop. Nipponzan's practice does not focus much on the reading of even the Lotus Sūtra. If you are to read at all, I encourage reading more of the writings of Ososhi-sama. After all, there is nothing more than Ososhi-sama's *Gomyōhan* to provide us with such an appreciation of the inexplicable sublimity of Na Mu Myō Hō Ren Ge Kyō. The Lotus Sūtra expounds on the merits of the Odaimoku. However, those who do not chant the Odaimoku cannot understand it.

The Tendai School does not chant the Odaimoku. Nor was the chanting of the Odaimoku the primary practice at Hōon-ji Temple[1] where I was ordained in Usuki, Oita prefecture. Rather, services to recite the Lotus Sūtra were held from morning till night. Nipponzan practices by chanting the Odaimoku. The recitation of sūtras and *Gomyōhan* as well as other learnings are all precursors to faith in the Odaimoku. Please practice with this in mind. I can attest to its truthfulness with absolute certainty. I have come this far in my life adhering to it. I trained under masters of various

---

1　法音寺.

schools until the age of 33, but ultimately cast aside everything I learned and have walked about chanting the Odaimoku. Now the Odaimoku has pervaded the entire world. It is not the Lotus Sūtra that spread, it is the Odaimoku of the Lotus Sūtra that has propagated. The Lotus Sūtra is only the exegesis of the Odaimoku. The *Gomyōhan* says, "The vast entirety of the eighty thousand teachings [of the Buddha] and the copious eight volumes of the Lotus Sūtra were all expounded for the purpose of revealing the five characters of Myō Hō Ren Ge Kyō."[2]

.

---

2 A citation from the *Shōgu-mondō-shō* [聖愚問答鈔 *Questions and Answers Between the Sage and the Unenlightened*] written by Nichiren Daishōnin in 1265.

108

The Identity of Myō Hō Ren Ge Kyō

August 30, 1982
Tama Dōjō, Tōkyō

WHAT IS THE IDENTITY of Myō Hō Ren Ge Kyō? What is it that is called by the name Myō Hō Ren Ge Kyō? The entity of Myō Hō Ren Ge Kyō is said to be everything that exists in the entire universe, everything that exists in the ten realms of existence from hell to the Buddha realm. *Jissō-shinnyo*[1] is the term used to describe it. The entire universe moves in complete order. This order is the entity of Myō Hō Ren Ge Kyō. All of the ten states of existence, be it the state of hell, of hungry spirits or any others, are quintessential entities of Myō Hō Ren Ge Kyō. Thus, it is a matter of course that everything can become Buddha. Attraction through evil karma creates illusions and manifests the evil path on which we suffer as human beings. Good karmic causality results in the Buddha, flowers or other pure states of joy. Yet, everything is an entity of Myō Hō Ren Ge Kyō, within which ten states of existence are embodied. To strive to do good and to be averse to evil is the manifestation of practicing the Buddha Dharma. All ten states of existence, including animals, hungry spirits and human beings, are embodiments of the sacred noumenon called Myō Hō Ren Ge Kyō. When we awaken to this, we are able to do good.

---

1 実相 真如. *Jissō* is the true state of all things, the ultimate reality, and the universal and eternal truth applicable to all things, the essence of all things. *Shinnyo* [*tathatā*] is thusness, suchness, the true form of things, reality.

109

A Religion for Universal Emancipation

September 13, 1982
Vienna Dōjō, Austria

I ALSO INITIALLY FELT that religion addresses issues of the heart and mind, thereby it suffices to focus on providing spiritual guidance specific to individual needs without being involved with political or other issues that affect people collectively. However, many of the issues today involve a huge institution known as the state, and on a larger scale, the globe. Unless the issues that concern the world change, merely striving for self-improvement at an individual level misses the point. Who can put right the misdirection of the state? The state of affairs of the world has changed such that it requires religion to not only work to mend the minds of individuals but, at the same time, correct the misguided direction of the state and the world.

When the world is made impure and is being swallowed up in billows, bringing serenity and transformation to the individual mind is not enough. A just life of an individual cannot exist in isolation. A just life of an individual exists in the just life of a country and the just life of the world. When the peoples of the world recognize and seek this, religion must be what actively works to create peace in the world. Nichiren Daishōnin set aside from himself the notions of personal salvation, such as going to the "Western Pure Land" [of Amida Buddha in the world hereafter as preached by the Pure Land School] or being reborn in Heaven. He brought to the forefront a religion that sets the goal of emancipating humanity and the world by advocating a just faith that brings forth *Risshō-ankoku*, secure and peaceful nations.

Disarmament

At the age of ninety-eight
I attend the Disarmament Session
Beating the drum
Proclaiming to the world
That all military, all nuclear weapons
Must disappear
One sky, four oceans
Entirely at peace

Nichidatsu

110

THE GREAT POWER OF THE INDIAN PEOPLE

October 25, 1982
Rajgir Dōjō, India

AT A TIME WHEN India's freedom movement was gaining momentum under Mahatma Gandhiji's leadership based on the principle of nonviolence, an incident occurred at a small village in Northern India called Chauri Chaura. Angered by the police firing at local protesters, the people responded by killing the policemen. Gandhiji felt he must answer for the violence in the independence movement and suspended his leadership of the movement. The people of India pledged to hold fast to nonviolence in order to once again have Gandhiji lead them for his leadership was irreplaceable in the cause of India's independence. The greatness of Gandhiji's thought on nonviolence is unquestionable. However, the fact that 400 million Indians endured years of tribulation, yet sustained complete faith in independence through nonviolence as called for by Gandhiji is a wondrous phenomenon. Gandhiji, who led the nonviolent movement, was truly a man of greatness. But the awesome power of the 400 million Indian people who put nonviolence into practice and won independence is even greater.

The world has now turned into a powder keg of nuclear weapons. It is only a matter of time before it ignites. The power to prevent it is in the hands of we, the people, not in governments or those in power. When the more than 4 billion people of the world take a stand for peace, embrace a new, international order of ethics and say we will not tolerate war; when we refuse to kill or to be killed but say we want to live together peacefully in nonviolence, then humanity will be following in India's footsteps and will successfully prevent the nuclear holocaust. The successful outcome of India's freedom movement provides a precedent that demonstrates the ability of the nonviolent movement to prevent the nuclear holocaust of tomorrow. The peoples of the world must take this to heart and rise to the occasion. Let us learn from India's independence so that we, too, can be victorious in preventing nuclear war.

111

Nipponzan Myōhōji

November 16, 1982
Patna, India

I NAMED THIS ORDER Nipponzan Myōhōji when I first stepped out abroad to spread the Buddha Dharma. Until this day, no matter where we go to spread the Dharma, we are known as Nipponzan Myōhōji. The Lotus Sūtra contains prophecies on how it would spread. During the first 2,000 years, it was to spread from India to China, Korea and throughout Asia.[1] It is also foretold that in the Era of Declining Dharma, 2,500 years after the Parinirvāna of the Buddha, the Lotus Sūtra would once again spread throughout the world from Japan. In this era, it is said that the hearts and minds of the people are impure and confused, the technologies of killing highly developed and that the world is on the brink of total consumption by the tools of war. In the Lotus Sūtra, the teachings of the Buddha meant for emancipating this age were enfolded in a single phrase and bequeathed to the disciples at the Divine Eagle Peak for transmittal in the Era of Declining Dharma. This single phrase is Na Mu Myō Hō Ren Ge Kyō. Na Mu Myō Hō Ren Ge Kyō is a teaching that did not spread anywhere nor was there any one to spread during the 2,500 years following the Parinirvāna of

---

1   i) Reference to Chapter XXIII of the Lotus Sūtra, *The Story of the Medicine King Bodhisattva*. ii) Kumārajīva's master Sutyasoma instructed him that, "The sun of Buddha has gone into hiding behind the western mountains, but its lingering rays shine over the Northeast. These texts are destined for the lands of the Northeast. You must make sure that they are transmitted to them." From these two sources, Nichiren Daishōnin inferred that the lands of the Northeast means Japan and that the Lotus Sūtra shall spread to *Jambudvīpa* [the entire world] from Japan.

Buddha Śākyamuni.

Various medicines are available and can be administered to cure minor illnesses. However, when the illness is grave and critical, a small medicine[2] that is easy to take, that contains the maximum dose of all available cures is what is needed to save a moribund person. When relief provided by Buddhism in the past is no longer adequate in benefiting the people, the single phrase of Na Mu Myō Hō Ren Ge Kyō is pronounced to be the medicine for extinguishing the flame that is about to reduce the world to ashes in this non-virtuous era. Based on his close examination of the sūtra, Nichiren Daishōnin, who was born in Japan, initiated the chanting of Na Mu Myō Hō Ren Ge Kyō. He took upon himself the mission to free humanity from the agony of extermination that is to come by warfare in the Era of Declining Dharma. This Buddha Dharma, which was chanted for the first time in Japan—Na Mu Myō Hō Ren Ge Kyō—must be spread throughout the world to quench the flames of modern warfare. As I stepped into the world to deliver this Dharma, I named the order Nipponzan Myōhōji,[3] which signifies the teaching of Na Mu Myō Hō Ren Ge Kyō that is to be transmitted.

---

2 The medicine consisting of the five or seven characters of Na Mu Myō Hō Ren Ge Kyō is a small pill condensing all the 69,384 characters of the Lotus Sūtra in one phrase. Chapter XVI of the Lotus Sūtra, *The Duration of the Life of the Tathāgata*, urges this medicine be taken.

3 Nipponzan is the *sangō* [山号 title of the mountain, i.e., temple]. Traditionally, temples were built in mountains, which frequently became the names of the temples. Guruji gave the name Nipponzan to represent the Buddha Dharma from Japan, and Myōhōji incorporating the *Myōhō* [Sublime Dharma, Na Mu Myō Hō Ren Ge Kyō], which is to be disseminated in the Era of Declining Dharma.

112

The Invaluable Life of Mendicants

December 27, 1982
Tama Dōjō, Tōkyō

The Japanese term *biku*[1] from the Indian language means mendicant. One day a disciple asked Lord Buddha what is the most difficult thing to do as a human being. Lord Buddha answered that it was to leave home and become ordained. What is difficult about becoming ordained? Lord Buddha responded that it is to shave one's head and sustain one's life through mendicancy. When one does not lack food, clothing and dwelling, the ordained is no longer an ordained. One no longer practices mendicancy and ends life in sloth. In this lies the decline of Buddha Dharma. It is not that the teachings became obsolete. Rather, it is caused by the monastics not leading a life of mendicancy. Things have somewhat opened up for Nipponzan today. This became possible because we have forsaken the path of sustenance and adopted the practice of walking.

An ordained person gives up adornment, taking nothing to decorate the body with. The life of an ordained originated with prohibitions on personal possessions except for a few items, including a mendicant's iron bowl, a walking staff and a patched-cotton robe. That was when the Buddha Dharma spread rapidly. When it spreads, magnificent temples like this are built and the monastic starts to lead the life of the laity. That leads to a carefree

---

1 比丘 *bhiksu* [Sk]. Male member of the Sangha, a Buddhist order, used here as a generic term for a monastic who shaves his head and leads a mendicant life.

life, which impedes practice. Nipponzan has a chance of preserving the life of Buddha Dharma of Japan owing to a few who practice throughout the world.

Jainism in India, born approximately the same time as Buddhism, still observes the mode of the mendicant life. It withstood political persecution and internal changes. Practitioners walk everywhere barefoot, even in major cities like Calcutta or Bombay. Vehicles are not used. This mode of life has both strength and weakness. Jainism faithfully guarded this life and so did not die out in India. On the other hand, Jainism could not develop into a movement to liberate the sufferings of the times because of this. Given these strengths and weaknesses of the mendicant life, we, monastics, should recognize that the Buddha Dharma would die out should we lose sight of what it means to be a *biku*.

The impasse in society and politics comes from everyone amassing materials out of avarice. This is the stumbling block in capitalism and equally in communism. I believe the error is in defining food to be of utmost importance to human beings. We will break through this misconception. The practice of mendicancy by which the ordained walks into communities is what illuminates the darkness of human beings. We are not in the business of merely going about to be offered food for sustenance. We are to be an example that reminds others of society's forgotten spiritual treasure. A life of joy is a spiritual treasure. With each additional persecution and hardship confronted, Nichiren Daishōnin's joy grew greater. At the time he was dragged to Tatsunokuchi to be executed by decapitation, Shijō Kingo-dono accompanied him crying. Nichiren Daishōnin consoled him saying, "Can you not smile at a time of such great joy for me?"

This spiritual treasure, this life of joy, exists regardless of the realities of this world. It is a world of its own. Peace will come to our societies when all the people of the world arrive there. Peace will not come no matter how much we produce and distribute unless we arrive there. Only strife befalls us. Our practice of leading the invaluable monastic life shall be the path to cure the illness of modern civilization: the blindness caused by competition over material things.

PART TEN

Our Grounds for Nonviolence

113

SPARE NOT YOUR VOICE

March 14, 1983
Sri Pada Dōjō, Sri Lanka

"VOICE PERFORMS DHARMA-WORK."[1] Na Mu Myō Hō Ren Ge Kyō must be chanted without sparing our voice. Our practice to provide the benefit of the Dharma to others[2] is to deliver the Odaimoku to the ears of others without sparing our voice. To chant the Odaimoku in the mountain in solitude is the practice for one's own benefit.[3] Our joyful voices chanting the Odaimoku must resonate in the ears of the multitude. It is our voice that plants the Odaimoku deep in the mind field of the eight consciousnesses.[4] "I, Nichiren, alone have been chanting Na Mu Myō Hō Ren Ge Kyō, Na Mu Myō Hō Ren Ge Kyō without sparing my voice."[5] Do not spare your voice. It is arduous. However, once we gain confidence in doing it, we will have a fairly good idea of what we can achieve in life. Our body and life will be dedicated to the single practice of chanting the Odaimoku. Whether we succeed in anything else is of no consequence. Building temples and stūpas are secondary issues. The essential matter is to chant the Odaimoku without

---

1 Citation from *Hoke-gengi* [法華玄義, *Fa-hua-hsüan-i*]. Dharma work is the liberation of sentient beings by the Buddha. 声為仏事[*Shōi-butsuji*].
2 *Keta* 化他.
3 *Jigyō* 自行
4 *Hasshiki* [八識], *astavijnānāni*. According to the teaching of Hossō school, sentient beings possess eight distinct faculties of consciousness; the first five corresponding to the five-sense perceptions of sight, hearing, smell, taste, touch; the sixth to the conscious mind; seventh and eight, broadly speaking, to the different aspects of the subconscious mind.
5 Citation from *Requital of Gratitude*, *Hōon-jō* 報恩鈔.

sparing our voice.

We all tend to spare our voice. It is hard to sustain it. It is written that Bodhisattva Never Despise escaped afar and continued to chant the twenty-four character *gāthā* aloud even after he was beaten because of it. Our whole life must be committed to one thing—chanting the Odaimoku. This is what Nipponzan's job is. We need not tend to anything else. Whether one is foolish or wise, knowledgeable or unknowledgeable is of no significance. You don't even need to know any doctrines. It does not matter if you do not know anything else. Simply be assiduous in chanting the Odaimoku. That is our practice. We chant because we must carry the Odaimoku to the ears of the people with whom we cross paths. If we were to spare our voice and stop chanting, eventually no one will chant the Odaimoku.

114

Spreading the Dharma

March 17, 1983
Sri Pada Dōjō, Sri Lanka

I HAVE TRAINED many disciples to this day, but those who are averse to fasting or who figure out ways to make it easy on themselves over time, for the most part, appear inclined to leave Nipponzan in their latter years. Be diligent knowing that this is a difficult practice for one's own discipline. Diligence in this practice does not yield any return of monetary gain or lay followers. Do not expect anything; practice for practice sake. Ordinary human beings like us must do the work of faithfully delivering Ososhi-sama's teachings and bring the prophecies of the Buddha to fruition. Even we can do fasting or chanting the Odaimoku, practices given to attain that goal. Neither the reading of sūtras nor research on doctrines of the denomination will do. Ososhi-sama's aspiration was to chant the Odaimoku to be fully prepared at all times to face any formidable undertakings. Nothing else.

Having a temple ties us down to run it and prevents us from achieving any Buddha-work throughout our life. The downfall of an institutionalized order thus begins. It can be averted by leaving the temple behind and by walking about chanting the Odaimoku. However, a temple to care for tends to tie us down for the rest of our life with things like replacing the roof or other maintenance and construction work. Our life then becomes no different from that of a layperson. Even worse is starting a family and having children. No one can neglect and leave them. It was not easy even for Lord Buddha. Leaving one's wife and children behind is an extremely hard thing to do. With a family, one's primary consideration is the children until they become self-sufficient, doing whatever possible so that they would not have a hard life. This remains the main focus all the way up to one's latter years. Even with an aspiration to spread the Great Dharma, it cannot be done with a wife and family.

The members of Nipponzan who are influencing the world today are those who have no such shackles to tie them down. The virtue and dignity of the Genuine Dharma manifest through them. Ososhi-sama taught that chanting of the Odaimoku is the one and only thing that will benefit the Era of Declining Dharma; even observing precepts is secondary to it. However, in spite of that, he created an order of tonsured, ordained disciples. We must carefully contemplate the significance of what this means. As an ordained disciple of Oshoshi-sama, not one of the six elders[1] ever possessed a family or temple throughout his life. All six elders embarked on dissemination of the Dharma. Ososhi-sama's entire life was spent spreading the Dharma. It was not spent building temples, stūpas or in acquiring lay followers. His life was one of hardship. That is what the life of a practitioner of the Odaimoku should be. If one fails to understand this crucial point, a single step in the wrong direction could result in an error for life. Whether this seems tedious or exciting, it is the invaluable obligation of the ordained to be free with nothing to bind us, so that we may go anywhere we need to, whenever we need to and do whatever we need to in our work for the Lotus Sūtra.

No words or academic learning are needed to spread the Dharma abroad. The one thing required is the practice of the Odaimoku of the Lotus Sūtra. In *Requital of Gratitude*, Ososhi-sama revealed the essential doctrine of *The Dharma of the Three*

---

1 The six eminent elder monks Nichiren Daishōnin designated on October 8, 1282 at Ikegami immediately before his death who were entrusted to serve as the guiding light in carrying the teachings forward.

Great of Mysteries,[2] which consists of the essential object of veneration depicted in the essential section of the Lotus Sūtra,[3] the platform of precepts depicted in the essential section of the Lotus Sūtra and the Daimoku of the essential section of the Lotus Sūtra.[4] A reference to these three gives the impression that they are three distinct and separate matters. However, they are all embodied in the single act of chanting the Odaimoku. In essence, they are facets of the mystery that eventually manifest through it.

---

2 *Sandai-hihō* 三大秘法.
3 *Honmon* 本門 the essential section is the latter half of the Lotus Sūtra, where the eternal nature of the Primordial Eternal Buddha is revealed.
4 Na Mu Myō Hō Ren Ge Kyō.

115

Kiyosumi

April 27, 1983
Kiyosumi Dōjō, Japan

THROUGHOUT MY LIFE I have been fortunate to be able to engage in the daily practice of Na Mu Myō Hō Ren Ge Kyō, which was left for the liberation of the virtueless age of the Era of Declining Dharma, turbid with the five decays.[1] I can genuinely identify with the words of Nichiren Daishōnin, "Truly, truly, this must mean that I have paid homage to ten myriad *koṭis* of Buddhas in the past."[2] There is no greater joy than this for someone born human. And it makes me proud as a human being that I can take joy in it. I committed my life to chanting the Odaimoku, and of all the places in the wide world, Mount Kiyosumi in Japan is the most treasured, incomparable place for me. This is where the Odaimoku was first chanted. I have always felt a special bond to this mountain and hoped to build at least a modest hermitage, but lack of financial resources prevented me. Moreover, at that time, the Kiyosumi Temple[3] here on the mountain belonged to the

---

1 *Gojoku* 五濁, *panca kasāyā* [Sk]. The five defilements of the present world: i) defilement of the kalpa, or era, things like war, natural disasters, pestilence, etc.; ii) defilement of views; iii) defilement through illusions; iv) defilement by exhausting good karma; v) the decay of life span.
2 Letter to *Jakunichi-bō* 寂日房御書, September 16, 1279.
3 Officially read Seichō-ji 清澄寺, also commonly known as Kiyosumi-dera, is the temple where Nichiren Daishōnin was ordained and where he first started chanting the Odaimoku. The temple was opened in 771 and was a Tendai School temple at the time Nichiren Daishōnin was ordained in 1273. Seventy years after his passing it converted to a Shingon temple and once again returned to the Nichiren School in 1947.

Shingon School, where chanting of the Odaimoku was not accepted as the right practice.[4] However, out of an earnest desire for a dōjō here where I could freely chant the Odaimoku, I finally built a hut. Eventually my ardent wish was heard, and the Kiyosumi Temple converted to the Nichiren School. A succession of deputy chief priests[5] with jurisdiction on this mountain kindly offered support and aid to Nipponzan's practice. We were grateful to receive their invitation to freely use any area on the premises that we so chose. The land on which this dōjō was constructed, likewise, belongs to the Kiyosumi Temple. It was offered to us unconditionally.

4 *Shōgyō* 正行.
5 *Bettō* 別当.

116

The Lotus Sūtra Practiced as a Physical Reading

April 27, 1983
Kiyosumi Dōjō, Japan

How fortunate would you say Nichiren Daishōnin was as a person? The circumstances he chose, relinquishing personal fortune and happiness, have won him the faith and empathy of many today. The persecutions at Tatsunokuchi,[1] Izu,[2] Sado Island[3] and Komatsubara[4] are all testimony to the life he lived. He was not fortunate, yet he was always joyous. Why? Because these events allowed him to "read" the Lotus Sūtra with his physical body, enabling him to practice it. Reading the Lotus Sūtra with one's body is to liberate the modern times with the Lotus Sūtra. The practitioners of the Lotus Sūtra who are to free the modern world have three formidable enemies[5] confronting them, imposing various hardships throughout their lives. When the Honzon is corrupted, Na Mu Myō Hō Ren Ge Kyō turns into a tool of greed.

---

1 Tatsunokuchi is the execution ground in Kamakura, where Nichiren Daishōnin was taken to be beheaded on September 12, 1271.
2 On May 12, 1261, Nichiren Daishōnin was sentenced to banishment at Itō village on Izu peninsula, current day Shizuoka Prefecture, and was pardoned on February 22, 1263.
3 Sado Island is the largest island of Japan in the Japan Sea and was where those who committed the most egregious felonies were exiled. Nichiren Daishōnin was exiled in October 1271. After the Mongolian invasion, Hōjō Tokimune issued an edict to bring him back in February 1274.
4 On November 11, 1264, Lord Kagenobu Tōjō of Amatsu and a troop of armed men attacked Nichiren Daishōnin and his disciples.
5 Persecution by state power, arrogant monks and lay people.

The object of greed varies with the individual. Some want money, some want clothes, etc. No matter how great they may be in number, those who misuse the Odaimoku cannot possibly bring salvation to humanity or to a nation. The essential teaching of *Risshō-ankoku* is lost without a trace when the Odaimoku is used as a tool for personal happiness. When personal happiness takes precedence over everything else, the issues confronting the nation lose their relevance and turn into idle talk.

117

Letter to Reverend Myōmitsu[1]

November 6, 1983
Darjeeling Dōjō, India

THE *GOMYŌHAN* we recited today teaches Ososhi-sama's heart and mind in chanting the Odaimoku. It is relevant to today's Nipponzan. "I am not the founder of any school." Just like Ososhi-sama, because I do not consider myself to be a founder of any school, I chant with due reverence. Just as Ososhi-sama says, it is as if I am chanting in my dreams, following in his footsteps without being fully conscious of why I chant as I do. He also points out that he is not the follower of another, older school; not a renowned scholar; nor leading a praiseworthy life of adherence to the precepts that is in any fashion different from the lives of ordinary people. With great modesty, Ososhi-sama refers to himself as "equal to a bull or sheep, not particularly wise." Nipponzan is a bunch of nincompoops and less than a bull or a sheep, which is fine. The problem is if we assume airs of being wise. That prevents us from chanting the Odaimoku, regarding it as something to be chanted by those of inferior capability. We don't know the reasons why the Odaimoku is invaluable, but chant it because we are taught and exhorted to do so. Accordingly, we wondrously chant it. We must never feign to be wise or scholarly. Ososhi-sama self-effacingly calls himself ignorant as a bull or sheep. In terms of wisdom, we are even lower than them, perhaps at the level of an earthworm or a mole. We must never forget who we are lest we

---

1 Refer to Guruji's *The Bodhisattvas Who Emerge from the Earth-1*, p. 72.

become arrogant. We have neither title nor rank. All we do is go about intently chanting the Odaimoku. Wherever we go, we are at the mercy of other's generosity in receiving food to eat. We are nothing more than that. That is where we need to place ourselves. When the Odaimoku is chanted, those who do not welcome it will speak ill of us. "Ultimately, whether it is a good thing or a bad thing. . ." Maybe it is not a good thing since there are those who are not joyous in hearing it. Yet, at the same time, there are those who are joyous. " . . . Neither I nor anyone else knows for sure." That's how it is. We don't know.

118

Commonality With Gandhiji

November 13, 1983
World Sarvodaya Assembly, Wardha, India

On October 4, 1933, I was able to meet Mahatma Gandhiji for the first time here at Wardha. That meeting lasted fifteen minutes. There was hardly time to say anything. I sat quietly facing Gandhiji while he intently turned the charkhā, spinning cotton yarn, oblivious to the visitor. I heard that the development in spinning machines enabled a single worker to produce enough yarn for hundreds of people. At one point I thought that if this is true, spinning yarn could be left to machines. Back at that time, Gandhiji launched a movement to remove European sovereignty through the spinning of yarn to create a free and independent country for the 400 million Indian people. Perhaps no one believed that an independence revolution could be achieved by spinning yarn. I was no exception. There have been political revolutions since long ago, but they were resolved by force of arms. There has been no precedent in history where a revolution for independence was achieved by spinning yarn. Whether it was feasible was doubtful. Mahatma Gandhiji's turning of the charkhā was based on his absolute faith in the single act of spinning the yarn in achieving India's independence.

I pondered on this. A single person producing enough yarn for 10, 20, a hundred people with a spinning machine could be, in a way, a miracle. However, if Gandhiji could bring a historically unprecedented political revolution—a free independent country for 400 million people with the spinning of yarn—it would be truly a miracle of all miracles. There is a passage in the sūtra,

> The Buddhas, saviors of the world, abide in their great transcendental powers, and in order to please living beings, they display immeasurable divine powers.[1]

This describes an invisible, non-material power in action. It didn't matter even if Gandhiji was the only person who believed in the success of the independence movement through spinning the yarn. There is no telling where help comes from in a world invisible to our eyes. I left Japan with the aspiration to bring tranquility to nations and peace to the world by chanting Na Mu Myō Hō Ren Ge Kyō while beating the drum. This became my life's work. If one asks whether a political revolution has ever been attained by chanting Na Mu Myō Hō Ren Ge Kyō and beating the drum, the answer is no. Nevertheless, I do it because I believe in it. I may be able to attain it. This is what I hold in common with Gandhiji who believed in India's independence revolution by spinning yarn.

---

1 Chapter XXI of the Lotus Sūtra, *The Divine Transcendental Powers of the Tathāgata.*

119

The Unity of Prayer

November 13, 1983
Sevagram Ashram, Wardha, India

Mahatma Gandhi believed that the goal of the independence movement can be achieved by spinning yarn and inspired 400 million Indians to unite in a common aspiration. Gandhiji taught and himself believed that spinning yarn is the prayer of the freedom movement and not about the quantity of yarn produced. It united the hearts and minds of the Indian people, providing a rallying point through prayer. In other words, the Indian people were able to share in Gandhiji's belief that the materialization of India's independence will come through spinning the yarn. Even without him, India would be able to produce its own cotton. Though people were unemployed, spinning yarn would allow them to clothe themselves. It did not require exertion or hard labor. Children, women and certainly men could spin yarn. It provided the unifying prayer, a spiritual knot that tied the people together in the independence movement. Gandhiji spun yarn wherever he went. Eventually this movement materialized a wondrous independence without historical precedence before our very eyes.

Today, Buddha Dharma of Japan has been introduced to India. Nichiren Daishōnin firmly believed until the very last days of his life that the Buddha Dharma of Japan would be returned to India. He left this belief in writing. However, during the 700 years following his passing, his words had not come to fruition. Should any prophecy remain unfulfilled for 700 years? Today, 700 years later, the Japanese government rejected Nichiren Daishōnin's "Buddha Dharma of Japan," claiming that it has no bearing on the policy of Japan. A dedication ceremony was performed for a stūpa on September 25 in Vienna, the capital of Austria. The Japanese ambassador to Austria was requested to attend, but the invitation was turned down on the grounds that religion has no relevance to the policy of the Japanese government. The Japanese government is currently attempting to secure the nation's defense through arms build-up. This is reflected in its offer to position US nuclear weapons on Japanese soil, allegedly to ward off a Soviet attack. Thus, Nichiren Daishōnin's teaching of *Risshō-ankoku* is still rejected in Japan today, while gaining credibility in Europe, the United States and India. Japan suffered defeat in World War II when it tried to defend the nation while rejecting this teaching. In spite of this, Japan still has not awakened and continues to prepare for war. *Risshō-ankoku-ron* calls to "promptly mend thy trivial faith and immediately embrace the single Truth of the Genuine Vehicle." India has indeed mended the trivial faith of defending the nation with arms and embraced "the single Truth of the Genuine Vehicle," the single true Way to live as human beings. India's independence movement possessed no arms. It depended entirely on the perfect employment of the spinning of yarn that served the people as the Dharma of prayer.

Similarly, the prayer by Nichiren Daishōnin was *Risshō-ankoku*, to achieve "ultimately peace in the world, peace and tranquility of the land." This aspiration is shared by all. Religion is meant to materialize it. The work of religion becomes meaningless when the nation falls, its people perish. Any religion that causes the fall of the nation and its people should not be followed. "When the nation falls and its people perish, who will venerate the Buddha, who will have faith in the Dharma?" There is no need to follow any such religion that does not serve in preventing the fall of the nation and its people from dying. Na Mu Myō Hō Ren Ge Kyō is the prayer that provides for the nation and its people to flourish.

Once chanting it, even those who have never chanted before will be inspired to pray. Where else is there a voice of prayer for world peace? Na Mu Myō Hō Ren Ge Kyō is the voice of prayer that will emancipate the current times. This is Buddha Dharma of Japan. At Wardha, Mahatma Gandhi employed it in India's independent movement.[1] Even after Gandhiji's passing, the Buddha Dharma of Japan, Na Mu Myō Hō Ren Ge Kyō, is spreading in India. Na Mu Myō Hō Ren Ge Kyō is a prayer for *Risshō-ankoku*—peace and tranquility of the nation, a path that leads citizens to peace and comfort. Without it, misfortunes ensue and tragedy by atomic and hydrogen bombs, nuclear weapons, is likely to befall humanity.

---

1 Gandhi incorporated Na Mu Myō Hō Ren Ge Kyō as the first prayer to be offered at the ashram's prayer meetings every morning and evening. Even to this day, national celebrations in India also start off with Na Mu Myō Hō Ren Ge Kyō chanted thrice following this tradition Gandhi started.

120

GANDHIJI

November 13, 1983
Sevagram Ashram, Wardha, India

ON OCTOBER 4, 1933, I was able to meet Mahatma Gandhiji for the first time at Wardha. Fifteen minutes was allotted for this meeting. There was barely time to convey anything of substance to Gandhiji. I was quietly facing Gandhiji, who was turning the charkhā, intently spinning cotton yarn as if oblivious to his guest. Spinning the charkhā symbolized Gandhiji's unshakable faith that this act would win India's independence. Our 15-minute meeting passed without a word spoken. In parting, Gandhiji said, "I met you today because Bajaji told me to meet you for 15 minutes. If he suggests seeing you again tomorrow for 15 minutes, I will. Come see me with Bajaji's permission." However, Gandhiji observed a day of silence once every week. His aide reminded him that the next day was his day of silence and that he would not be able to speak, even if the bhikshu from Japan visits. Gandhiji countered, saying, "That is true. I may not be able to speak, but I enjoy the drum the Venerable beats. All religions use instruments for prayer; the prayer of Japanese Buddhists is indeed valiant." He then picked up the drum and beat it. This was the first prayer drum of the Buddha Dharma of Japan that was beaten in India by an Indian person. I have met many people from different counties, but never have I met anyone as delighted as Gandhiji by the sound of the drum and prayer voice of Na Mu Myō Hō Ren Ge Kyō. The Buddha Dharma of Japan was in this way transmitted to India through this very person. The Odaimoku of the Buddha Dharma of Japan, and its

Honzon, the stūpa, have taken root in India. Stūpas and temples are now built in different parts of India, and the Odaimoku is being chanted. If you go to Rajgir, you will see up to a thousand visitors daily. There is no distinction of religion or schools of religion. They resonate with the faith of the Indian people.

121

Our Grounds for Nonviolence

November 15, 1983
Wardha, India

THE POWER INDIA DEMONSTRATED to the modern world is the power of nonviolence advocated by Mahatma Gandhiji. When we read *Remonstration with Bodhisattva Hachiman*[1] it says, "The Era of Declining Dharma is replete with formidable enemies of the One Vehicle. What counters them is the divine benefit by Bodhisattva Never Despise." What did Bodhisattva Never Despise do? He dedicated himself to the practice of *tangyō-raihai*. He stopped reading sūtras and instead walked about, bowing to others in reverence. In response, people used force against him. They spoke ill of him and beat him. He would then go away and continue to venerate them with palms together saying, "I bow to you because you all shall become the Buddha." The nonviolent movement is a legacy that was to be practiced by the disciples of Ososhi-sama, but no one stepped forward. Instead, Mahatma Gandhiji did. Nipponzan is currently propagating the movement of nonviolence in the world. The earlier mentioned teaching of *Remonstration with Bodhisattva Hachiman* is the grounds for it. Bodhisattva Never Despise cast aside everything else and engaged in *tangyō-raihai*. This practice is the most explicit expression of a nonviolence movement. It is not a passive act of refraining from violence, but actively exercising nonviolence.

---

1 *Kangyō-hachiman-shō* 諫暁八幡鈔. Written by Nichiren Daishōnin on December 16, 1280 at Mount Minobu.

Nipponzan promotes the movement of nonviolence throughout the world, opposing war and armaments. Our practice is predicated on nothing other than *Remonstration with Bodhisattva Hachiman*. We must practice *tangyō-raihai*. Nipponzan is not blindly emulating others but rather follows the precedent set by Bodhisattva Never Despise. Japan, as a nation, did not follow in his footsteps. The Nichiren School did not follow in his footsteps. It was India's Mahatma Gandhiji who came forward and followed in his footsteps in the Era of Declining Dharma. He was uncompromising in his rejection of violence and held reverence for all. There was not a single person he despised. This was what made it possible to resolve the struggle with Britain without going to war. Bodhisattva Never Despise went about venerating others with palms together because they were to become Buddha. He venerated them in the face of violence uttering, "You shall all become Buddha." This is the essence of nonviolence.

122

RISSHŌ-ANKOKU-RON
TREATISE ON GIVING RISE TO THE TRUE DHARMA FOR PEACE AND TRANQUILITY OF THE NATION

December 4, 1983
Kiyosumi Dōjō, Japan

"TO FIRST PRAY for the nation, it is imperative to give rise to the Buddha Dharma" is how I have you read this passage. It has been commonly misread up to now as "first pray for the nation." I am not certain how the guiding marks are placed beside the kanji characters[1] in the modern version of the *Gomyōhan*, but the erroneous reading of the passage as "first pray for the nation, and to that end, it is imperative to give rise to the Buddha Dharma" is interpreted to mean that first and foremost prayers be offered for the nation and chant the Odaimoku to that end. It places the nation first. The imperative of Buddha Dharma is relegated to second. Buddha Dharma thus became used as a tool. The nation is the subject, and Buddha Dharma subordinate to it. This is a misreading of this passage. How, then, is the word "first" used, and what does it give precedence to?

Another passage in *Risshō-ankoku-ron* says, "If one wishes to have peace for oneself, first pray for the tranquility of the

---

1 The original manuscript written by Nichiren Daishōnin was in Chinese characters known as *kanbun* 漢文 without guiding marks between characters or marginal notations on the left-hand side of the characters to instruct the reader on the order in which a sentence is to be read in the Japanese word structure. These marks that assist reading Chinese text in Japanese are called *kunten* 訓点 and were developed with the introduction of Buddhism and Chinese translations of its scriptures.

world."[2] When personal issues of the individual are given priority, one tends to become less concerned about compelling issues that could cause national ruin. The fundamental issue is the nation, not the individual. As the title of *Risshō-ankoku-ron* indicates, the essential issue is "*ankoku*," the nation; our individual, personal issues rest on it. The desire to bring peace and tranquility to the nation must take precedence over the desire to achieve individual tranquility. That is what "first" is referring to in "To first pray for the nation..." What is done? "It is imperative to give rise to the Buddha Dharma." It is taught that faith in Buddha Dharma should not be in pursuit of personal happiness at the expense of security of the nation.

In fact, Nichiren School that chants the Odaimoku erroneously reads *Risshō-ankokou-ron* to say, "First pray for the nation." Buddha Dharma is considered a secondary issue. The fact that the nation is given priority is fine, with that much I agree. However, when Buddha Dharma is made subject to the state, it fails to be the prayer in the interest of the nation. Buddha Dharma is the substance. The rise and fall of a nation is dependent on the Dharma. The error made by those who advocate *kokutai-ron*[3] is in slighting Buddha Dharma with the notion that the state reigns supreme over all else. The Nichiren School misinterpreted Ososhi-

---

2 The original word here is *shihyō* 四表, meaning i) the four directions of a nation, ii) between heaven and earth, i.e. the world.

3 国体論. Theory of National Policy, but literally the theory on "the national essence." *Kokutai* is a framework in defining what it is to be Japanese. It served in different interpretations as a unifying idea from the Meiji Restoration to the end of WWII. *Kokutai* is the national government based on the Japanese system of the supreme authority of the emperor. The system utilized a democratic form, yet turned out to be more of an absolute monarchy. The center of the system was put down in *Kojiki* [*Record of Ancient Matters*], the oldest surviving historical book on ancient Japan. It held that the emperor was a direct descendant of Amaterasu Ōmikami, the sun goddess. This belief included unity of state and church. Those who advocate *kokutai-ron* are the theorist and promoters of this notion, and Guruji's reference here is specifically pointing to those advocates within the Nichiren School and its sub-sects.

sama's *Gomyōhan* to cater to *kokutai*.[4] Which of the two would bring liberation to the people? Is it the state, which is considered supreme, or the Dharma? The Dharma is a spiritual issue. The Dharma is what determines the rise or fall of a nation. The nation prospers when the Dharma is given precedence, when True Dharma is sought. Misguided doctrines bring the nation to ruin. Thus, the very title of *"Rissho-ankoku-ron"* exhorts to first give rise to the True Dharma, which results in the peace and tranquility of the nation.

4 When Japan sought to become a modern state with the Meiji Restoration having established Shintoism as its spiritual pillar, some in the Nichiren School and its sub-sects aligned themselves with the government policy, and by the early Showa era [Showa era was 1926-89] became a constituency that had significant influence on national policy.

123

A Single Grain of Rice

December 21, 1983
Kiyosumi Dōjō, Japan

SPRING IS YET TO COME. *Sōdō* at a Zen temple is where young monks practice. I also practiced there. The Zen School practices *takuhatsu*[1] [mendicancy] on the streets. Monks live on offerings including rice, vegetables or monetary donations received from the households as they walk about in this practice. It also allows the practitioners to forge karmic connections to the benefactor in handing down the teachings of the Buddha. Comparable to the practice of *takuhatsu* at Nipponzan Myōhōji is the practice of *gaitō-shugyō* [chanting Odaimoku and beating the drum on the streets].[2] This practice is strictly observed. The Zen practice of *takuhatsu* is still observed in places like Kyōto. Vested in a single unlined kimono tucked up high wearing *zōri* [Japanese sandals] on bare feet, the practitioners intone "Hō—" instead of "Na Mu Myō Hō Ren Ge Kyō."

Treading on ground covered with frost, the cold nipped at our hands and feet. Although we were wearing *tendai-gasa* [a headwear made of woven reed], it was still extremely cold for a shaved head. Despite the cold, someone eventually came out from one of the houses to offer rice from a small plate to each monk as he walked by. When it was my turn, the young lady, shivering from the cold, gently but hastily placed rice in my *zuda-bukuro* [a sack carried by the monks to place scriptures and other necessities

---

1　托鉢.
2　街頭修行.

284

as well as offerings received]. Grains of rice accidentally spilled to the ground. It might have been just one or two grains, but the *hikite*, a monk with the role to guide us, who was standing by my side, said, "Pick up the rice." There is a phrase: "The preciousness of a single grain of rice is as weighty as a massive mountain." That is what people in the old days taught us. A single grain of rice may not be considered a big deal, but one must receive it with a mind that it weighs more than a mountain. From that perspective, not to collect the grains of rice soiled in mud cannot be justified. "Pick up every grain." I picked up every single grain. "The preciousness of a single grain of rice is as weighty as a massive mountain." When this is taken to heart, as I did on that occasion, the debt of gratitude to all sentient beings shall be felt as weighty as a mountain.

Nowadays when money seems to come around easily, one loses a sense of gratitude no matter how much one has. For a monk who has nothing, an offering of rice sustains his life. Whatever sustains his life is extremely precious. No one could be disrespectful out of gratitude for anything that sustains his or her life. Just like Nipponzan Myōhōji, Zen temples do not have many lay supporters and devotees. Nevertheless, they thrive in Kyōto or Kamakura owing to the practice of *takuhatsu*. They walk in the cold shivering. There are no complaints even if no one gives. There may be a single household out of the tens or hundreds of homes they pass that happens to make an offering.

"The preciousness of a single grain of rice is as weighty as a massive mountain." It is a good phrase. I came to appreciate it on that occasion. If we were to take lightly the offerings made by others, we will pay for it and find ourselves in needy circumstances throughout our lives. The only reason Nipponzan is able to do decent work even though we do not cultivate, have a business nor solicit help from others is because we have not forgotten to be grateful, keeping in mind that "The preciousness of a single grain of rice is as weighty as a massive mountain."

The life of a monastic is to take a single bowl of rice, or

even a single cup of tea, with debt of gratitude. Buddha Dharma will never decline as long as the ordained know a debt of gratitude towards offerings made. Those who offer to such a person can give joyfully. No one would give to those who know no debt of gratitude, who act as if they're taking back money they loaned. We do not hold a debt of gratitude just to receive from others. Offerings come spontaneously when we know to be grateful. This is the reason behind the Zen School thriving with many monks. Nipponzan is not thriving as much because offerings are taken for granted. Offerings are made by the volition of the giver. It is not something we ask for. The Zen School practices *takuhatsu* and walks around town persevering in the cold, but not many give. Occasionally one household out of several hundred would make an offering. They are grateful for that single grain of rice offered.

Those accustomed to receiving large sums of money do not know how to be grateful. They are inclined to think that money comes easily if solicited, as if drawing freely from their own savings. If we do that, no one would want to give. That is what would happen. If we are grateful for even very small offerings, they will be bestowed on us. Because of the very nature of the teachings we practice, Nipponzan is an order that cannot survive without being indebted to the kind offerings from others. If we were to be wasteful in the way we spend money and fail to remember a debt of gratitude for the offerings we receive, this order, Nipponzan, will cease to exist.

124

The London Stūpa

December 29, 1983
Kiyosumi Dōjō, Japan

BUILDING THE LONDON STŪPA will not be the work of only a single city or, for that matter, the work of a single country. Rather, it shall set the stage where the global disarmament movement challenges the momentum of military build-up in the world. Its location is England, the cradle of modern civilization. It shall command major international attention because the good medicine that eradicates the venom of modern civilization is about to be introduced there. I believe that Japan is also looking on with astonishment to see a stūpa being built in England. Just like the U.K., Japan is taking part in the nuclear arms build-up through its alliance with the United States. The people do not seem to support it. Yet, simply not supporting it is not enough. We must be resolute and dignified when presenting an opposing view that makes plain their error. This task must be spiritual in nature. Already, the work is underway in England. Milton Keynes was its first step, and the London Stūpa shall become the heart of this campaign for peace. I believe that the eyes of the people will be opened by it. This has nothing to do with policy; it is spiritual power. I believe that the spiritual power that manifests will consequently shatter the misguided beliefs harbored in their minds and hearts. We are a small band of maybe four or five individuals, as you can see, without worldly power. Yet, we are committed to putting our lives on the line to see this through to fruition. We shall see to it that we succeed and will not let you down. This shall become the pillar for building peace in the world.

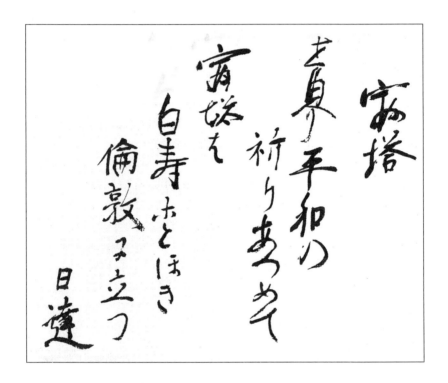

The Origin of the London Stūpa

January 16, 1984
Osaka Dōjō, Japan

ACTUALLY, IT WAS an Iranian Muslim[1] who presented the idea of building a stūpa to the Greater London Council. He deals with cars. Nipponzan occasionally borrowed his car, and that's how he came to know us. This Muslim person shot a documentary of the dedication ceremony of the Milton Keynes Peace Pagoda. The general public has no interest in this kind of film—a small number of us were probably its only audience. However, it just so happens that an acquaintance of his[2] attends the Greater London City Council meetings, and Sadegh suggested that if the Greater London City Council were seeking a Honzon for peace, why not show the documentary of the Milton Keynes Stūpa dedication ceremony at its council meeting. He said, "Fine." The film was shown to the City Council. The City Council also said, "Fine." A stūpa was hence planned for the city of London. Matters wondrously opened up for us from unexpected places without our asking. A film taken by a single Muslim supporter of Nipponzan led to the decision to build a stūpa by the Greater London City Council. There is no knowing from where the divine invisible power of the Buddha will come.

---

1 Sadegh Moghadas.
2 Alan Tomkins, member of the Art and Recreation Committee of the Greater London Council. The two met at a maternity ward where their wives were delivering their babies.

126

THE TEACHING THAT UNITES THE WORLD

May 29, 1984,
Hotel Okura, Tōkyō

THE WORLD MUST COME to exist as one nation. How? Neither power nor war can achieve it. The heart and mind of the people must be transformed. The misguided views that rely on nuclear weapons must be mended. The work of mending the heart and mind of the peoples of the world is the work of religion, for it is religion that transforms the heart and mind. What provides the core of religion is called Honzon [principle object of veneration]. It is an acknowledgment of the sacred with ultimate spiritual authority. This is what Honzon is. A Honzon that peacefully unites the world is needed now more than ever. The Honzon of the Dharma of Three Great Mysteries by Nichiren Daishōnin has thus been revealed. The world must be united under this Honzon. However, whether in Japan or any other nation in the world, there are various religions and Honzons. What is the Honzon of the Dharma of Three Great Mysteries in relation to them? Existing Honzons have served to create the current perilous situation, but lack the power to resolve it.

Prevalent religions like Christianity or Islam are monotheistic and have a history of eradicating any god that is not the One believed in. This was what God commanded; therefore, no other religion was allowed to exist where Christianity spread. Islam destroyed Buddhism in India, the land of its origin, without a trace. Indigenous religions were destroyed where Christianity spread. It may serve the purpose of uniting the people under one

God, but the fact that violence, which is antithetical to the very nature of religion, was used leaves an internal seed of conflict after other faiths have been eradicated. Today we see such examples of killing among Christians in Northern Ireland as well as cruel killing among those of the Islamic faith. All this goes to show that a religion that resorts to violence cannot be employed in creating future peace in the world.

The religion for the future must be a religion of absolute peace, the ultimate, noble religion of the world, with expansive capacities of emancipation, unity, perseverance and power. It is the religion that teaches the way to absolute peace and, for the past 2,500 years, has exerted power to stem acts of war throughout the expansive region of Asia. The dissemination of Buddhism was the reason very few international wars were waged in Asia. The Honzon of Buddhism—the teachings of Buddha Śākyamuni—will now create peace in the world. For this very purpose, Buddha Śākyamuni entrusted Nichiren Daishōnin with the dissemination of this teaching in the remote past of 2,500 years ago. True to this mission, now that it has come to pass "when all the living see, at the kalpa's end, the conflagration seemingly burning," we must spread this teaching and bring to realization Buddha's words "tranquil is this realm of mine." This is the reason why this religion was left and its Honzon revealed. This is the teaching of Honzon in the Dharma of Three Great Mysteries.

127

WHERE IS NIPPONZAN?

December 7, 1984
Atami Dōjō, Japan

As NIPPONZAN COMES to possess things like temples and stūpas, it becomes no different from other established organized religions. Nipponzan would then no longer be what it is. Monks of institutional orders do not practice spreading the Dharma even to nearby places, let alone abroad. I am concerned that unless the institutional order within Nipponzan is removed, Nipponzan will no longer be what it is. Among you are people who have temples, families, stūpas and devotees. You have created a separate order from Nipponzan. When I say Nipponzan now, I mean a group of four or five young monks in Sri Lanka. I have never instructed them on what to do. They have made their own decisions and acted accordingly. Their work is now moving the world. Contemplate on what you must do as a person of faith. Our only concern should be to bring emancipation to the people, sparing neither our bodies nor our lives. Look around to see where Nipponzan is now. You would have to go to Sri Lanka to find Nipponzan as I know it. Staying in a place like this will turn you into monks making a living out of monkhood.

128

KAIDAN OF HONMON

Summer 1984
From *The True Meaning of the Dharma of Three Great Mysteries*
– Treatise on the Precept Dais [1]

NA MU MYŌ HŌ REN GE KYŌ chanted without sparing one's voice is the time when the great precept of the essential section of the Lotus Sūtra is proclaimed and expounded. The place where Na Mu Myō Hō Ren Ge Kyō is chanted without sparing one's voice, in other words, this very domain, is the kaidan [precept dais] [2] of the essential section of the Lotus Sūtra. *Dan* [3] signifies the domain that provides dependant reward, [4] a reference to the enlightenment of the domain we live in. [5] It is by no means a

---

1 三大秘法正義-戒壇論 *Sandai Hihō Shōgi*. This is the last treatise written by Guruji in the summer of 1984 before his passing on January 9, 1985 at 100 years of age. It is the sequel to *The True Meaning of the Dharma of Three Great Mysteries– Treatise on the Principle Object of Veneration*, which was written in early 1984 and publicly presented for the first time as the key note lecture on May 29, 1984 on the 70th commemoration of the founding of Hokkekai. Guruji's final treatises reflect his ultimate belief that differs with the conventional interpretations on the subjects of principle object of veneration and precept dais, critical matters facing the Nichiren School, and go to the very heart of these crucial issues.
2 Kaidan 戒壇 is the precept dais or platform where the precepts are conferred and where the initiated accepts the Buddhist precepts.
3 壇 of kaidan.
4 *Ehō-no-kokudo* 依報の国土. The part of the reward on which one's existence depends; the secondary and circumstantial part of the reward which one receives in this life as the result of acts in previous lives, such as a house, possessions and surroundings. A term contrasted with *shōbō* 正報, the reward proper, the principle reward one receives in life, namely one's own body and mind.
5 *Kokudo-seken-no-jōbutsu* 国土世間の成仏, also can be translated as the enlightenment of the realm of non-sentient beings.

structure.

Bodhisattva Never Despise, who practiced in the past, did not seek validation through imperial command or decree, nor did he build a kaidan. He went out on the streets alone, bowed and venerated whoever passed him with palms joined together enunciating the essential phrase consisting of twenty-four characters.[6] He fled from assailants and continued to venerate them from afar and to recite the essential phrase aloud. This is how the benefit of the Lotus Sūtra is bestowed in the Era of Declining Dharma. The public streets were the kaidan for Bodhisattva Never Despise. It is not a specific physical location where the people of the world are congregated for the initiation of precepts.

The people's capacity to be initiated to the precepts [by the Bodhisattva Never Despise, ushering them to the path of enlightenment] is of the era characterized by the non-virtuous possessing distorted views who slander the Dharma out of arrogance, and not the penitent who atone their wrong.[7] The method of conferring the precepts is what Tendai called "imposed poison,"[8] which is the active conferring of precepts to unwilling recipients. It benefits recipients by provoking anger in their hearts and minds, eliciting from them verbal abuse as well as aggression with swords, clubs and sticks. This act sows the seed of Buddhahood,

---

6　The twenty-four Chinese characters, 我深敬汝等, 不敢軽慢, 所以者何, 汝等皆行菩薩道 in Chapter XX of the Lotus Sūtra, *Bodhisattva Never Despise*. "I deeply revere you. I dare not slight or despise you. For you all will walk the Bodhisattva path and are to become Buddha."

7　In the Era of Declining Dharma, the Bodhisattva Never Despise engages in the practice of venerating all people precisely because their capacity is non-virtuous. The seed of Buddhahood has been destroyed, and this act of veneration seeks to restore this Buddha-seed.

8　而強毒之 Referenced in *Hokke-mongu* 法華文句, *Fa-hua-wén-chu* [Chin.] *Hokke-mongu* is a ten or twenty–fascicle commentary on *Miao-fa-lien-hua-ching-wén-chu*, also known in short as the *Fa-hua-ching*, It was composed by Tendai and written down by Kuanting of the Sui Dynasty. One of the *Fan-hua-san-ta-pu* 法華三大 is *dokku* 毒鼓, poisonous drum, as opposed to *tenku* 天鼓, celestial drum. Here it is a similar analogy of offering the sound of the drum as means of planting the Buddha seed in unwilling recipients who are provoked to anger and irritation when hearing it.

which is one of the three benefits of conferring karmic relationship: they include sowing the seed of Buddhahood,[9] germination[10] and reaping the fruit of Buddhahood.[11] Our founder, Nichiren Daishōnin himself, proclaimed he followed in the footsteps of Bodhisattva Never Despise. The streets of Kamakura[12] were the kaidan revealed in the essential section of the Lotus Sūtra. The Daimoku that consists of the seven characters of Na Mu Myō Hō Ren Ge Kyō was the precept to be conferred. No other rituals, such as the construction of the physical platform for conferring the precept, were required. In the past, be it Buddha Śākyamuni's Era of Declining Dharma or Buddha Candra-sūrya-pradīpa's [Buddha Sun Moon Brilliance][13] Era of Declining Dharma, the precept-conferring dais of the essential section of the Lotus Sūtra has always been the entire domain, the dependant reward land in which people live. It is not a noumenal kaidan,[14] but a phenomenal kaidan.[15] This is the true teaching[16] [in the essential section of the Lotus Sūtra], which opened the way to bring enlightenment to the domain we live in.[17]

---

9 *Shu* 種.
10 *Juku* 熟.
11 *Datsu* 脱.
12 Kamakura was the seat of power during the reign of the Hōjō shogunate where Nichiren Daishōnin engaged in his practices.
13 A Buddha described in Chapter XXIII of the Lotus Sūtra, *Bodhisattva Medicine King*, who expounded the same sūtra innumerable kalpas ago.
14 *Ri-kaidan* 理戒壇.
15 *Ji-kaidan* 事戒壇.
16 True teaching revealed in the essential section of the Lotus Sūtra as opposed to earlier, provisional teachings.
17 *Kokudo-seken-kaie-no hōmon* 国土世間開会の法門.

SELECTED BIBLIOGRAPHY

SOURCES IN ENGLISH

A Dictionary of Chinese Buddhist Terms. 1st ed. Taipei, The Republic of China: Ch'eng-Wen Publishing Co., 1975.

Anesaki, Masaharu. *Nichiren: The Buddhist Prophet.* 2nd ed. Gloucester, MA: Harvard University Press, 1966.

Christensen, J.A. and Nichiren Buddhist International Center. *Nichiren, Leader of Buddhist Reformation in Japan.* 2nd ed. Fremont, CA: Jain Publishing Company, 2001.

Hooker, Richard. "The Japanese Constitution." *Ancient Japan.* 1999. Washington State University. 8 Jan 2007 <http://www.wsu.edu/~dee/ ANCJAPAN/CONST.HTM>.

Hurvitz, Leon, trans. *Scripture of the Lotus Blossom of the Fine Dharma,* Translated from the Chinese of Kumārajiva. 2nd ed. New York: Columbia University Press, 1982.

Inagaki, Hisao. *A Dictionary of Japanese Buddhist Terms.* 5th ed. Kyoto: Nagata Bunshodo, 2003.

Japanese-English Buddhist Dictionary. 2nd ed. Tokyo: Daitō-shuppansha, 1979.

Kato, Bunnō, Yoshirō Tamura and Kōjirō Miyasaka, trans. *The Threefold Lotus Sūtra.* 6th ed. New York & Tokyo: Weatherhill/Kosei, 1984.

Murano, Senchu, trans. *The Lotus Sūtra, The Sūtra of the Lotus Flower of the Wonderful Dharma,* Translated from the Chinese. 2nd ed. Tokyo: Nichiren Shū Shimbun Co., Ltd, 1991.

Prince Shotoku. International Buddhist University. 8 Jan 2007 <http:// www.shitennoji.ac.jp/ibu/english/ibuprinceshotoku.html>.

Sarvasthananda, Swami. *Contemporary Gujarati Literature III*. Sri Ramakrishna Math. 8 Jan 2007 <http:www.sriramakrishnamath. org/magazine/vk/2006/04-4-1.asp>

Sayadaw, Mahasi. *A Discourse on Dependent Origination*. Association for Insight Meditation. 8 Jan 2007 <http://www.aimwell.org/ Books/Mahasi/Dependent/Becoming/becoming.html>.

Swanson, Paul. *Foundations of T'ien-T'ai Philosophy, The Flowering of the Two Truths Theory in Chinese Buddhism*. 1st ed. Berkeley, CA: Asian Humanities Press, 1989.

Watson, Burton, et al, trans. *Letters of Nichiren*. 1st ed. New York: Columbia University Press, 1996.

Writings of Nichiren Shōnin, Doctrine 1. Ed. Kyōtsu Hori. Tōkyō: Nichiren Shū Overseas Propagation Promotion Association, 2002.

Writings of Nichiren Shōnin, Doctrine 2. Ed. George Tanabe, Jr. Tōkyō: Nichiren Shu Overseas Propagation Promotion Association, 2003.

Writings of Nichiren Shōnin, Doctrine 3. Ed. Kyōtsu Hori. Tōkyō: Nichiren Shū Overseas Propagation Promotion Association, 2004.

Sources in Japanese

『織田仏教大辞典』　織田得能、1983 新訂6刷、大蔵出版（株）

『撃鼓宣令－葉山法難録』藤井日達、第三編1928、日本山妙法寺

『昭和定本日蓮聖人遺文』日蓮宗電子聖典、2003、日蓮宗

『日蓮聖人御遺文』加藤文雅・霊艮閣版、重刻新版1967、山喜房佛書林

『日蓮宗事典』、1981、　日蓮宗宗務院

『藤井日達聖人全集』1994-1999、隆文館

『仏教と世界平和』藤井日達、1980、社団法人日印サルボダヤ交友会

『法華経』上中下、坂本幸男・岩本裕注釈、第8印発行2004、岩
　　波書店

『法華辞典－山喜房仏書林　広説仏教語大辞典』中村元著、2001、
　　東京書籍

『わが西天開教』藤井日達、1974、春秋社

『わが非暴力』山折哲夫編、1975、春秋社